Trinia 2-15-20

Light a can[illegible] turn on relaxing m[illegible] and grab a glass of your favorite beverage of Enjoy your copy of Silhouette Changes! Hope you enjoy the steamy scenes <wink>

Toni 2020.

SILHOUETTE CHANGES

T. R. Gray

T. R. GRAY

SILHOUETTE CHANGES

BY T. R. GRAY
Editing and Interior Layout by Urban Book Editor
Cover Design by Bowman Artistic Design

Published by T. R. Gray
Printed in the United States of America.
ISBN-13: 978-0-578-43779-8

10 9 8 7 6 5 4 3 2
First Edition

Warning: Explicit Content. Mature Audience Only.

SILHOUETTE CHANGES

T. R. Gray

Acknowledgments

To my mother Melodee Gray, and both my fathers, Hayward Lowe and Dave Gray Jr. [R.I.P]. Thank you for your unconditional love. Your examples of love kept me going, even when life got tough.

To my eldest daughter, LaToyia Carroll, I appreciate your guidance and honesty. Your passion for finding one's Authentic Self has been uplifting.

To my youngest daughter, Tiera Terry, thank you for being a true inspiration on how to stand my ground and fight for what I want.

To Mr. Travis Wood. Thank you for supporting my vision. You are much appreciated.

To Michele Barard of Urban Book Editor. It has been a pleasure working with you. You have been more than an editor. At times, a writing coach! You have taken this project from good to great. I can't wait to work with you again.

Dedicated to Anyone
Facing a Crossroad

TABLE OF CONTENTS

Silhouette Changes

In the loud silent night
A boisterous quiet fight
Tough fragile walls
A mind to dismiss all
The unsung calm rage
Heart delicately clangs
Wild conservative views
Outrageous shy cues
Mind deluged and subdued
Angelic lies…Nightmarish truths
Silhouetted Hues

By T. R. Gray

CHAPTER 1

LEXY
Friday - 7:03 p.m.

Sirens echoed through the June summer night as law enforcement tried to move human obstructions. The chanting grew louder as the number of unruly, sweaty protesters increased, and the people melded into one massive, throbbing unit. The mob blocked traffic, shifting defiantly like an angry swarm of bees preparing to strike.

"Justice is a must. Justice is a must. Justice is a must!" They demanded justice for the ongoing national trend of increased minority deaths by law enforcement.

Lexy stared out of her office window at the police officers trying to control the riotous crowd in the downtown Minneapolis intersection. Their efforts seemed futile. Consumed with her own affairs, she began pacing the floor, deeply inhaling her cigarette, and blowing smoke high in the air, leaving a locomotive trail of haze behind her for the ventilation system to suck up. "I don't give a damn what he wants; I pay through the nose as it is! I've worked hard for this business, and now I'm just supposed to let this relic from the past fuck it all up!" Stopping at the desk, she crushed the stubby cigarette out and lit another one. "Dammit, Marcus; I thought you were on my side!" She scowled at her immaculately dressed friend of twenty-two years with her small, narrow, deep-brown eyes ablaze with anger, and her button nose flared with irritation.

Marcus sighed. Upsetting the boss was not his goal. He looked away with unease and then back at her. "I know it's not about the money for you. Are you going to take the meeting with him?" he asked apprehensively and then pretended to pick lint from his tailored suit.

Lexy stood in front of an oversized one-way mirror that overlooked the French Boudoir styled club below while smoking her cigarette and thinking about her conundrum. As much as she loved the decor of the club, she was looking forward to the completion of the ongoing renovations, which were just in time for the annual White Out Ball. Now, she was beginning to wonder if it was time for her own personal re-invention. Vincenzo's organization's increasing presence in her club meant they were conducting illegal activities. For years, The Family had left Lexy's alone, but something changed. Because of their history, he expected her to ignore the obvious. But, Lexy could not follow the ancient idealization of trying to keep an old lover from stirring up trouble out of respect for their past and his ranking in organized crime. Her French manicured acrylic fingernails drummed on the glass, playing an orchestra in her head that did not match the muffled thumping of the club music below. At the same time, Chi performed her famous pretzel bend on the main stage as a customer beckoned her on with a twenty-dollar bill.

Against the backdrop of the red and gold decor surrounding her, Marcus could not help but admire how exquisite Lexy looked in her red fitted evening gown. She had swept up her auburn micro-braided hair extensions into a French twist. His middle-aged eyes roamed over her caramel-colored muscular back—lightly dusted with small freckles and moles. His gaze ended at her firm rear end. A stirring in his groin began, so he refocused his eyes up and watched her red rouged lips take a pull off her cigarette. He noticed her square-shaped jaw muscles tighten and relax repeatedly—a habit she no longer realized she did. Hearing no response from her, her club manager spoke again, "Well, are you going to meet with him? He expects a reply by tonight. He has been waiting. I should be there, right?"

Her fingers stopped drumming.

"Yes, I'll meet with him, but I'm still dealing with the audit. I need more time. This has been extremely difficult. Be patient, Marcus. We're almost there..." she trailed off and then whispered, "Shit, I've got to do something."

"Baby Doll...," he began.

"Why don't you check with security?" she said, dismissing him.

He stood. "You seem a little tense." Marcus walked over and placed a hand on her shoulder. "Uh...should I come over tonight?" he asked cautiously, hoping she would say yes.

* * *

Marcus and Lexy met when he attended a financial meeting with his coworkers at The Gold Mine—now Lexy's Gentlemen's Club. The conservative executive, who did not own a pair of jeans, had no interest in the exotic location of the meeting until he saw Lexy. Soon after, he made it a point to frequent the establishment to get to know her. It took months and patience on his part. When she finally let him into her private life, they began to navigate the sexual world of the strip club industry as a couple. The two were inseparable until the typical couple thing happened, and they resolved to transform the relationship into an everlasting friendship based on mutual respect. Over the years, he had become her confidant, her advisor, her business partner, and her lover. Most of all, Marcus was her best friend.

* * *

"No. I'm going to call it an early night," she said, reaching across her chest and touching the hand that was on her shoulder. "I'll call you in the morning when I'm done working out." Tilting her head up, she accepted a kiss on the cheek.

"Please be careful when you leave. Not all protestors out there are here for the right reasons. You know, people can be opportunistic."

"I'll be careful," Lexy replied. She sipped her wine, watching Marcus take leave in his well-tailored suit and harmonious accessories. Lexy often thought he missed his calling and should have had a career in the fashion industry. Then, turning her attention back to the activities below, she watched Kat stroll down the walkway. "Damn, Kat. You're looking good tonight," she mumbled, focusing her expressionless eyes on the dancer.

Lexy had been eyeing Kat, stage name Angel, for the last three years, but kept her thoughts to herself. Dating an employee was a recipe for disaster, as well as opening oneself up to a sexual harassment case. Tired of the stress of the club, Lexy picked up the phone and dialed her lover, Lisa.

KAT
Friday - Earlier That Evening

Kat—legal name Katherine Renay Olson—dealt with her own dilemma before going to work that night. The open hand slap caught her off guard. She had no time to brace herself. The force of the blow caused her to spin around, sending her wiry, tall frame careening to the floor like a sack of potatoes. Tyrone Terrell Li—referred to by his sobriquet TL—stood above her, his six-foot-four-inch frame casting a shadow over her slim body. "Bitch, you don't know when to keep your fuckin' mouth shut! What tha fuck's wrong with you?" he shouted, not caring if his baritone voice carried through the condominium walls.

This was not the first time TL had hit her, so she knew, even in her confusion, not to answer the rhetorical question, nor make any sudden moves. The room spun; her head throbbed. Blood oozed out of the corner of her mouth as she gazed unsteadily at the pant cuff of his jeans and athletic shoes with her honey blonde hair hanging down around her heart-shaped face.

"What the fuck you got to say now, bitch? I'm not hearing you," TL challenged. His masculine, ebony-colored face twisted in rage as his eyes narrowed, his teeth clenched, and his thick top lip curled up at the corner in a snarl.

"I'm sorry," she said with a quiver in her voice and then sniffed, causing blood to go down her throat as she gazed at the floor.

He took a step back while keeping his eyes on her. Then, bending down, he reached a manicured hand towards her face. Kat flinched and turned her head slightly while sucking the side of her lip that did not hurt, not sure if the sting of another slap would follow. He cupped her narrow chin, drew her head up, and leaned his face inches from hers. "That was some stupid shit inviting your Bible-thumping friend when I told you not to. I don't need some goody-two-shoe bitch in my business. Fuck around, and I'll put her punk ass to work. Is that what you want?"

Kat shook her head no.

"Who has been in your corner…huh? That bitch sure ain't."

His deep voice flowed like silk over his smooth lips as his eyes softened. He was strikingly handsome. Kat could smell cologne drifting into her nostrils. She wondered how someone so rotten could smell so good.

"Y-You've been," she answered with inaudible words.

"What?" he calmly asked.

"You have," she answered louder in a soft voice.

He glanced at the specks of blood on the white carpet and reversed course. "Get that shit up and pull yourself together! You can't go to the club looking like a broke bitch!" he barked.

Kat cringed closer to the floor at the force of his words.

"You know I need my money. Game on," he said and winked.

The ringing of TL's cell phone interrupted the silence that followed his command. As he strode across the room to answer it, the twenty-one-year-old pushed back tears and pulled herself off the floor to go gather cleaning supplies.

* * *

Kat and TL had been together for three years. They had met at a challenging time in her life. Her relationships at home were unstable—an alcoholic stepfather and a fanatically religious mother. When TL met her at a bus stop on Hennepin Avenue, she was vulnerable. He knew at once she was a thoroughbred and strung the fair-haired teenager along for six months until she was legal, which was an easy task for him. TL possessed the qualities of patience and a gift for gab. Kat believed him when he promised her the stripping was temporary. Now three years later, it was apparent things were not going the way she had expected.

The handsome man in his mid-thirties had a chiseled face, exotic, slanted eyes, a perfectly proportioned nose, prominent cheekbones, and thick, wide-set lips that would make any woman take notice. He kept his naturally curly hair cut close in a fade on the sides with minor volume on top and sported a clean-shaven face. He wore the trendiest clothes on his basketball player type physique, and on average, the jewelry he wore cost more than the average car. TL preferred not to acknowledge the Asian side of his genetic makeup and considered himself African American. Despite this mindset, his baby-soft hair and slanted, tight eyes were a dead giveaway that a DNA test would reveal a mixed heritage.

The hustler of women did not drink liquor, smoke cigarettes, or use mind-altering drugs, which was a rarity for someone in his profession. His high came from earning money via his investments. When not managing his women, TL spent his time investing in Wall Street, playing golf, lifting weights, playing basketball, or spending time at sports bars gambling at pool tables. He never ate fast food and seldom watched television. When he did, he watched International news or stock market channels and did not partake in social media. For a pimp, he was unique.

* * *

In the bathroom, Kat's personal sinkhole seemed to swallow her whole. Looking in the mirror, her wide-set, large pale blue eyes, with muddled makeup from crying, stared back at her with misery and despair. She ran her fingers across her over-tweezed eyebrows, which caused her to wince in pain when she touched a sore spot. She then ran them along the slightly crooked path of her pencil-thin nose—an irregularity received two months before when TL had broken it—before pulling strands of her long hair from dried blood anchored to the corner of her mouth. Finally, she touched her left cheek, which bore a red handprint that would require foundation cover-up. Kat surveyed her figure—a six-foot, thin frame with tiny, perky breasts, a smooth, flat stomach, and long legs that looked more suited for a fashion runway than a stripper's catwalk.

Kat contemplated how things had gotten out of control. The distraught girl began to quietly cry, suffering silently so as not to bring on another round of wrath from the giant in the next room.

* * *

From an early age, Kat never felt she belonged. In high school, the boys had studied her from afar as if she were a rare gazelle in the jungle of the school hallways. They were not sure of how to approach the pretty, introverted girl. Other than her best friend Beverly, Kat did not socialize with anyone. Even with Beverly's love, a pain existed in her heart, and she never understood why. Often, the thought of suicide plagued her. Now, years later, the same unstable emotions haunted her.

On the other hand, TL had been there for her when no one else had. He bought her beautiful things, encouraged her to finish high school, and had been her first and only lover. Most importantly, he helped to replace the emptiness when Beverly moved to California. Initially, romantic pillow-talk of marriage dominated many lustful nights with the man of her dreams, but, as time passed, the talk faded. With a long-running history of low self-esteem, despite her angelic beauty, Kat valued herself through the perceived love of TL. Over time, TL introduced her to his other investments. It was during that phase she had begun to numb her emotions with drugs and alcohol.

* * *

Kat dug in her purse and pulled out a blunt. TL forbade her to smoke in the apartment, but she thought, *Fuck 'em,* and lit up. Then, she turned on the shower and the exhaust fan to displace the smoke. Sitting on the toilet, she took a deep drag of the drug. As the thick smoke filled the air, she stifled a cough. A calming effect engulfed her until paranoia that TL would smell the weed hit. Kat snuffed out the blunt, dropped the rest of it inside an empty medicine bottle, and sprayed a neutralizer before brushing her teeth and stepping into the shower.

Feeling sorry for herself was not the answer to her problem. Getting beautiful was the way to fix things because it meant making more money. The more money she saved, the further away she could get from TL. This was the plan. Running her hand over the "*TL$*" tattoo on her right, bony hip, she realized time was running out. She decided she should contact Beverly and make an excuse to cancel the visit. As much as she wanted to see her best friend, protecting

Beverly was the priority. Even if TL could not bring forth his threat of "putting her to work," he could bring misery to them both. TL had nothing better to do than orchestrate being God in someone's life. That was his job; that is how he made his living; that is what he was an expert at. Yes, she would have to call Beverly and try to stop her from coming.

BEVERLY
Friday - 5 p.m. Pacific Time

Twenty-one-year-old Beverly Lynn Carlson hummed happily to a gospel song as her white, convertible Mercedes Benz sped along coastal highway 101 with the sun shining bright. With natural, manicured nails, her slender hands held the steering wheel steady as she made mental notes of final preparations for her trip home to Minnesota. With most errands complete, she had a few hours left before going to the airport. As the tail of her white scarf fluttered in the wind behind her, she began singing happily, speeding along, and enjoying the warm California weather.

On the other hand, Beverly's agent, Arlene, did not approve of the impromptu trip. With modeling opportunities available, she wanted Beverly to remain in California to continue working on her burgeoning career. Beverly begged to differ and pushed her personal agenda with her broker. Over the past year, many things had happened in her life, and she needed a break. Her fiancé had broken up with her, and she had recommitted herself to Jesus Christ. Beverly had stopped going to nightclubs, drinking liquor, smoking weed, and having sex outside of marriage—all lifestyle choices that went against moral, spiritual, and ethical codes ingrained in her since childhood. Her path had gone crooked, but now, renewal efforts yielded positive fruit. Visiting home would allow another repair in her life. Over the last three years, Beverly and her best friend had lost touch. She and Kat used occasional calls, texts, and social media to stay connected. Still, it was not as intimate as the face-to-face interactions the girls needed. Letting Arlene derail the visit was not an option.

* * *

Beverly and Kat met when they were ten years old. Joanne, Kat's mother, a single parent of one child, moved into the Selby Dale area—an African American neighborhood in St Paul, MN—across the street from Beverly's middle-class family. When the two girls met, they hit it off instantly. At that time, both adolescences looked awkward, nothing like the beauties they were now. One was honey-blonde, blue-eyed, tall, gangly, and often struggled with her lanky limbs. The other was almond-colored, hazel-eyed, two inches shorter than the former, and waif-like in size. Both appeared as if they suffered from anorexia or bulimia, which neither did. Because of their height, the two looked like middle school students rather than fifth graders. Some of their peers took note of their sweet and enduring personalities and embraced them; other classmates bullied them with cruel taunts and jeers, which only made their friendship stronger.

* * *

Beverly eased down her Eucalyptus tree-lined street without noticing a missed call on her cell phone. She pulled into a small parking lot and secured a spot in front of a set of yellow-flowered Bird of Paradise plants that lined the walkway. Laden with packages, she negotiated her way into her apartment. Her cat, Jetta, met her at the door. The feline yawned, advanced out of the shadows of the hall, and gave her a where-have-you-been look as Beverly set pet supplies on the kitchen counter. Jetta followed her down the hall, past the bathroom, and to the back of the tiny apartment's only bedroom. Jetta jumped on the bed and surveyed the opened luggage, stepping into each one to test a potential future sleeping spot. Beverly shooed her out and closed the baggage.

It did not take Beverly long to dress for the flight. With above-average looks, she wore no makeup other than face moisturizer and lip gloss. At five feet eleven inches and one hundred and twenty-five pounds, she carried an athletic build that made even her jeans and t-shirt look high fashion. Her exquisite doe shaped, hazel eyes contoured by thick eyebrows and round pouty lips could melt the heart of even the most narcissistic personality. These natural attributes, coupled with a permanent smile and sweet demeanor, attracted people to her often causing them to have an unexplained desire to cater to her every need. Beverly grabbed her belongings and headed to her neighbor's apartment to give her the extra key and last-minute instructions for Jetta's care.

* * *

On the plane, Beverly checked her messages.

"Miss Lady, I've got good news! I booked a job for you in Minneapolis on Tuesday, June 5th, with Voy. I'll send the information. Thank you, love. Toodle-loo!" her agent's cheerful voice ended the voicemail. Beverly smiled. *Leave it to Arlene to find work for me while I'm on vacation.*

The plane began to pull from the gate, so she checked the last message. "Hey, you, it's me," Kat's delicate voice purred like silk on a ribbon, "Something has come up. I need to see if we can reschedule. Tomorrow won't work. I'm sorry. I'll pay your re-scheduling fees. Give me a call when you get this. Love you!"

"Excuse me, Miss. You'll have to turn your cell phone off," a flight attendant informed her in a stereotypical candy-coated voice; but her facial expression denoted something different.

Beverly nodded and complied. Since they had both confirmed the trip a few days ago, she wondered what was going on and noted that Kat had the arrival date wrong. As the plane began to taxi down the airstrip, Beverly knew she would have to ask Kat in person.

* * *

Well after eleven p.m., Beverly arrived at The Bellows Hotel in downtown St. Paul. After assuring her anxiety-ridden mother that she had arrived safely, she called her friend. Kat's sexy, prerecorded voice came on, "You reached the number you dialed. Please, leave a message."

Beep. "Hi, Bird, It's Bev. I'm at The Bellows; room ten eighteen. Call me, girl."

Knowing it was too late to call friends, Beverly showered and ate a late-night snack. Near midnight, donned in a white spa housecoat—compliments of the hotel—she spent time gazing out the picturesque hotel window that overlooked the Mississippi River. Conflicting emotions swirled in her heart. It felt lonely being in Minnesota without her primary family unit. Her parents lived in El Paso, Texas, with her twin brothers who were in their senior year of high school. But she felt excited to be home to see Kat and believed something special would happen on this visit, something good. Feeling the strain of travel, Beverly retired for the night, making sure to pray first.

"Father, God, thank you for being my Savior. Thank you for seeing me safely here. I pray the Holy Spirit guides my footsteps. I'm grateful for your love, mercy, and grace. I pray that my personal relationship with you will grow stronger, and you will use me to help others through your love. In Jesus's name, I pray. Amen."

She got in bed with her Bible and reread scriptures from the seventh chapter of Matthews, which reminded her to not judge others. Her spirit received the words. She thought about Kat stripping, having sex outside of marriage, drinking, and drugging. Beverly promised herself that she would try to talk to her friend about her lifestyle without coming on too strong or be too judgmental. There were skeletons in her own closet, so she had no justification to point an accusatory finger at her best friend. It was taking time for her to work out her own salvation. Her thoughts went back to Kat's attempt to cancel. They both seemed equally excited about the trip. Realizing there was no way to figure things out until she spoke to Kat, she set her Bible on the side bed table and went to sleep.

CHAPTER 2

LEXY
Saturday - 6:30 a.m.

Minnesota loons cried out for attention on the bodies of water scattered throughout the City of East Lake. Humid morning air supported the meteorologist's prediction of an impending muggy day. In one of the opulent homes, two women lay in bed as the sun struggled to push through the custom blinds and blackout drapes of the master bedroom suite. Soft music played from a satellite radio station and evidence of after-hour activities littered the room—overflowing ashtray with two different lipstick colors on cigarette butts, half-filled wine glasses, empty wine bottles, sex toys, and edible lubricants. Lexy's caramel-colored, shapely legs were wrapped around Lisa's cream-colored petite legs, their bodies entwined as one. The elder of the two lay still, listening to the younger's soft snores. She held her girlfriend from behind with her nose nestled in the back of her neck, breathing in the intoxicating aroma of rose petal cologne.

Peeling their bodies apart, Lexy got out of bed and went to the adjoining on-suite to run a bubble bath—fussing at herself for not removing her make-up before passing out earlier that morning and wishing she had gotten more than three hours of sleep. Once in the hot water, an extensive hygiene ritual ensued—soak, shave, exfoliate, cleanse, and moisturize—which made climbing back into bed tempting. But back in the room, she moved about like a ninja on a stealth mission, quietly putting on clean loungewear and grabbing her business tablet so as not to wake Lisa.

Dressed in a short, black silk robe and wearing no-nonsense slippers, Lexy entered the modern kitchen from a set of stairs that allowed access from the back part of the front hall foyer. Any other time, the bright sun through the skylights of the cathedral ceilings and the musical notes of natures' feathered friends outside would have been welcoming. This morning's hangover did not agree.

"Fuckin' birds," she muttered, frowning as if they were the cause of her inability to drink responsibly.

The result of the consumption of too much wine now felt like a war raging in her head. Her stomach fared no better. It felt like a Viking ship rolled through it as if on rough seas, nausea in the pit of her stomach, making it impossible to think of breakfast.

Through squinted eyes, she surveyed her surroundings. She felt no connection to the upscale restaurant-grade kitchen with all the bells and whistles a chef could want. Sustenance for her was simple—water, protein shakes, raw fruits and vegetables, cigarettes, and lots of wine; therefore, the dream space went unused. Sitting at the breakfast table with a warm tea mug between her hands and the steam from it lingering around her face, her jaw muscles tensed and relaxed as she absent-mindedly clenched and released her teeth. She set the cup down and fingered faded scars around her wrist—a reason her jewelry collection consisted of many thick bracelets to cover them.

Why is he fuckin' with me?

Partnering with Vincenzo was something she could not let happen. Collaboration would inevitably mean losing control of the club and her personal life. The fact that she had been careful through the years to abide by industry rules, both legal and illegal while avoiding major scandals, was one reason, among others, she was upset. The disrespect infuriated her to no end. "Fat bastard!" she said to the walls around her and crinkled her button nose.

Long ago, when Vincenzo was svelte and moderately handsome, it had been easy to be his secret lover. At that time, he was needed and wanted. Fifteen years post-relationship, the decision on how to eradicate his increasingly intrusive actions into her life, without bringing herself down, or the club, was the priority. It also boiled down to principle.

* * *

The path to success for Lexy did not come without challenges. After leaving home at the age of sixteen and living on the streets for two years, the headstrong teen found herself at the Goldmine Strip Club. From there, her journey to becoming a businesswoman ensued. After suffering a miscarriage—Vincenzo had fathered the baby and promptly abandoned her when she revealed the pregnancy—she resolved to take control of her fate. After years of dancing and receiving mentorship from a wealthy client, Lexy covertly bought shares in the struggling club, which created legal opposition from the white male partners. Over time, stakeholder buyouts left her with a run-down, seedy club.

Once in control, Lexy revamped the dark, perverted atmosphere into a sophisticated man's paradise. Backyard bartenders were replaced with professionally trained mixologists. All staff underwent background checks and drug screening, and an elaborate security system was installed. These measures did not stop all unwanted illegal activity, but it did start her employees with a clean slate and gave her peace-of-mind.

Next, Lexy addressed the entertainment. She knew men wanted options. They wanted what they would not openly admit to, variety. She sprinkled enough diversity to make a statement without taking too many Caucasian dancers out of rotation, which set her club apart from the others. The soon-to-be mogul brought the club out of an archaic time-period with Marcus by her side. Marcus received a stake in the business and was appointed general manager. He was paid a hefty salary with bonuses and benefits, which he grew into his own small fortune. Unfortunately, the one benefit she could not give him was marriage, which he had asked for three times over the last twenty-two years.

Once she modernized the club, her aggressive management style remained consistent. Considering she grew up in poverty and dropped out of high school, things had worked out well for her. Now, with the trend of the industry becoming franchised and Vincenzo's intrusion, Lexy had to develop plans to keep her club on a continued trajectory of success. In the past, these types of decisions had been easy but now seemed draining.

* * *

Is it time to walk away? Was I wrong for not franchising? Should I be investing capital in renovations? God, I don't want to deal with Vincenzo!

The throbbing in her head roared, causing concrete thinking to elude her. Through bloodshot eyes, she looked around at her plush surrounding and wondered why emptiness haunted her. Something was missing.

Do I need children? She frowned. *No, I'd make an awful mom. Do I need God? Shit, no amount of God can erase my sin card.* Lexy sighed. God was an ambiguous figure to her. Pursuing a relationship with God left her radar during her childhood. Her opinion on the matter was neutral, neither against nor for. Spirituality was a foreign subject to her.

If there is a God, please take this God damn headache away so I can get on with my day.

Lexy moaned. The addict in her wanted a cigarette, which she knew would make her head hurt more, so she opted not to pick up the cancer stick—a rarity. Standing and stumbling slightly, the hungover woman realized it only made sense to get back in bed.

Back in her room, Lexy slipped into bed with Lisa and slept through her nine-a.m. workout, her noon massage, scheduled errands, and a multitude of calls from Marcus. When Lisa awoke, she found a small box with a note sitting on top of her clothes. The note read, "Lisa, have a good day. This is for you. Kisses, Lexy!" Lisa lifted a three-carat tennis bracelet out of the rectangular box and marveled at its beauty. After kissing Lexy on the forehead, she let herself out, making sure to set the security alarm.

BEVERLY
Saturday - 9:20 a.m.

"Hey, you!" Beverly said, cheerfully answering Kat's phone call.

"Whazup, girl!" Kat responded with a voice no more than a

gentle whisper. At the sound of each other's greetings, the girls giggled like teenagers.

"So, what's up? I didn't get your message until I was on the plane. Did you have my travel dates mixed up?"

"Oh, it was nothing," Kat replied, trying to sound casual, then pulled her lower lip into her mouth before releasing it. "TL didn't think the condo was ready for a guest, but everything is fine now. I told him you were staying at The Bellows. Everything is fine," she repeated.

Beverly did not believe her. The sound of Kat's voice told her something was wrong, but she kept her suspicion to herself.

"So, Bev," Kat teased, "Are we going to hang out like old times?"

"Old times, what's that supposed to mean?" Beverly shot back in the same playful manner.

Kat's voice took on a more serious tone. "Well, I know you've made some changes in your life."

Beverly scoffed. "Are you referring to the fact that I have accepted Jesus Christ as my Lord and Savior?" Before receiving an answer, she continued, "Bird, we will always be sisters. Nothing will change that. Just because I quit drinking and smoking doesn't mean I can't have fun."

"Yea, you didn't do much of either of those things, anyway. You were always such a goody-two-shoe. But, hmmm…," Kat searched for the right words, "I-I just can't see you not clubbing, not listening to good music…you know, hanging out…blowing off steam. I just can't see it."

"Wow!" Beverly exclaimed, "It's not that bad. I get high off life. I dance at church, pray when I get upset or exercise to blow off steam, try to eat right, you know, healthy ways to unwind. I take that same energy from my old lifestyle and spread the gospel…hashtag, win souls for Christ."

"Hashtag? Really, Bev? Does anyone say, 'hashtag' anymore?"

"See," Beverly said, "That's why I'm settling down. I'm not cool anymore."

The girls laughed in unison.

Kat feigned exasperation. "And sex? Please, don't tell me you've given up sex!"

"For now, until I meet my husband," Beverly replied, sounding as if she needed convincing herself.

On the other end of the phone, Kat sat on her bed in a white t-shirt with her long legs folded under her like a young colt and her hair cascading down her sides in two loose pigtails. She mimicked putting a gun to her head and then pulled the imaginary trigger. "Pow!" she piped into the phone and rolled over backward, landing on a mound of pillows. "I'd shoot myself first! No sex!" Looking at the ceiling, she scolded, "Alright, Mother Theresa, I don't want you trying to convert me on this trip. I'll never give up sex!"

This was a strange statement, considering she rarely got sex from TL. He had a multitude of women to sleep with, whereas Kat was faithful to him.

"Well, I can't guarantee what the Holy Spirit will do, but we're definitely going to make up for lost time."

The girls continued chatting, often finishing each other's sentences in the process. Their conversation flowed effortlessly as if three years had not passed. They finished their talk by agreeing to meet at noon.

Beverly hung up, feeling energized. She slung a workout bag over her shoulder and headed to the lobby, where she learned the hotel gym was closed for maintenance.

The concierge apologized. "I'm sorry for the inconvenience, Miss, but I can offer you a complimentary pass to a facility not far from here. It's well equipped and just about a mile from here." Beverly smiled and accepted the pass.

* * *

The weather was brisk, and the air was calm. The rising sun emitted a promise of a warmer day as the rays shined through between the high-rise buildings. Feeling rested and relaxed, Beverly used the walk as a cardio warm-up, ignoring the admiring looks of passers-by. When she got to the gym, she was pleased. It was luxurious, making her want to call Arlene and scold her for being negative about her trip.

When Beverly entered the weight room, men and women snuck glances at her as they pretended to busy themselves with their workout. A couple of people smiled, and she returned the gestures. Stares from others made her feel uncomfortable. She felt self-conscious, not fully understanding the impact of her beauty. People had complimented her and stared at her all her life, but she never took her appearance for granted. The more people stared, the more Beverly reverted into a self-imposed shell.

Exercising helped Beverly tune out the prying eyes. The young woman started her workout at the Roman chair, worked her way through the back-extension and seated row equipment, and lastly, to the back-pull-down machine. While doing her pull-downs, she got a whiff of a familiar men's cologne. Turning to look behind her, she was face-to-stomach with a smooth chocolate six-pack. Following the reverse route of a single drop of sweat, her eyes traveled upwards to an impeccable chest and then to a set of deep brown eyes set in a handsome dark face.

"Morning. I was wondering if I could work a couple of sets in with you. This is the last machine on my list," a man with a smooth, masculine voice asked.

Beverly looked at him in silence while willing herself to speak. His looks were striking. His small, tight eyes had thick lashes, his bone structure like that of a marble statue. She was accustomed to working with good-looking men; however, this specimen was one of the most stunning she had ever seen. Had he not been so handsome, the intrusion into her personal space would have been annoying.

"Sure," she replied, smiling and trying not to stammer, "but you'll have to add more weights."

They exchanged places, and she stood back and watched him from behind. She noticed how precise his haircut was and how well-manicured his nails were. His back was a perfect inverted triangle, and his muscles contracted as he squeezed at the end of the pull-downs. With each repetition, the veins began to bulge in his well-defined biceps. After each squeeze of his back muscles, he let out a grunt and then returned the weights to their starting position. She wanted to make small talk, but he seemed focused on his workout, so they continued taking turns in silence. During their exchanges to share the equipment, she could not help but notice how close he seemed to brush past her.

After her third set, Beverly said, "That's it for me. Enjoy your workout."

"You too," he replied, flashing a row of white, straight teeth.

Whew! That smile! She thought.

It was a welcome relief to get on the treadmill. Beverly wanted to get her mind off the handsome man. She had not had sex in a year. This was her first temptation, and it disturbed her. She yearned for the deep-voiced man to sweep her up and carry her into a romantic fantasy. As she began to put more effort into her strides, she forced herself to push through her childish thoughts and refocus to ignore her flesh. Beverly prayed a brief prayer to God, asking for spiritual strength.

* * *

Alert and sharp, he had stridden into the weight area with his head held high and his back erect, commanding attention with each step. Within seconds, his eagle eyes had made a reconnaissance of the room. As he walked towards the cardio equipment, he gave customary nods to gym regulars intending to keep his eye on her. Eventually, their workout paths led them to occupy the same space in the fixed machine area, and he sat one aisle over, watching her at the pull-down equipment.

Surveying Beverly, TL noted she had a toned physique and appeared to either work out regularly or carried good genes. There was something about the attractive young woman that made her look wholesome. He had noted her perfect B size breasts, narrow waist, and firm round butt. Dollar signs floated in his head. He walked over and stood behind her, knowing she would turn around. When she did, he forced himself to control his excitement at the beauty of her light hazel eyes, round pouty lips, and flawless complexion.

Patience. Ignore her. Don't be too attentive, he thought.

Her stares penetrated him from behind, so he made extra efforts to contract his back and bicep muscles and made sure to come into her personal space during each exchange. At the end of her set, watching her walk away, he searched his memory. TL knew all the gorgeous females in the metro area, but this one, he could not recall.

Upon leaving the facility, he did some lip service to the semi-cute girl at the main lobby desk. He leaned in and touched her hand lightly to butter her up and get personal information on his target. He was not able to learn Beverly's name, but he did find out she was staying at The Bellows. He left the gym, leaving the just-turned-eighteen-year-old counter attendant believing there was hope for a date with him. Within no more than two steps away from the gym employee, the minimum wage girl became irrelevant to TL.

KAT & BEVERLY
Saturday - Noon

The smell of freshly baked bread filled the air in Café Grand on Grand Avenue. It was a small cafe with large picture windows that overlooked the historic tree-lined street of Summit Hill, a gentrified section of St. Paul. Walking into the cafe was like walking into dessert heaven. Cakes, chocolate bars, pies, and goodies lined the shelves of a glass casing, which also served as an ordering counter. The smell of freshly brewed coffee, soups, and other lunch food delicacies dominated the air, filling the café with mouth-watering aromas.

Beverly spotted Kat sitting at a table in front of one of the picturesque windows and could not help but notice how breathtaking her friend looked. Wearing a short, flowered sundress, Kat stared out the window, her waist-long hair swept into a loose bun on the top of her head, with long tresses randomly framing her thin face. Kat's thick kohl makeup made her ice-blue eyes pop and her delicate nose less prominent. She wore bright red lipstick on her thin, wide-set lips, which matched her extremely long red acrylic talons and her red toenail polish. Gladiator styled white sandals snaked around her never-ending legs, and gold rings adorned most, if not all, of her fingers. Two gold chains on her neck completed her look. It all seemed excessive for Beverly's taste, but nevertheless, she felt her friend looked breathtaking. Beverly approached the table.

"Oh, my God!" Kat exclaimed as she stood to give Beverly a hug. "You look great, Bev!"

"Not as good as you, Bird!" Beverly exclaimed and hugged back tighter.

"Man, it's good to see you!" Beverly took a step back and admired Kat.

"I know," Kat responded with a broad smile, showing teeth and gums, and stepped back, too.

They stared at each other in silence with smiles anchored on their youthful faces. After a few seconds, they broke out in a boisterous laugh. Patrons from a nearby table glanced at them, causing the young women to stifle giggles as they sat down.

The waiter brought water, and the girls asked for more time to review the menu. Upon his return, Beverly ordered a Mediterranean lentil salad with a light vinaigrette and water, and Kat ordered a small salad, fried shrimp, garlic toast, a vanilla shake, and chocolate cake. Avoiding serious conversation, they chatted until their food arrived, and the waiter reluctantly left the presence of the stunning women.

"You're glowing, Bev. Are you in love or something?" Kat cocked her head to the side and looked at Beverly's sun-kissed face.

Beverly flashed a thought to the dark, handsome man at the gym. "No, I'm loving myself these days," she said with bright, well-rested eyes, concealing the truth of her disturbing attraction to the stranger. "I got good sleep, that's all." Beverly beamed.

"Alright, if you say so." Kat moved a long hair ringlet from in front of her eye. "Okay. You go first. What's been going on?" she asked.

"Well, Ms. Katherine…"

Kat rolled her eyes.

Beverly mimicked the dramatic eye roll. "Alright, Bird," she relented, "the condensed version is that, as you know from some of our talks, I had a few rough starts when I first got to California, but now, I've finally got my act together. You know the cliché. Girl moves to Hollywood. Girl falls in with the wrong crowd, and then girl has harrowing experiences that sober her up. Voila!" Beverly snapped her fingers to simulate her miraculous transformation.

Kat stopped eating and held her fork mid-way between her plate and her mouth. "Go on."

"I fell in with the wrong industry crowd and began partying too much. It started out innocent, you know. A drink here, a drink there, but eventually, by the end of my second year, I started losing control. I began missing auditions, and, at times, I would show up looking a mess. Man, I even started getting a bad attitude."

"Really? Not you?" Kat said and placed her fried, jumbo shrimp down before clumsily wiping the crumbs from the corner of her mouth with her hand. "Nothing seemed wrong, other than the regular stuff we griped about when we talked."

"I know. I know. I was good at hiding things. I was ashamed." Beverly wiped the corner of her mouth with a napkin and then perked up. "But, praise God! At a photo-shoot lunch break, I met Sister Sarah. I began attending her and her husband's home Bible study sessions, and it helped me understand the word of God in a renewed way. Different than what I learned at church with you and your mom." Beverly hastily added, "I don't mean to offend. I loved going to Sunday school and all the programs we were in, but..."

Kat held up her hand and interrupted, "No offense taken."

Beverly smiled before taking a sip of water. "I'm rebuilding my life. Things are great. I still have challenges, but I handle them different now."

Kat frowned. "I'm gonna need the verbal blueprints?" and then proceeded to use her tongue to lick rogue food from around her mouth, removing most of her lipstick in the process.

"I'd be happy to share my testimony with you, but first, please, tell me how you've been doing? I promise. I'll share details later."

Kat absentmindedly pushed the ignored salad around the bowl and cleared her throat. "Uh, n-nothing fantastic like a-a modeling career; I'm still dancing at Lexy's. That's all."

"Wasn't that The Gold Mine?"

"Yep," Kat looked down at her plate and fiddled with the napkin in her lap.

"So...are you okay?" Beverly prodded.

"Yes...no...I don't know. It's all I know. I don't have skills to do anything else, and I don't think I can go back to school."

Kat's posture shrunk.

"You know me. School was never my thing. Even with your help, I barely graduated. Besides, I've got bills." Pausing to slurp her milkshake noisily, she continued speaking in a low volume. "It's getting harder to dance, though. Some days I can't stand the men looking at me, and those bitches…oops…I mean them girls. You know what I'm saying." Kat fumbled with her napkin and anchored half of her lower lip between her teeth. "I mean, I like the money and all, but I'm tired of having to be someone else, cheerful and sexy when I don't feel like that. I don't know," Kat murmured and looked down at her lap. "I can't work without getting a buzz on first. Shit, I drink and smoke so much weed that if I did try to go back to school, I probably couldn't remember nuthin."

Beverly wanted to say many things, but her spirit told her to listen. Silence filled the space between them as she waited patiently.

Kat spoke again, taking her time, causing her whispery voice to take on a sexy tone. "But on the other hand, I make good money. I have the best of everything. I can buy what I want. I like sleeping in and having my biggest decision of the day be whether I'm going to go to the spa or going shopping. I meet celebrities, and I'm always on someone's VIP list," Kat concluded as if campaigning for herself.

Beverly reached across the table and cupped her friend's hand while trying to search for the right words that would not sound too preachy, hoping the Holy Spirit would guide her. After a moment, she spoke. "Bird, what about your future? How will you live when new, younger girls push you out?"

"TL has a plan," Kat blurted out. "He has made investments for us. I know things will work out."

"What if things don't work out with you two?" Beverly asked.

Kat was thankful for the waiter's interruption; it allowed her to dodge the question.

"You could come to California and live with me. I bet Arlene would love you. We could save for a dance school or a modeling agency. I know we could partner in something fantastic."

"Leave momma, Bev? The church is the center of her world, and you know she is committed to the hospital. I can't imagine her anywhere else," Kat replied, reverting her eyes back down to her plate.

Beverly ignored the weak argument.

"You are talented, Bird. I know you would do well in the modeling industry."

Kat looked up; her eyes brightened. "You really think so?"

"Absolutely! Of course! You have the personality, the height, and you have the looks. Anyone would be happy to work with you. Looking a little more serious, she added, "You'll need to quit smoking weed, and you really should stop drinking, that stuff will ruin you physically, emotionally, and spiritually."

"I know," Kat sheepishly replied.

"Are you doing any other drugs?" Beverly asked casually before taking a bite of the salad she was still working on.

"Nothing else," Kat replied, quickly shaking her head no. "Just weed."

"Well, I'll be here 'til next Sunday. We have a little time to figure things out. I know Jetta would love having you around."

"You still have Jetta? Isn't she about a hundred years old?" Kat asked with a mouthful of chocolate cake.

"That's my baby, Bird," Beverly replied.

Both girls looked at each other and laughed without constraint, which garnered irritable stares from a group of middle-aged, obese women at a neighboring table. After composing themselves, and Beverly wiping off the cake Kat sprayed on her, Beverly noticed Kat's mood changed.

"What's wrong?"

"Well, …um…TL. I'd hate to leave him."

Beverly frowned. "Are you hearing yourself?" she said in an aggressive tone, her voice rising slightly. "How can you worry about someone who doesn't treat you with respect! I don't understand!"

Accusatory glares came from the same group of weight-challenged women.

Beverly lowered her voice.

"I'm sorry, Kat. That was out of line."

Displaying remnants of chocolate cake stuck in her lower front teeth, Kat grinned.

"Whatcha grinning about?"

"You, it's like hearing my old friend. I knew this new goody-two-shoes girl couldn't squeeze my real girl out!" Kat grinned wider.

"Oh, girl, I never said I wasn't human. Besides, serving Christ doesn't make you perfect. On the contrary, you're more conscious of sin. You don't want to commit sin, and you strive to be more Christ-like.

Kat continued eating her cake, not bothered by the outburst.

"I'm really sorry," Beverly said with sincerity and then motioned to Kat that chocolate cake sat lodged in her lower teeth.

"Apology accepted," Kat replied, regaining her light-heartedness before dipping her napkin in her water and running it across her teeth. "I can't deny the thought of starting fresh hasn't crossed my mind. I don't know why I just don't do it. I guess I'm waiting for the right time. Sometimes I'm ready to take off, and sometimes I'm not. I know you don't think much of TL, but I do love him, Bev."

"How do I get to know someone I've never met?" Beverly stated. "Seriously, Bird. The pics I've seen involve him skiing, horseback riding, and golfing. He is wearing hats and sunglasses, and none of them are close-ups. I could pass TL on the streets and not know who he is."

"Alright, Mother Theresa, I'll introduce you to him before you leave."

"Thank you. I'm hoping I'm wrong about him, but something tells me I'm not. I wish you'd just leave him. Heck, the man doesn't even have a social media account. He is old, Kat," Beverly frowned to reinforce her feelings.

"Bev."

"Okay, don't look at me like that. I'll back off, but you've got to promise me you'll consider me and Jetta as an option."

"I promise. Really, I will," Kat said, perking back up and hiding her sorrow behind a radiant smile.

Observing the pile of napkins around Kat's area and the food surrounding the table around Kat's plate, Beverly nodded yes. She then glanced down at her neat area and smiled. Kat had not changed, still beautiful but untidy.

The rest of the afternoon was relaxing for the two women. They strolled down Grand Avenue arm-in-arm, window-shopping among the renovated Victorian homes—repurposed specialty boutiques—occasionally patronizing a store to buy a gift for one another. Other shoppers stared at the two lovely women, but neither noticed. They were too busy enjoying each other's company. Sauntering along, the girls discussed their Sunday plans. Kat said she would consider church service and agreed if she did not go, that they would meet after service for a mid-day dinner at the condo. As early evening approached, they walked back to the café parking lot where they embraced and said their good-byes.

"I'm so glad you're here, Bev!" Kat said and wrapped her long limbs around Beverly's shoulders.

"Me too, Bird. Me too!"

When the girls parted ways, Kat felt happy. Beverly's visit gave her hope. While getting into her vehicle, Kat's cell phone rang. She viewed the number on the caller I.D. "Oh shit! Shit, shit, shit!" Her hands balled up, causing her acrylic nails to dig painfully into her palms.

CHAPTER 3

KAT

Kat's happiness converted to worry. Sitting in her vehicle on a side street off Grand Avenue, she debated while the phone continued to ring. It went to voicemail. Her heart raced, and an acute desire to have a bowel movement overtook her. She lit a piece of a left-over marijuana blunt to see if that would help, but the warm fuzzy feeling that washed over her did not quell the desire to use a more potent drug. Kat returned the call.

"Hey, girl, waddup?" Kat asked.

A deep, husky woman's voice replied, "Shit, I got some fire shit for you. I hear ya back online," the woman speaking slang spoke slower than necessary.

Kat knew this was a lie and that no one told Taz she had started using cocaine again because she never told anyone she stopped. A dealer's game now started playing out.

"Where you at?" Kat asked, no longer feeling distressed, having shifted into a different mode.

"At Big Mike's, but not for long. Uh'mm, uh'um," Taz said, clearing phlegm from her throat. "I'll wait a spell if ya hurry."

"Give me 'bout thirty. I'll be there. Same as usual, ok?"

"Bet."

Without a proper goodbye, Taz hung up.

* * *

In thirty minutes, Kat was knocking on the back door of a small brick duplex in North Minneapolis. While waiting, she nervously looked over her shoulder at the darkening alley. The sun was going down, and she knew the area was not safe. A white pit-bull tethered to a thick metal chain, bolted to the base of a tree, in the yard next door motionlessly eyed her, taunting her with a death-like stare. It seemed an eternity before someone came to the door, but it was only a few minutes.

Without saying a word, a black male in his early thirties, with wooly, knotted dreadlocks, and stained clothes, escorted her past a kitchen door and down a flight of creaky, worn basement stairs. The man's pungent body odor trailed behind him, causing Kat to frown her nose in disgust and to tilt her chin down to smell the perfume from her dress. The descent into the basement brought her into a deeper level of musk. The silent man and Kat walked down a dark hallway, passing a room that had a washer and dryer, old furnishings, and several large, black garbage bags. Their path ended at the rear of the basement in front of a closed door. After knocking and responding to the reply to come in, he opened the door. He waved his arm for her to enter, releasing more body odor in the process, before turning and disappearing back into the dimly lit hallway.

Feeling a blast of heat engulf her, Kat stepped into a cell-sized room. A haze of thick, smoke hung in the air, saturating the dingy walls. A dirty—once white—sunken couch filled the space to the right of the door; a black crate with a broken mirror served as a coffee table, and another over-turned crate was used as an end table. The makeshift end table housed a disc player that no longer worked. An occupant of the room named Big Mike sat in a metal folding chair positioned under a small casement window next to the crate and the disc player. The window had a towel nailed up like a curtain and an adjacent window—the one over the couch—was boarded up. A miniature tabletop fan, its blades covered in dirt, struggled to circulate the warm air from one corner of the room.

Kat addressed a white woman sitting on the floor in front of the littered crate table, "Hey, Jackie."

Despite new clothes, the woman looked far from pulled together. Her greasy shoulder-length hair, sagging pale skin, and body odor contradicted the fresh look of her attire. With a harsh voice that sounded like acid burnt vocal cords, Jackie replied, "Damn glad to be alive; son of a bitch Big Mike damn near killed me, threw me out the motherfuckin' car! Broke two ribs, damn bastard!"

Jackie paused to glare at Big Mike, took a drag of a cigarette, and blew a cloud of smoke in Big Mike's direction. "Shit, a bitch can't get a motherfuckin' break! I'm better now, tho. Sure nice to see you, tho. Can ya' help me out?" Jackie tried to smile, but the residual effects of a previous stroke prevented one side of her mouth from moving.

From her position on the couch, Taz lazily said, "Aw, shut the fuck up. I'm tired of that same 'olé story. You talk too fuckin' much." She shifted her red, glossy eyes over to Kat. "Why can't you have a sweet voice like Kat?"

Kat looked at Jackie and wondered how she managed to stay alive. Her body looked anorexic, her head appeared too large for her petite frame, and her mouth looked like it smelled of rot.

"Your voice sure is pretty," Jackie agreed with vocal cords that sounded like they could cut stone.

"Thank you. Uh, hey, Big Mike."

Big Mike sat in the chair, staring through space, and twirling a blackened crack stem in his hand, oblivious to the fact that Kat addressed him. He put the paraphernalia down and picked up a homemade pipe, pulled it apart and scraped residual drugs from the bottom with his figure hunched over the makeshift table like a mad scientist. This disgusted Kat but not enough for her to walk away from the scene.

* * *

It had been two months since Kat had indulged in crack. The last beating from TL over her smoking had nearly killed her, and Lexy had given her an ultimatum to straighten up or lose her job. After several days in the hospital, Kat had vowed to quit. Up until this point, staying clean had happened by sheer will power and ignoring calls from slippery people. The only problem was that she never told the slippery people that she had quit, nor had she changed her phone number. She never went to support meetings or sought additional resources to help with recovery. That was her biggest mistake. Dealers would periodically call her, which kept her connections going.

* * *

"Uh-hum." Jackie cleared her charred voice.

Kat ignored her.

"You gonna parallel park, or what?" Taz asked with a marijuana weighted voice.

Taz weighed two hundred and fifty pounds and stood at five feet, two inches tall. Taking up half the couch by slouching at an angle, with a short, squat head, a boy's crewcut, and dressed in men's clothes, it was hard to ascertain if Taz was a man or a woman. In her hand, she held a red bandana, which she used periodically to wipe the sweat dripping from her chunky forehead before it could slide down on her round, summer-baked face.

"What's your plea-sure?" the drug dealer asked.

"I'll take fitty candy and fitty salad," Kat replied, purposely saying fitty instead of fifty.

The sound of Kat's voice was like a splash of ice water on Big Mike's face. He jerked his round—badly in need of a haircut—head up, which glistened with sweat. Big Mike was not actually big anymore, but a fraction of the size of the man he used to be due to years of abusing drugs. With an intense look in his wide saucer-shaped eyes and his large black and pink lips set in a tight line against his dentures, Big Mike watched Kat and Taz; his eyes darted back and forth to watch every move between them.

Taz pulled out small square plastic bags with the word "Vegas" stamped in red on each one and extended her tattooed sleeved arm, opening her palm to give Kat a pick from the tiny bags of crack. Kat hesitated, wanting to pick the biggest, but realized they all looked the same, causing her to give up and blindly grab one. The desire for the drug was too strong to waste time being meticulous.

"Get ready to go to Vegas," Taz said exhaustedly, folding her flabby arms across her chest and settling deeper into the couch.

"Does anyone have something I can use?" Kat asked Jackie and Big Mike, now not caring that they both suffered from lack of oral hygiene.

Immediately, Jackie produced a beat-up looking glass smoking stem. Kat sat on the edge of the dirty couch and dug a lighter out of her purse, making a mental note to make sure no one pocketed it. After dropping a piece of the drug on the stem, Kat put fire to it and inhaled. A crackle and pop sound temporarily displaced the white noise of the inadequate fan as Kat inhaled the melting white drug.

The hit of the drug gave Kat a slight ringing in the ears, and a feeling of euphoria flooded her body. Everything felt calm for a moment. Kat wanted another hit to feel the exhilaration again. She handed Jackie and Big Mike a nice-sized piece of dope; they both inhaled their pieces and then turned their hungry eyes back on her, wanting more. Kat's next hit began to make her chatter rapidly, talking about anything and everything. Jackie stayed attentive, hoping this would cause Kat to give her another piece. The air grew thicker from Jackie and Big Mike chain-smoking cigarettes. Kat did not seem to notice. After some time, she looked at her cell phone and exclaimed, "It's already eight o'clock!"

"So," Taz replied, her eyes low from marijuana and her face glistening from the sweat she no longer tried to wipe.

"I've got to be to work at nine…hmm…let me get one more fitty, and then I'm outie."

Kat handed her the money without waiting for an answer, wishing she had liquor to calm the slight queasiness in her stomach. Taz knew Kat was on "go" to chase her high and would not be going anywhere. Taz lit a blunt and settled into the filthy couch, glad Kat would prevent her from running around making deliveries. It was too bad that Taz was right. At nine p.m., Kat still sat on the edge of the couch, smoking drugs. When her cell phone rang again for the umpteenth time, she turned it off.

CHAPTER 4

LEXY
Saturday – 8:34 p.m.

Lexy opened her eyes to darkness. The bedroom curtains were still closed from the previous night, and the sun had just begun to go down. Wiping her swollen eyes and rubbing her tense jaws, she emerged from her luxurious bed with her lingerie twisted around her torso as if she had slept in it for weeks.

The room was a mess from the Friday night/early Saturday morning rendezvous with Lisa, which was the reason she lost a day. Stepping over the clothing on the floor, she made her way to the bathroom with her cell phone in her hand. "Damn," she said, looking in the mirror and wiping her hand across her petite nose, "I look like hell." Checking her cell phone, she saw that she had several messages and an equal number of missed calls. "Shit! Call Marcus," she spoke hoarsely into her phone, activating a voice dialing feature.

He picked up on the first trill. "Baby Doll, are you alright? I've been calling for hours."

Setting the phone on the bathroom countertop and placing it on speaker mode, she replied while placing eye-drops in her eyes, "I'm fine, Marcus."

"I've been worried about you."

"Damn," she muttered, as she reached for an aspirin.

"What's wrong?"

"Nothing, I need to get dressed. I'll see you shortly."

"Did you set up the meeting?"

"No!" she snapped.

Realizing her loss of time was not his fault, she softened her voice. "I'll see you in a few."

Once again, Lexy performed an extensive hygiene ritual. An hour later, looking refreshed, she was on her way to the club dressed in a black pantsuit, leopard print bodice, black pumps, and a set of small pearl earrings. Her braid extensions pulled back into a single ponytail at the base of her neck made her look younger than her mature years. She got into the waiting limo so she could work during the forty-minute ride to Minneapolis. She had planned to call Vincenzo during the ride, but she got sidetracked when she started checking her email.

* * *

A little after ten p.m., Lexy arrived at the club. A black limousine and several luxury vehicles were waiting for service at the valet. Security staff greeted guests and kept foot traffic moving by tactfully ushering wannabes past the venue. Treated like a queen, security escorted her under a scarlet-colored awning—which covered the walkway—and up cement steps that lead to a set of massive double oak doors. Beyond the giant, highly glossed doors, she stepped into a grand foyer where another set of oak doors were, along with cameras disguised in an exquisite French chandelier.

Upon entry through the second set of doors, country music met her ears, which indicated either Sunshine or Baby were up. On stage, Baby, a voluptuous chestnut-brunette, twirled a lasso as her double D breast swung in unison to the sound of the music and the catcalls from the men in the shark pool. Lexy stopped at the reception desk to check in. While talking to staff, Marcus came up from behind and touched her shoulder.

"Hey, Baby Doll," he said.

She turned to face him. "Hey, you," she replied, and kissed him lightly on the lips, trying to make up for snapping at him earlier.

He gazed at her with concern. Even a stranger could tell Marcus' heart belonged to her.

Reading his expression and ignoring the puppy dog look on his face, she replied, "I'm fine, Marcus. So, what's going on? How are we looking?"

Pushing back his personal feelings, he began his report as they walked. "Friday night ended well. Some of the girls complained about the increase in house dues, but seeing how the club is undergoing a facelift, I told them to shut the fuck up or go work elsewhere.

Lexy stifled a grin. It was unlike Marcus to cuss. He was terrible at it, so she found it hard to take him seriously when he did.

He continued, "The two new limos will be here next week. I'm still working on the funding for the last two. Within a few months, we'll have a new fleet. I hired a new bartender. The flash drive is in your box. Cookie quit, and Kat hasn't shown up for her shift." He finished by taking his over-priced glasses off his face, something done more out of habit than necessity.

They bypassed an elevator and walked up the staircase to reach Lexy's office. Marcus closed the door behind them, causing the music to become a muffled, distant rhythmic succession of "thumps."

Marcus watched her settle in behind her desk, light a cigarette, cock her head to the side, and rub the side of her neck. While massaging, she looked down and away with her eyes closed. Marcus began to feel sexually turned on at the unintentionally seductive way she moved. Despite having vaginas around him all the time, he wanted to make love to her and only her. It had been three months since they slept together, and he was beginning to wonder if this really was the end. Lexy had warned him many times but had always come back to him. Now, something was different.

Her voice pulled him away from his private thoughts.

"I said, would you like a drink?"

"Oh, sorry…uh no, I'm fine. I'm on water tonight." Without offering any explanation, he headed to the minibar to pour her one.

Lexy eyed him. He always had a drink with her at the start of her shift.

"So, wasn't Kat scheduled to come in late? An out of town friend, right?" she asked.

"Yes, that's what's weird about it. She didn't have to come in until nine. I tried calling, but I didn't get an answer."

"Did Cookie say why she quit?"

"She mentioned something about trying her luck in Vegas." He handed her a glass of wine and then walked over to the security monitors to survey the club.

"I see. Well, if Cookie stays in contact, let her know she is welcome to come back. I wish she had given proper notice, but she was a good employee. I'll let her back, assuming her looks and her frame of mind are intact. You know how that Vegas thing goes. As far as Kat is concerned, she knows she's walking a fine line. Call a few girls off the blonde list and see if someone can come in, just in case. I don't want to risk being short a blonde on a Saturday night."

"Yah betcha, Baby Doll," he said in a mocked Fargo accent before departing and leaving a light trail of cologne behind him.

As he walked away, she admired him. His presentation spoke first class. He was older than her, but at the age of fifty-five, he was holding his own. Exercise was not his thing, so his waistline was beginning to match his hip-width, which made him appear shorter than his five-foot-ten-inch frame. His hands were soft—a sign he never did a day of hard labor in his life—and his heart even softer. Though average in looks, his immaculate choice of wardrobe and meticulous attention to personal hygiene made him dashingly handsome. This, along with his intelligence, conservative manners, and kind demeanor, was more appealing to Lexy than most of the arrogant, rich men she hosted.

Despite not wanting a committed relationship with Marcus any longer, Lexy could not imagine life without him. He was the only man she trusted. Now, more than ever, she needed her second-in-command.

Lexy sipped her Pinot Noir and took a drag of her cigarette, irritated at herself for her unhealthy habits, yet, desperately needing the dysfunction. Even though she was more in control than in the past, she knew addiction plagued her. No matter how rich she was; no matter how much her exterior screamed success; and no matter how cool, calm, and collected she appeared on the outside, inside she screamed for mercy from the many bottles of wine; from too many cigarettes; and from too many nights of lack of sleep over the last twenty plus years. The body and the mind could only take so much, and she knew it.

Lexy tucked away her thoughts of Marcus and her assessment of her issues and dialed Kat's number. If Kat answered, she hoped TL was not near. Yes, he supplied good dancers for the club, but she did not care for his character and the way he strong-armed his women. Lexy understood his legacy—being born of a pimp and a prostitute—

nevertheless, he left an above-average bitter taste in her mouth. TL's fake charm and heartlessness did not escape her; however, he was an expert at what he did, and she surrounded herself with experts. It was what it was.

Kat's voicemail came on. "You reached the number you called. Please leave a message."

She thought, *Fuck this bitch!* But, within seconds, tried calling and texting several more times. On her last attempt, the ringer went straight to voicemail. This was too bad. As much as she liked Kat, it was time to let her go.

Taking a pull of a newly lit cigarette, she sat for a moment looking at the security monitors. As she watched, her breathing came heavy, and she contemplated the effect cigarette smoking was having on her health. She promised herself that after the details of the club were worked out, she would quit. On one of the monitors, she watched a burly security guard escort a drunken patron out of the club.

The office phone rang.

"This is Lexy," she said in her signature, monotone voice, believing it was Kat calling her back.

"This is Rick, ten forty-five in the dressing room!" the assistant manager exclaimed with urgency.

"Did you call 911?!" she replied while bolting out of her office with the phone still in hand.

"Yes, they're on their way!"

Without missing a beat in her heels, Lexy took the stairs down like a river overflowing a dam. When she reached the bottom, she used the railing, flung herself in the direction of a door, and burst into the employee dressing room, breathing hard and scanning various sections of the spacious room. A group of dancers stood at the far end. Snatches of conversations reached her ears as she ran towards the crowd.

"That bitch dead," one of them said, her hand sitting high on her hip, the other hand waving back and forth with her head and eyes rolling in unison in an, "I told you so" manner.

"Yea, told that idiot to leave that shit alone," another dancer with butt implants sneered.

As Lexy broke through the crowd, Rick came into view. He had begun placing external defibrillator patches on the fallen dancer's bare chest to analyze for a shockable rhythm. No rhythm existed. The bluish tint of the girl's face and the heroin clinging to her nostrils said it all. Nevertheless, Rick and Lexy began CPR. The pair took turns trying to create enough cardiac exchange to bring her back. Sweat trickled down Lexy's face while she worked and counted, "One and two, and three, and four, and five and six..." *Where are the medics?*

After a full minute, Rick shouted, "Pulse check!"

No pulse. They continued their efforts.

Lexy recognized the fallen dancer, Sandy—stage name Wisdom—a girl from the affluent city of Minnetonka, west of Minneapolis. Sandy had wanted to get away from her wealthy family, and all they represented, but had no "true" hard luck or tragic story to explain why. Considered the "black sheep" of her siblings, she had jumped into the sexual entertainment lifestyle feet first, especially embracing heroin and ill-advised hook-ups with customers. This was the result. Her green dilated pupils stared up at Lexy as if to say, "I didn't know!"

By the time the paramedics arrived, Lexy knew there was no reviving Sandy. Of the dozen or so times Lexy had been in a CPR scenario, most victims had not survived. The few that did were the reason she never gave up administering aid. Laboring to catch her breath, the exhausted woman stood and backed away from the body.

"Fuckin' cigarettes," she muttered. Her sweat-soaked jacket clung to her back and she tasted makeup foundation, mingled with salty sweat, dripping onto her lips. "Damn, damn, damn!" she cursed through gritted teeth.

Emergency personnel began entering the dressing room. Making their way to the back, they tried not to glance at the almost naked women but failed. Bending over the deceased, a medic clicked his teeth as a flat line displayed on the heart monitor device. He checked in a second lead, but there was no change. His partner could not palpate a pulse. Neither medic was surprised at the outcome.

Sandy's death was only the beginning. It would be a long night filled with police statements, mandated city reports, and Sandy's family, if they chose to come. Lexy was relieved that Sandy's collapse had not occurred out on the floor with clients watching. Behind her, Lexy heard Marcus barking orders to the women standing around. He made his way to her side.

"And where the hell were you?" she asked in a flat tone.

"Madam, I was orchestrating the extraction of some heathens off the premises," he said, trying to sound upbeat. "So, who was it this time?" he asked, watching Lexy set her mouth in a hard-pressed line.

"It was Wisdom. I mean, Sandy Hill."

Marcus took off his glasses and wiped them and then took a second look. He whistled and then said, "Ewwe! Isn't she the rich kid?"

"I'm afraid so," Lexy responded warily.

Marcus noticed a few girls nearby trying to eavesdrop.

"I'm sure some patrons out there would like a dance. Who's up?!" he snapped.

Heeled feet scattered and bared breasts swung. The aroma of body wipes, lotion, and perfume mingled in the air with the odor of death as the girls busied themselves to get back to work. The dancers eased around the body on the floor. One woman commented that she did not want the stench of Wisdom on her and that the dead woman's ghost would make her lose money, so she headed to the showers. Two dancers argued over who would take the deceased girl's locker while a new employee walked away in horror. No one seemed to care about Sandy. Lexy glanced around the posh boudoir styled locker room that hosted spirits of other women like Sandy and then back down at the outline of the body, which was now covered with a sheet.

Did you need me? Did I miss something? she wondered and turned to Marcus, scared to ask the question. Still, she had to. It felt irresponsible if she did not. "Did we know she was using?"

"Lexy, don't." Marcus turned and faced her. "Don't do this. He tried to take hold of her hands. Irritated, she pulled away from him.

He sighed.

"There were some rumors. No more than any other whispers about what happens around here."

It bothered her that she was wondering if Sandy's death was her fault. In the past, these thoughts had never crossed her mind. Setting morality and ethics aside, everyone had the right to make their own decisions if they did not physically hurt someone else. Being a product of dysfunction herself, Lexy recognized, at times, her thoughts were irrational.

"Rest in Peace, Sandy Hill," she said, looking at the outline of the sheet.

"Rest in Peace," Marcus whispered.

For a moment, the activity around them disappeared. Then, Marcus disrupted the sullen moment. "Aren't you tired of all this?" he asked, tilting his head down and looking up over his glasses to look at her downcast eyes and then back at an officer taking a witness's statement near them.

"Not now, Marcus. Not now," she firmly warned and walked towards the police officer, leaving Marcus looking forlorn when a commotion at the dressing room door caught his attention.

A male voice cut through the air. "Don't touch me!"

"Sir, this is a crime scene. You cannot come in," the first responder told a man in his mid-thirties with strawberry-blonde hair.

"Don't you fucking touch me!" the man yelled.

An older woman dressed in refined clothing stood behind him with a blank expression on her face and tight lips.

"Can I help you?" Marcus asked as he approached the group.

"No! This place has done enough!" the man shouted, causing the police officer taking Lexy's statement to walk over to the group.

"Where is my sister? Where is she?" the irate man yelled.

"Sir, lower your voice," the officer commanded.

Wide-eyed, the man belted out, "Where is Sandy?"

"Please, let's step into my office," Marcus said and attempted to place a calming hand on the man's shoulder.

The physically fit man slapped Marcus' hand off his shoulder as he jerked his body away as if dodging a boxer's jab.

Sandy's mother broke her silence and firmly said, "Jason, let's go. We will meet them at the morgue. Let our lawyers handle this," and turned and walked away.

"This is not over!" he shouted before turning and following her.

Marcus watched them take leave. He did not know why, but Jason made him feel uneasy.

It was well after one a.m. when the dancers were allowed back into the dressing room. Pending the autopsy report, all physical evidence pointed to an overdose. Lexy's adrenaline rush was gone, and she felt tired and hungry. Because of the emergency with Sandy, the scheduling of the meeting with Vincenzo had been put on the back burner. Lexy told herself she would contact him after getting some rest.

CHAPTER 5

BEVERLY & SISTER SARAH
Saturday - 8 p.m.

Freshly showered and wearing a pair of white pajama shorts and an oversized pink t-shirt, Beverly sat on her queen-sized bed, finishing her scripture readings. She looked around the room, appreciating the eco-friendly decor of the Oriental bamboo theme, which felt calming and relaxing. It did not bother her that she was in bed early on a Saturday night. On the contrary, the long afternoon with Kat had provided emotional and physical fulfillment. Getting into bed early felt like a positive way to end the night.

After talking with her mother and checking her social media accounts, Beverly settled in and started channel surfing. Nothing of substance was on television, so she decided to call her prayer partner, Sister Sarah. Praying was not on the top of her agenda; however, she felt it was better than watching mindless TV. Plus, the incident at the gym weighed on her mind, which gave her another valid reason for prayer. Just as she was going to hit the TV power off button, a newscaster announced the upcoming White Out Ball at Lexy's Gentlemen Club. Media footage played from last year's ball.

Beverly watched Lexy pose on a red carpet wearing a white, fringed roaring twenties flapper's dress. "Wow!" she said in disbelief, taking in the woman's physique and sophisticated aura. Her cell phone rang on the bedside table, taking her attention away from the story about the ball. "Hi, Sister Sarah, I was just about to call you."

"Hi, sweetheart, the Lord told me to call you, too. I see we are on the same spiritual path." The elderly woman chuckled heartily before continuing. "Well, praise God. How is your trip going?" Another hearty chuckle followed.

"Things are going great! I'm enjoying time with my best friend. I've picked up some modeling work, and I'll be attending my childhood church in the morning. God is truly blessing!"

"Amen! Amen!" Sister Sarah agreed.

"How is your family?" Beverly asked.

"We are doing well. John is at a deacon's convention. The kids are out back. I was just sewing on the children's church program costumes and cooking dinner."

"Oh, I don't want to hold you up," Beverly said apologetically. I was going to call to say hello and to see if you would pray with me. But if you are busy…um."

"Honey child, nonsense, nonsense. I surely don't mind any, just as the sun don't mind rising each day. It's never a bother to do the Lord's work. Besides, I need a break. The meatloaf is in the oven, and I'm 'bout done with these robes. Lord, Jesus, my eyesight and crooked hands need a break." Sister Sarah followed with her standard hearty chuckle. "What's on your heart, baby?" she asked, her Southern accent extra heavy on the word "baby."

Beverly stammered. "Err…well…umm…today, at the gym… let's see…I-I've had my first struggle with…my flesh. He was so handsome and smelled so good. It was difficult to be around him."

"I see. I see. Sister Beverly, hold on a moment, honey."

There was a brief pause as Sister Sarah set the phone down and grabbed her Bible. Upon returning, Beverly could hear pages turning. When Sister Sarah finally picked the receiver back up, she asked Beverly to write down Corinthians 10: 13 and Romans 6: 11—13.

"Ok," Beverly replied, as she jotted down the scriptures on a hotel note pad retrieved from the nightstand.

Then, without warning, Sister Sarah began to pray, so Beverly placed the cell phone on speaker mode, closed her eyes, and lifted her hands.

"Lord, we come to you humbly, giving thanks that your communication line is always open. We know, Father, that your son has shed his blood for us, and we are grateful…"

Sister Sarah continued praying, and Beverly occasionally added an "amen" or "yes" to support and acknowledge the prayer. By the end of the prayer, both women's voices had gone from a hushed whisper to enthusiastic shouts, with intermittent interjections of halleluiah. This went on for a few more minutes, and then Sister Sarah's volume began to decrease, which in turn prompted Beverly to lower her tone. Sister Sarah ended the prayer with, "…keep her pure in mind, body, and spirit, Father. Lord, give her the strength to withstand the temptation of her flesh. Give her strength, Father, because she wills to do your work. We thank you, in the mighty name of Jesus. Amen."

Eyes closed and hands extended to the ceiling, Beverly repeated, "Yes, Lord. Yes, Lord."

After the emotions of the moment died down, Sister Sarah stressed again for Beverly to study the scriptures and then bid her goodnight.

Beverly glanced at the clock. It was nine p.m., and she was sure that's when Kat said she had to start work. Before settling in for bed, she said a special prayer for Kat and then turned out the lights. She was glad she had been obedient and called Sister Sarah.

* * *

When Sister Sarah hung up, she knew her praying was not over. First, she called her boys in from the backyard to eat dinner, fixed their plates, and instructed them not to disturb her for a moment. The children knew their mother was going into her prayer closet and knew this was not a time to misbehave. Impeded by her weight and age, slowly and carefully, she went in the basement, lit a candle, and knelt before a table covered with white linen, a Bible, and a bottle of anointment oil. Sister Sarah had a strong faith and belief system, so she was not sure why she had such an uneasy feeling in her stomach. Something did not feel right. Kneeling at the table, she began to pray for Beverly.

TL & MARIA
Saturday - 9 p.m.

With a full moon anchored high over the city of Minnetonka, a shiny, black Bentley drove slowly up a long gravel road, which eventually gave way to an asphalt driveway in front of a Cape Code styled mansion. When the machine parked, an attendee opened the door and assisted Maria out of the hand-stitched leather seat. Her large breasts lead the way, followed by TL.

Upon entry into the impressive house, soft music from the talents of a young man in a black tuxedo who played soothing music on a Baby Grand piano greeted the ostentatious guests. Subdued chatter from the conservative elite competed with the music as staff dressed in black and white moved throughout the space attending to the guests. Most of the hundred-plus guests were Caucasian, except for a sprinkle of minorities. TL and Maria were two of those sprinkles.

The couple went through a receiving line in a massive foyer like one would expect at a palace. Wait staff took their invitations, received Maria's summer shawl, offered hors d'oeuvre, handed out beverages, and gave directions to the facilities. TL and Maria stood out—he in a black-on-black semi-formal suit and she in a scarlet floor-length gown that clung to her curves. Their elegant dark clothing contrasted against the bright colors of the light summer causal suits and Easter styled spring dresses the other attendees wore. Despite the couple appearing like they did not get the dress code memo, the other guests looked out of place. One might have thought TL and Maria were the hosts.

* * *

Maria had come to Minnesota, via Albuquerque, New Mexico, to help her sister care for their terminally ill grandmother. TL, ulterior motives prevailing, had locked in on the unsuspecting Latina in a convenience store and followed her to the pharmacy department. Not only was she beautiful, but also needy, vulnerable, and jobless, three factors that worked harmoniously in his world of investments.

Immediately, he set out to become Maria's new boyfriend, coming into her and her sister's lives like a savior on a white horse. TL paid medical bills and bought the highest-quality medicines and supplies insurance did not cover for the ailing elderly Gonzalez. Maria's older sister, Estelle, had viewed the handsome black man, whose teeth seemed a little too perfect, with skepticism. However, when she saw measurable improvements in her grandmother's hospice care, she conceded and allowed him to continue helping to preserve their grandmother's quality of life.

It had been three months since TL came into their lives, and over that period, Ms. Gonzalez's illness had started taking its toll. Since the grandmother would not be around much longer, TL decided it was time to set Maria up for the long haul. The idea of her returning to Albuquerque to rejoin her family was of no concern to him, nor was he concerned as to whether Maria would choose her family over him. He had a good track record of becoming a woman's everything. With an audition secured at Lexy's for her, he was positive a new stream of income was on the horizon.

* * *

The glamorous home they were in belonged to a wealthy real estate developer by the name of Jordan Glass. TL believed the party would be an effective way to see how Maria performed around socialites. So far, except for making her throw away her gum, she was doing well. At nineteen, he could not expect perfection from her. Spotting Jordan across the room, TL steered Maria by her elbow towards the billionaire. "Just follow my lead, and don't say anything stupid. You feel me?" he whispered in her ear.

Nodding, Maria followed. In her head, her heavy Spanish accented voice rehearsed what TL had instructed her to say. Equally important, she had to remember that her stage persona was Jordache.

"Jordan, my man!" TL's confident voice boomed out, followed by his thousand-watt smile. "Everyone that's anyone is here! Yes, indeed!"

Jordan replied with equal enthusiasm, "TL!" and accepted TL's outstretched hand.

"Glad you and…" Jordan smiled at Maria, holding the suspended handshake on pause between them.

"Aw," TL said slyly, noting the excitement on Jordan's European face as the wealthy man looked at the young woman before him. "This is Jordache. Jordache, this is Mr. Jordan Glass."

Jordan's smile grew wider as he pulled his shoulders back and chest out to impress the young girl with his cosmetically enhanced body parts.

"Hello, thank you for having me in your home. It is a pleasure to meet you, Sir," she demurely stated in hard to understand English, holding her hand out for him to shake, which caused him to drop TL's hand and take hers, instead.

He ceremoniously bent down and kissed the top side of her hand and then said, in a quasi-perverted tone, "Jordan and Jordache, I like, I like…" Rising back up, he brought her hand to his mouth and kissed it again before saying, "…hmmm, but, please, none of that sir stuff. I'm already a man of a certain age. Let's not speed up the train."

Maria let out childlike giggles, which caused her milky breast mounds to bounce with each succession of laughter. Her round, youthful face glowed, and her large brown, gold-flecked eyes sparkled. She cocked her head down, demurely looked up at Jordan through black, silk laden mascara lashes. Jordan's gaze traveled down her smooth face and took in her full mouth, briefly fantasizing about her cherry-colored stained lips giving him a slow, sensual blowjob. Watching her delicately licking her lips, his penis hardened.

TL laughed, "You look like you want to discuss business." He smirked, enjoying seeing the hustle unfold.

"Definitely, definitely," Jordan responded, still holding Maria's hand, and not taking his eyes off her.

TL turned towards her and tenderly said, "Baby, excuse us for a few minutes. Go try some of the expensive food Mr. Glass has floating around this palace.

"Okay, Papi," she cooed and kissed him on the cheek, then tossed her long thick, wavy black hair with the upper side of her hand.

Sauntering away from the two men, Maria unknowingly gave Jordan a reason to get further excited when he viewed her peach-shaped plump derriere. The aroma of vanilla musk lingered after her. Jordan struggled further to control his erection.

"So, are we going to talk business, or what?" TL asked, taking bottled water off the tray of a passing waiter.

"Yes, most definitely," the real estate tycoon said before leading TL to a back office.

* * *

After his meeting with Jordan, TL found a comfortable seat in a lounge area in a corner of the main room. Having sent Maria out to mingle, he watched her from afar, careful to watch the men's expressions as she made her way around the great hall. The men, he noticed, tried to hide their attraction to her. At the same time, their women hung protectively on their arms, unaware that the perceived threat—Maria—would be the reason the middle age couples would go home and have the best sex they have had in years. And, as instructed, Maria told the men—out of earshot of their significant others—to come to see her dance at Lexy's.

Glancing at his diamond watch, TL realized the time allocated for the event had expired. He caught Maria's eye and nodded for her to return to his side. He pulled her close and nuzzled her neck, causing her to throw her head back with a throaty laugh. He could not wait to get her back to the hotel.

"Baby, I don't want this night to end. Let's go celebrate," he whispered in her ear, even though no one was within earshot.

"You know I like notten better, Papi," she replied in her thick accent.

"You know what time it is," he whispered and steered her by the waist towards the coatroom.

* * *

It was midnight when TL and Maria arrived at the Ambassador Suites Hotel. Once in the room, they enjoyed a sensual shower, during which time TL enjoyed her oral skills. After the shower, she donned a red camisole and thong set he had bought as a gift he decided red would be Maria's professional working color.

As they sat on the bed, the exotic scent of her Moroccan wash wafted through the air, sending an inviting erotic cue to the masculine man. The champagne coursed through her veins, giving her a warm, fuzzy feeling, thus making her receptive to anything the pimp had to offer. He pulled her into his arms and buried his face between her well-endowed breasts, working his way with light kisses up her soft neck. Maria's world erupted into a passion-filled fantasy. She tilted her head back to soak in the pleasure of his full lips. He trailed tantalizing kisses back down to her breast. Her nipples got hard.

With his left hand cupped behind her neck, he guided her down onto the bed. His right hand began traveling downwards while his fingers stroked her body. Maria's breaths came short and fast as moistness began to seep between her thighs. She let out a gasp as his fingers stroked between her legs through the fabric of her thong.

His penis swelled and throbbed against her leg. She arched her back and thrust her body against his fingers. Readjusting his hands, TL held Maria by the head and forced her gaze up towards him as they lay across the bed. The soft whisper of his deep voice took her out of her dreamlike daze and grabbed her attention. "You know you're mine forever, right?" he whispered.

"Yes, Babee! Yes! Please!" her passion-filled, husky voice begged, "Please, you make love to me, Papi?" she whined. Then, she reached for his penis while simultaneously guiding two of his fingers into her open, moist mouth. Maria began seductively sucking his fingers as she stroked him.

As he watched her red lips go up and down on his fingers, his erection grew larger, harder. Not wanting her in charge of the contract closing, he withdrew his fingers from her mouth and embraced Maria in a long, deep tonguing session. Their lips locked as they explored each other's mouths. He separated from her, leaving her writhing on the high-count bed sheets and donned a condom.

Her gasp echoed in the room when he entered her. Slowly, he began stroking while embracing her and placing all his weight on her. TL gently locked her head in his muscular arms and began whispering passionately into her ear, making sure he continued with the purposeful slow, deep stroking. "You so good, girl." His words were soft, yet manly. "Yes, it's good, baby, hmm. It's good, baby," he said, his words coming out like a low growl. "There is no turning back. You're mine. Do you hear me? Mine."

He continued stroking in silence.

"Jess…oh…jess…, baby, jess," she gasped, barely able to speak; her English not translating well in the heat of passion.

Speaking directly in her ear, he whispered, "Tell me." He entered her deeper.

"Yes, babe, I'm chours. I'm chours!" she relented as her pelvic rhythm caught stride with his, and they began to pump in unison.

"Don't let anybody in my pussy. You feel me?" TL said while raising Maria's legs up over his shoulder and giving her the rest of him.

"Oh…jess, babee, jess…Luv me!" she conceded.

TL continued to do what he did best, giving Maria multiple orgasms, making her feel like she had the sweetest sex in the world, and stroking her body through the night, which she enjoyed immensely. This was TL's profession; he did his job well. During the wee hours of the morning, as she drifted off to sleep, TL called out her name in the darkness.

Before he could ask, she groggily replied in Spanish, "I know, babee. There's no turning back. I'm chours."

TL smiled. *Kat had better get her shit together.*

Thirty minutes later, with Maria's back to him, and his body pressed against her plump butt, he began to get an erection again. He put a condom on and glided back into her still warm box as if he had been there a thousand times. A moan escaped her lips, and she pressed back to meet his thrust. He buried his face in her warm sweet neck and reached around to cup her oversized breast. *God, she feels good!*

On this round, TL finally satisfied himself, having completed the task of satisfying Maria several times that evening and well into the a.m. hours. Upon completion, he drifted off to sleep feeling content, calculating financial increases as he did.

Meanwhile, Maria lay next to him, faking sleep.

Finally, a man worth marrying and having babies with!

She believed him to be a man that would love her unconditionally and take care of her better than any of the locals she grew up with in

Albuquerque. In her mind, dancing at Lexy's would be temporary. The focus of her life was to take care of her grandmother and, now, take care of her new man. If dancing helped their relationship, then she decided it was a transient phase worth entering and justifiable because it was not prostitution. Despite knowing about Kat and believing there were no others, Maria felt the lovemaking that night assured her he would be letting Kat go.

After making sure TL was sleep, Maria got out of bed. She retrieved the used condoms that had been carelessly discarded on the carpet and the side table, something she had done many times over the last three months when she slept with him. In the bathroom, she prepared the needleless syringe. Yes, Maria had plans for TL.

CHAPTER 6

KAT
Sunday - 5 a.m.

With the task of smoking complete, Kat could no longer tolerate the environment. The walls of the room felt smaller than when she entered. Humid dampness and smoke clung to her clothes, skin, and hair, making her feel suffocated and dirty. After looking at the time on her phone, she tried stretching her long legs, which were cramped between the space of the sunken couch and the pseudo coffee table, while pulling her sundress down and holding her purse protectively against her body.

Rumbling snores from Taz, which were slightly louder than the acid tone of Jackie's rambling, one-way dialogue, permeated the hazy room. Big Mike stood looking out the small, filthy window by pushing aside the contaminated curtain towel. Out of the corner of her eye, Kat watched a large roach scurry with confidence across the cracked, cement floor.

"You guys hear that?" Big Mike asked, standing on his toes to peer through the dirty window. When no one answered, he turned to the occupants of the room and repeated, "You guys hear that?"

This annoyed Kat, and she wished he would sit down. Jackie continued holding her solo conversation. Kat had no idea what she was talking about, nor did she care. She only knew that her head was beginning to hurt, and she was through getting high.

One more smoke.

It had been twenty minutes since her last toke, and she was hoping the feeling of euphoria would return. Kat took the hit and felt nauseated at once. In the meantime, Jackie droned on, debating the pros and cons of the best type of drug paraphernalia to use for various substances. The oblivious woman did not notice Kat holding her hand to her mouth to stifle vomit.

"I'm going to get going," Kat said aloud and then stood up slowly to leave the toxic room.

Jackie said good-bye, Taz snored louder, and Big Mike continued looking out the window.

* * *

The morning chirping and chattering of the communicating fowl of the air set the blueprint for a beautiful summer day, a stark contrast from the dark atmosphere from which Kat emerged from. Squinting, the fair-skinned woman dug around her purse for sunglasses. She exited the somber home, fearful the canine next door had gotten loose from his restraint. Having spent the last several hours barking, the dog slept next to a large tree, no longer concerned with his job of intimidating the community.

Once in her vehicle, Kat sat for a moment with the windows down and took several deep breaths. Then, despite needing fresh air in her lungs, she lit a marijuana cigar to calm down the cocaine-induced paranoia. The stimulant in her system had agitated her, and Kat could feel her heart palpitating in her chest. Within a few moments, the mellow effect of the marijuana rolled over her, and she felt a little better. Before driving out of the urban-decayed alley, she turned down the volume of the already low music and put a piece of gum in her mouth. As she drove, the pain in her head continued, and the reality of what she had done began to fully dawn on her.

"Dammit," she muttered while creeping down the barren side streets—regular nighttime residents of the poverty-ridden neighborhood having just gone to sleep themselves, which gave the Northside an illusion of safety.

Frustrated at having blown two hundred dollars on crack, which had now given her a two-hundred-dollar headache, Kat pondered the consequences of her reckless behavior. She had lost her job and had set herself up for a beating by TL. Stubborn tears swelled on the rims of her eyes, but the numbness of the drugs prevented an unchecked deluge of salted water from coming forth. Emotional instability continued to seep into her psyche during the anxiety-ridden drive Eastbound to St. Paul, towards the sun, and into her prestigious upper-class downtown community near the Mississippi River. Jumbled thoughts tumbled in her head as she pulled into the underground garage.

It took ten minutes for her to find the courage to get out of her vehicle and navigate her way through the garage and back lobby to the elevator. Spending a minute standing outside her front door, angling her body away from the fixed cameras in the hallway while pretending to search for the keys in her purse, she let out a long breath and prepared to enter.

Kat crept in and closed the door softly behind her. She scanned the dining and living room areas, using the emerging light from the wall to wall smart glass windows—concerned TL would appear from the shadows and hit her when least expected. With her heart racing and the pain in her head returning, Kat tiptoed. Her movements resembled that of a deer in a forest that had just heard leaves crunched, which resulted in a series of minute inches forward due to her anxiety. Standing at the bedroom door—with nausea returning in the pit of her stomach—the back and forth debate began again, ending with the decision to go in and face the music. Her hand went to the door handle.

What was that?

The rhythmic sound of her own blood in her ears dominated the silence of the moment.

Is that movement, or is that my imagination?

Kat turned the knob and opened the door slowly. Through the crack, she peered into the blacked-out room. It took a moment for her dilated pupils to adjust to an even darker environment. There was no way of telling if TL was in bed. It was now or never. Kat slipped into the room, walked a few steps forward and tripped on high heels carelessly left on the floor, thus, falling forward and landing on the bed. Scrambling, she jumped back off the bed in two quick motions, bracing herself for an angry outburst. To her astonishment, there was none.

Kat turned on the light, revealing an empty room. Hesitantly, she made her way towards the bathroom and stood at the door, listening to the heartbeat in her chest and glancing around the edges of the door looking for light. The seals of the door were dark. "TL," she whispered and entered the bathroom, exposing a vacant bathroom.

Kat responded quickly to her newfound situation like a track star running for gold by stepping out on the balcony of the high rise and taking a couple hits of a joint to help her sleep and rejoicing that she had avoided another beating. It had not crossed her mind as to where TL was or what time he had left. A check of her voicemail revealed Marcus and Lexy had left messages, but no word from TL. After taking a quick shower and running a toothbrush across her smoke coated teeth, she decided to take a gamble and return Lexy's call.

"Hello, Lexy, this is Kat. Did I wake you?"

"What time is it, Kat?" Lexy groggily asked. Kat could hear her fumbling and muttering under her breath.

"Oh…um…, Lexy?"

Lexy spoke calmly and expediently, catching Kat off guard.

"Kat, there isn't anything to discuss. Clean your locker out."

Kat's headache came back.

"I can explain, please," Kat begged, hoping she did not sound high.

"I've had enough of your shit," Lexy replied, careful not to raise her voice.

"Please, Lexy," Kat whined, "I can't lose my job, not now…"

"You should have thought about that when you were missing your shift."

Kat started sobbing.

On the other end of the phone, Lexy frowned. "Dammit, Kat. Meet me in my office at ten tonight. I'm warning you." Her voice rose, "If you're not on time, don't show up. You're barred. Don't come in Lexy's again!"

"Oh, I promise…"

The phone went dead.

It was seven a.m. Kat lay in bed, tossing and turning, contemplating what to do about Beverly and the scheduled three o'clock meal with her. She reasoned she could get six hours of sleep, get up at one, and order Chinese takeout for delivery—contingent on

TL not breezing in and ruining her day. Reflecting on what she had been through that night, she promised herself never to return to Big Mike's place. The remorseful woman climbed out of bed and went to the kitchen to retrieve a glass of water to take a sleeping pill. Looking in the bedroom mirror at her bloodshot eyes and down at the *TL$* symbol tattooed on her bony hip, the pain of living felt unbearable.

Why am I so weak? Why? Damn crack... I need sleep. I need help, I need help. I'm so tired. No point of living...just do it!

Not sure if the front door opened and closed, she slipped back into bed. Lying in the darkness, the feeling of sadness consumed her. Her thoughts shifted randomly from subject to subject.

I don't want to live anymore. How am I supposed to see Beverly? I'm tired. I'll never be normal.

Kat lay in bed with tears rolling from the corners of her eyes and into her ears. Her body began wracking with grief as the effort to hold back muffled anguish escaped from her tightly pursed lips. Rolling over to TL's side of the bed, she pulled a revolver from the end table drawer and sat up. Slowly, fueled by drugs and alcohol, the despondent woman raised the gun.

"I'm sorry, Momma!" she cried out.

With the barrel to her temple, she closed her eyes and squeezed the trigger.

Nothing happened.

Confused, through weary eyes, she looked the gun over and then took the safety off it before placing the weapon back to the side of her head. Her hands trembled and shook violently, causing her trigger finger to put stress on the trigger.

"Oh, God! Help me!" she cried out, letting her hand fall, and releasing her grip on the handle. The gun slid to the bed. Kat took her pillow and stuffed it in her mouth and screamed, choking back as much despair as she could that erupted from the depth of her soul.

This went on for several minutes before the energy to sustain the emotionally draining activity tired her out. With swollen eyes and a flushed face, Kat picked up the gun. *I can't even do this right.* She placed the weapon back in the drawer on TL's side and then lay back in bed, letting the sleep medication take control.

BEVERLY
Sunday - 8 a.m.

As Kat drifted off to sleep from her failed suicide attempt, Beverly had just returned from a two-mile jog along the Mississippi River. The vacationing woman turned off the timer on her smart watch and sat on the plush carpet in her room to stretch through various yoga poses. When she got to the meditation part of the Hindu practice, it did not go well. Beverly could not concentrate. She kept seeing his smooth chocolate face, so she abandoned the spiritual science and began to prepare for church. The problem also plagued her in the shower. The warmth and steam lulled her away into dreamy subconscious thoughts. Her mind flashed an erotic image of her and the man from the gym caressing each other in the shower. Beverly shuddered.

Trying to ignore her mounting pent up sexual frustrations, she exited the shower sooner than she would have liked and slathered herself with baby lotion before putting on a white, cotton short-sleeved dress and low-heeled white sandals. Beverly hurried through a continental breakfast and then headed out the door with her Bible tucked under her arm.

* * *

The church, a large dull-white two-story building, resembled a renovated government facility, rather than a house of God, and looked in need of an exterior paint job. Beverly proceeded up the thin, slightly lop-sided cement steps and approached a set of whitewashed doors attended by two smiling ushers. Inside, from the twenty-foot ceilings supported by Roman-style pillars, to the double-wide marble steps that led to the main sanctuary, and the wall-sized portraits of the pastors on the walls, the interior design did not match the exterior and appeared to be overkill.

On the upper level, and inside an outer hall, an elderly woman in a pink suit handed Beverly a bulletin, and a male usher, who she recognized from her youth, escorted her to her seat. He extended his white-gloved hand towards the row for her to sit in and whispered, "Hello, Sister Beverly."

Beverly smiled. It felt safe and comforting in the sanctuary, which reminded Beverly of her youth. Stained glass windows surrounded the occupants, and rays of colorful light beamed into the angelic space. From the white lilies and potted plants lining the stage to the twenty-foot crucifix suspended in the air on invisible wires above the podium, the interior of the church showcased an old-world charm filled with history.

Looking up, Beverly examined the peaked ceiling and smiled as she took in the beauty of the intricate art carvings. She imagined it must have taken years of detailed labor to construct. During their childhood, Beverly and Kat had made it a game to count the patterns on the ceiling whenever the sermon for the day was too long and articulate for the two-elementary student's attention span. This often occurred on the first Sunday when communion took place, and the youth of the church remained in adult service.

The lyrics of the song "He Is My Rock" played on cinematic monitors positioned on each side of the stage. Beverly took a few minutes to take in the atmosphere, absentmindedly clapping to the song, letting her spirit settle in. After a moment of taking a few discreet glances around, she joined the others and sang along with the congregation.

The leader of the five-person praise team broke rank from the other praise singers and stepped forward to encourage participants, "My rock when I'm tired, my rock when I'm sad, my rock when I'm lost!" The singer's tempo picked up, and the band caught its stride. This went on for several minutes; people began to leave the pews and dance freely in the aisle and in front of the stage. Up front, a loud, "Yes, Lord!" rang out. A woman began jumping up and down, flaying her hands about like a demonic spirit possessed by an angel. Ushers fanned the emotionally charged churchgoer and aided her back to the pews as the merriment atmosphere of clapping, swaying, shouting, and rejoicing continued. Moans, pleas, and random hallelujahs from the men and women swirled with the mixture of the band's effort and the powerful vocals, which created a cult-like atmosphere.

The abandonment of a structured service continued well past the allotted time as the congregation praised and worshiped in unison. A row of conservative Caucasian students, visitors from a neighboring Christian college, looked on in both awe and concern while the African American churchgoers moved about unconstrained in their response to the pulsing of the live instruments.

Slowly, the music pulled back to a soft rumble until it subsided, a cue for a staff member to approach the podium and begin morning pleasantries, visitor recognitions, and announcements. To Beverly's delight, the announcer welcomed her home and encouraged her to address the congregation. Humbly she stood, thanked the Lord for being there, and gave respect to the pastors and the congregation before gushing about how happy she was to be back. Next, the dance ministry leader introduced a special guest.

The lights went dim; the sanctuary became quiet. A spotlight illuminated a young African American woman dressed in a tight fitted, long-sleeved white chiffon bodice with an overabundance of laced petticoat under a full white skirt, white satin gloves, and white satin ballet shoes. With her hair in a severe bun, the dancer looked like a professional performer from a world-renowned ballet company. The pre-recorded song "Whiter than Snow" began, and the woman's arms moved gracefully to the music.

As Beverly watched the dancer use pantomime, sign language, and ballet to bring the song to life, she held her breath and kept her eyes glued to every movement. The praise dancer mouthed the words to the song and began gliding from her position in the middle of the stage; the spotlight followed and continued to illuminate the expressions on her face. The audience silently watched.

As the music progressed, the princess gowned figure's movements became explosive. When the song peaked, so did the praise dancer's movements. Her motions became twirls, leaps, and kicks, each expression on her face matching the pleading of the singer's voice. Parishioners jumped to their feet. The desire for cleansing from sin evoked personal responses from many of the faithful and hopeful church members. Awestruck, Beverly reminded herself to breathe. Applauses continued to go forth as the performer illustrated the strong points of the song, ending by dropping to her knees and holding her tear-stained face to the ceiling, thanking the Lord for the gift of ministry.

Beverly's heart swelled with emotion. The movements of the dancer and the song conveyed many of her personal feelings. She longed for the absence of sin from her life, the desire to be a better person. The congregation stood and gave thunderous applauds, shouting "Glory" and "Hallelujah." Beverly stood, too, not registering the tears that slid down her own face until they dropped onto on her tightly clasped hands. Joining the others, she clapped enthusiastically with an open and raw heart.

The rest of the service went well. The Pastor's sermon, "Are You Living as an Example for Christ?" gave Beverly something to meditate on. Beverly took notes in the space provided in her bulletin, so she could study the sermon points later that evening. After service, Beverly spent time saying hello to members she knew—and smiled at those she didn't—before heading back to the hotel to freshen up for her lunch with Kat. Beverly looked forward to sharing the enjoyment of her morning with her sister. Three o'clock could not come fast enough for her.

LEXY
Sunday - 1 p.m.

The front doorbell chimed back to back. On the other side of the etched, frosted tempered glass, stood Marlene. Lexy opened the door. "Damn, girl. You trying to break my doorbell?"

Marlene sang out, "Good morning!"

"Whoa on the volume, chick," Lexy said, cupping her ear with one hand and holding the doorknob with the other.

Marlene leaped into the foyer. "Ah, just feeling good and ready to hit it! Do you want to run or lift first?" she asked, ignoring her sister's sour demeanor.

Lexy forced a grin. "You know I like to lift first. Come on; let me knock some of that spunk out of you."

* * *

When it came to Lexy's siblings, Tina, the eldest, and Marlene looked nearly identical—both were slimmer and taller than Lexy, while Lexy's physique had more density and detail—Lexy looked like the fraternal twin of the two. They all shared the same high angular cheekbones, square jawline, small, narrow set eyes, button noses, and nondescript lips. People often mistook the three as triplets despite the two-year age differences between Tina and Marlene and the twelve months between Marlene and Lexy—the latter being the youngest of the three.

Lexy preferred the company of Marlene over Tina, due to Marlene's non-judgmental attitude; whereas, Tina had assumed the unofficial role of the mother of the other two and tended to come off as prudish. Lexy considered Marlene to be her best female friend.

* * *

The women went through the kitchen and down into the finished basement, which consisted of both a theatre area and a complete mini gym, including a dance pole. They got on treadmills and began their ten-minute warm-up. Talking above the sound of the mechanics of the machines, Lexy asked, "How's the job going? You haven't been pissing and moaning lately."

"Not bad since that old fool Hanks left. You'd think we were slave labor the way that man had us working overtime. I'm glad we've updated our system, but he was paranoid. He kept saying that after his retirement, the Security and Exchange Commission would come after him if we didn't pass the audit."

"You know you need to speed that thing up."

"I'm getting there, Miss Olympic." Marlene pressed a button, and the treadmill picked up speed. "Anyway, he was running around, acting like an old ass. Hell, he barely knew how to get around the software, let alone turn his computer on." Marlene threw her arms up in exasperation, almost losing her balance on the equipment. "At the rate he had us going, I knew I'd never date again. Being in the office twenty-four seven was putting a cramp in my game."

"What game? Girl, your couchie got cobwebs. You know it's been a century since you had sex!"

Marlene frowned with disapproval and shook her head. "Couchie? You're not authorized to say that." The women laughed heartily, and then Marlene continued, "Oh, as if you're getting some. And, Marcus don't count. He's old news."

Wiping small beads of sweat from her forehead, Lexy replied, "Marcus and I are just friends."

The sisters walked in silence for another minute before Marlene spoke again, "So, are you still with, you know?"

Lexy scowled.

Marlene regretted the question, but since it was out there, she decided to pursue the answer.

"Well, are you?"

Irritated, Lexy shot back, "Why can't you say her name? It's Lisa!"

"Don't get your feathers in a tether girl. I know her name. You know me. I don't care about alternative lifestyles. I just want to attend your wedding and have a niece or nephew from you. I'm just being selfish."

"Yes, I still see Lisa," Lexy warily replied, stepping off the treadmill and walking over to the squat rack. "And we can have a wedding and children."

Marlene raised her eyebrows. "Is it that serious?"

"I'm trying to figure that out."

"What's to figure out? Either you know, or you don't."

"It's not that simple."

"Why not?"

"I'm not sure if she can handle the pressure of the lifestyle. I'm her first."

Marlene stepped off the treadmill. "Well, just tell her how you feel."

"I…plan to…um, there is so much going on. I'm waiting for the right time."

Marlene stepped under the iron weight bar and lifted it onto her upper back and shoulders. "Say, you know, Aunt Lilly has been asking about you."

Lexy did not reply.

"Don't you think things have gone far enough? I bet she doesn't remember the fight."

"Are you going to lift or talk?"

Marlene squatted, slowly. Lexy tapped under her chin, an indication for Marlene to lift her head and improve her form.

"She is ill, Lex. It's time you two patched things up. Aunt Lilly did the best she could to raise us when mom ran off."

Lexy added forty pounds to each side of the forty-five-pound bar. Concentrating on her form, she did not reply. After reaching a full squat, she stood up slowly, contracting her gluteus maximus through the entire range of motion.

Marlene tried again. "This is ridiculous, you know. We are family."

Bam!

Lexy forcefully placed the weighted bar on the holders and took an aggressive step towards Marlene.

"Oh, you think I'm being ridiculous?" Her tiny eyes narrowed. "Ridiculous is an aunt who plays favorites with her nieces! Ridiculous is an aunt who doesn't bat an eye when one niece gets pregnant at eighteen but shits a cow when I get pregnant at twenty-two just because of my profession! Let me give you ridiculous! How about an aunt who takes money from you but doesn't ever bother to say thank you! Don't get me started about her always going on about how mom let her down and what a shitty father we had as if I put the needles in their arms! Realizing her aggression, Lexy released her balled up hands and took a step back.

"Lexy…I'm…"

Lexy's perfectly arched eyebrows knitted together in irritation. "You're what? Sorry? You're always sorry. Why do you apologize so fucking much?"

Sheepishly, Marlene looked down.

"Just forget it, Marlene. Just forget it," Lexy said, sounding like the wind had left her sails. "You guys have selective memory of our shitty childhood, especially mine. Denial. Always in denial. Why couldn't I have been raised by a grandmother like most children with fucked up parents?" she muttered.

Marlene shoved her hurt feelings aside and placed her arm around Lexy's shoulders. The two sisters said nothing. After a few seconds, Lexy slid from beneath the arm and walked over to the heavy bag area where she secured her wraps and donned her gloves. Marlene hesitantly joined her, putting on her gear, too. Lexy took a boxer's stance and began punching the bag with powerful blows.

Whack! Whack!

Marlene, intending to fix things, tried to start a different conversation, but, in typical Marlene fashion, chose the wrong subject.

"Do you remember Grandma much? You were young when she passed. I barely remember her."

"Yes, I remember her a little. A few images here and there," Lexy said, realizing Marlene was trying to smooth things over. "I've told you this before," Lexy said.

Marlene tried taking jabs at the bag, while Lexy held it, and hurt her wrist in the process. Lexy looked on in amusement at her sister who tried to imitate her boxing technique and strength. The tension in the room eased and the women finished their workout while avoiding inflammatory topics. Afterward, Lexy opted out of having a protein smoothie with Marlene so she could send her along her way.

* * *

Later in her bedroom, Lexy found a yellow sticky note on her dresser that read Wood Hill Nursing Home. She recognized Marlene's scratchy handwriting and sighed out of annoyance. Marlene would not give up. Shaking her head, she went into her on-suite to take a hot bath. The gray and white marble floor pressed cold against her manicured feet as she stepped into the oversized garden bathtub filled with lavender-scented bubbles. A multitude of candles lined the marble ledge on the side of the tub under a large window, and Billie Holiday's melancholy voice played throughout the bathroom and the master suite. Inching herself slowly into the water, Lexy grimaced as the uncomfortably hot water touched her taunt, defined skin.

With her eyes closed and her head leaned back, she listened to the soulful sad music and mused over the bluesy song, wondering which of her personas—Alexandria or Lexy— matched its misery. Lexy's love-hate relationship with herself created constant inner conflict. Alexandria had a wonderful public persona in Lexy's professional life, but in her heart, Alexandria represented weakness and emotion. It was ironic that Lexy also knew that Alexandria was the cover to protect her from letting people know how awful Lexy really was. If they knew the real Lexy, the city would have run her out of the metro area long ago. She needed to manage her dual personalities to create balance to survive.

Damn, she thought, reflecting on some of the misfortunes of her life with the lyrics of the misfortune of the song while sinking further into the tub so that the water came up to her collarbone. Sweat dripped down her face and mingled with the wetness of the steamy water as the smell of the perfumed bubbles floated up to her nostrils. An hour felt like a minute in her favorite place to be.

Why is it that when you don't have time to soak, the water always feels the best?

Locking the world away is what she really wanted to do, but with her mind on the club, among other things, there was no way to do that. Eventually, she sat up and lit a cigarette. Her thoughts kept going back over the events of the last few days. Sandy's overdose was a serious matter, and she was sure she had not heard the last of it. She had to call Vincenzo. Then, there was Lillian. Despite her indifference towards her aunt, Lexy knew Lillian was the reason she had survived in the streets, and a part of her felt obligated to stand by the only mother she knew. She decided that it would be best to visit her, if for nothing more than to settle her own conscience, and check Lillian off her "to do" list. Retrieving the phone from her bath side table, she voice-dialed Vincenzo.

"Yeah!" Vincenzo gruffly answered.

"Hey, Vin. It's Lex."

"Yeah."

"Sorry, I'm late calling," she said apologetically.

"Yeah, let me get this straight. You missed the sit down twice, and now you call like it's okay, yeah? Who's the wise guy here, me or you?"

Lexy did not remember it that way. There was no scheduled "sit down" but a missed timeline; however, she knew not to bring up such a minute point.

Sounding as sincere as possible, she tried to smooth things over. "Vin, I have a lot going on. I didn't stand you up on purpose. There was a death at the club, and I have a family situation I'm trying to handle. I apologize. Can we talk this evening?" Listening to his heavy breathing, she waited for a reply.

"Oh, my Bella Bambino, I'd like to do more than just talk. You know what I mean?" He laughed at a joke he did not make.

Lexy frowned.

"But for now, business. If you don't fucka-with-me. You know what I mean?"

"Ah, come on, Vin Baby, it's me. We've shared these zip codes for twenty years. You know I'm a straight shooter."

The tone of her voice remained sincere. By using their long-standing relationship and stroking his ego, she knew she could buy time to keep herself safe; however, this approach would not last long.

"Midnight. The club," he stated with authority.

"Yes, I'll be there."

"Don't screw with me!"

"See you tonight, Vin."

Lexy sighed. Something was not right. Vincenzo managed a string of mediocre strip clubs from which he ran a lucrative prostitution ring, had a large stake in the drug trade and owned a couple of five-star restaurants. Why, out-of-the-blue, would he be interested in Lexy's? Were his legitimate operations not enough for money laundering? Her mind flashed back to the hardships that she had endured through the years and simmered anger boiled in the pit of her stomach.

Her cigarette had burned out, so she lit another, and then drank half of the bottle of water sitting next to her smokeless ashtray. The vein in her left temple throbbed intensely. Feeling it, she loosened the pressure of her jaws and caressed each side of them with her left hand, keeping the right hand high enough to prevent the bubbles from putting the cigarette out. Her thoughts swirled around the repeated concept of hurting him before he hurt her.

"Call Marcus," she spoke into her phone.

He picked up on the first trill. "Hello, Baby Doll. How are you?"

Skipping pleasantries, she got straight to the point. "I have a meeting set for Kat at ten, and Vincenzo will be by at midnight. Can you be in my office after Kat?"

"Yes, of course."

“Thanks. Okay, I’m going to get going. I’ll see you later tonight. Wish me luck. About to do a drive-by. Aunt Lilly.”

“Ouch! Aunt Lilly, whew! Make sure you have your bulletproof vest on.” He chuckled. “And don’t drink anything she offers you.”

Lexy smiled at their inside joke. “So noted. I’ll see you tonight.” She hung up the phone, pulled the hair tie off her braids, and slowly submerged under the water’s surface. Her micro braids fanned out like a peacock halo around her head.

I’m a dragon blowing fire underwater. I got this. After coming up, she laid her head on the edge of the tub and thought, languishing in the last of the warm water before getting out. *I need some rest. The Cayman Islands…Cayman…hmm! I’ll fix all these problems and then get rest…recharge…Lisa. Maybe invite Lisa.*

Again, she dunked her head under the water and lay with it submerged up to the corners of both eyes, causing the braids to fan out, making her look like an exotic mermaid resting near the surface. Feeling like life issues were beginning to form into workable chunks, Lexy started lathering up to finish her bath.

CHAPTER 7

KAT & TL
Sunday – Noon

TL barged into the bedroom and flicked on the light switch. The brightness invaded the darkened room as if the sun itself announced its presence. He did not see Kat in the bed. With sure steps, he picked up the window remote and opened the drapes and turned off the transition shade in two presses of a button. The noonday sun flooded the room and revealed Kat huddled under the blanket; her long limbs coiled into a ball like a butterfly in a cocoon. Even when he noticed her, he made no effort to be quiet. He never did.

Kat's eyes popped open in surprise, and her breathing stopped as if the lack of oxygen would make him disappear, and then resumed when the carbon dioxide in her lungs forced her to take a breath. A knot formed in her stomach from his presence. She waited for a barrage of questions to come her way, but the sound of heavy, retreating footsteps left her alone to agonize over expected confrontation.

TL turned on the shower.

As she lay in the bed, the downtown cathedral church's bell clanged to remind churchgoers that the sermon of the morning had ended.

Kat could hear TL singing as she pulled the covers off her head and peeped over the edge. His smooth vocals carried from the bathroom, revealing he was in a good mood. "Morning, Babe!" she called out.

"You alive, Pony?"

"Yeah, I'm sorry, I didn't get in till late. Me and a few girls went out and had drinks," she said with a raised voice so that he could hear her through the bathroom door.

"You have fun?"

Since when did he care if I had fun?

"Yeah, we did. Of course, Jade drank too much. I had to drive her home. Driving to Apple Valley was a pain."

Oh, shit, did I say too much?

"So, Babe, what did you do last night? I didn't hear from you."

Kat waited a minute or so for his reply.

"Jordan's event."

"How was it?"

"You know Jordan, classy."

Kat bit her lower lip. "Say, Babe, Beverly will be here at three for lunch. Would you like to meet her?"

He did not respond. TL always took his time to answer her; Kat waited patiently.

What's so hard about the question?

The door opened. TL stood dripping with his towel tossed over his broad shoulder, and his large penis swinging freely as he stepped to the double vanity sink where he took a moment to dry off. Kat watched him lovingly, forgetting last night's ordeal and how mean he could be. She admired his hard body and large organ, which appeared semi-erect despite being flaccid. Watching him shave, she forgot she was waiting on a reply; her brain was still foggy from the previous night's activity.

"So, that bitch came anyway?" he said casually, not missing a beat with his shaving. "Thought we talked about that shit."

Talked about it? You kicked my ass!

"Yeah, Babe, I tried leaving her a message, but she was already on the plane." Kat hesitated and then stammered, "I…I…know you'll like her. Bev won't be a problem. I promise," she said, and then looked down at the blanket.

TL continued shaving while Kat sat stressing, wishing he would answer. Finally, he said, "Naw, I'ma track down that dirty bitch, Cookie…up and quit Lexy's. Talking that shit ′bout going to Vegas and doing her own thing. I invested too much money in that bitch for her punk ass to just jump up and leave. That bitch owes me!"

Kat knew Cookie had been loyal to TL over the years, and he had gotten all his money back from her and then some. Saying he invested in a girl was his standard excuse to keep them. From his point of view, Cookie would owe him for life.

"My connect in Vegas tracked her down," TL said while continuing his grooming. "Shit, I'll probably have to fuck that stupid bitch all night."

Kat cringed.

Normally, it would not have bothered her to hear TL talk about the business, but lately, it was getting under her skin. The realization that she had never had a man to herself penetrated her heart like a red-hot fire poker. She no longer wanted to have her eyes shut wide open and felt exhausted from pretending her situation with TL did not manifest heartache.

"I gotta go to sin city and get that bitch," he said, wiping the last of the shaving cream off his neck with a white hand towel.

Kat inhaled sharply. A sense of relief washed over her but then turned to panic. Not sure what to do next, she sat in the bed feeling paralyzed because she did not want to say or do the wrong thing and create a negative situation with him. Unstable emotions surfaced, and sadness warmed over her.

I need a blunt! I need a smoke, shit!

Taking a few deep breaths, Kat unfolded her long legs from beneath her and slid gracefully out of bed, followed by her Rapunzel hair. The room spun. Using the king-size leather headboard, she steadied herself before making her way to the bathroom. With fear, she walked timidly past TL and stepped into the still moist shower that smelled of his body wash. Having had only four hours of sleep, the effort to cleanse felt laborious, which made her wish she had gotten more restorative rest. Kat made a pledge to herself to take a power nap after her lunch with Beverly—before her meeting with Lexy. The thought of her boss made her groan.

BEVERLY & KAT
Sunday – 3:05 p.m.

Impressed by Kat's living community, Beverly stepped out of her rental car and handed the keys to a young valet before continuing to a secured area between the external and internal lightly tinted doors. At the sound of a chime, the thick glass parted, and she stepped into a highly polished jade tiled atrium with four glass walls that seemed to disappear into the skylight, making it hard to discern between where the tempered glass ended, and the sky began.

On the right side of the lobby, an infinity waterfall streamed down the wall, giving the lobby a resort-like feel; and on the left side, an obnoxious sized fish tank dominated the space. From the soft music flowing through invisible speakers to the welcoming fragrance in the air, the spa-influenced lobby exuded serenity and peace.

A security guard sitting at a miniature command post checked her in and then directed her to the elevators located in the center of the atrium. Standing in front of one of the gleaming doors, she used her reflection to check her appearance—a white t-shirt, jean shorts, and a pair of white tennis shoes. Anyone looking at the young woman could have mistaken her for a teen. The elevator door glided open, and she stepped in for the ride to the penthouse level. Once at the top floor, the doors opened onto a professionally decorated commons area that looked like someone's living room surrounded by circular walls that housed four doors, one of which was Kat's.

Kat watched Beverly via security cameras. Several times, she checked her appearance in a mirror.

Do I look like a junkie?

The nervous host placed red relieving eye drops in her eyes and reapplied her already saturated lips with more red lipstick than necessary. Dressed in a yellow halter-top and yellow shorts and barefoot, Kat headed to the door wearing her freshly washed hair pulled back into a single ponytail. Large gold chandelier earrings dangled from her ears, she wore a total of six spiral gold rings on her fingers and a gold chain on her left ankle. Taking a deep breath, she put a big smile on her face and opened the door to the penthouse.

"Hey, Bird!" exclaimed Beverly, embracing Kat in the threshold of the door.

Once they broke apart, Kat guided her in with her arm around Beverly's slender waist.

"Wow! Look at this place!" Beverly stood near the front door taking in the panoramic view of the open-concept space bathed in black, white, and gray hues. The home looked like it floated on air due to the floor to the ceiling windows. "Can people see in here at night? I mean like if your lights are on and, let's say, someone has high powered lenses?"

"Nah, the windows are like one-way mirrors, and they transition to reduce the glare of the sun, depending on how we set them. We do have blinds in the bedroom, though. Sometimes at night, the city lights can be annoying."

"It smells good in here. Is that sweet and sour?"

"Yes. Sorry, though, it's take-out. I worked late and slept in, so I didn't cook," Kat partially lied and gave an apologetic look.

"No, that's fine, I'm famished. Church was great, but it sure can make you hungry. Girl, I don't mind takeout. You know that."

Kat bowed and waved her arm, motioning for Beverly to follow her. "Well, My Lady, I'll show you our humble abode, and then we'll feast."

After a quick tour, the first five minutes of the meal occurred in silence. Beverly's light breakfast and long morning contributed to her hungriness, and Kat had not eaten since her meal with Beverly the day before at the Grand Café. Once past the famished phase, with a mouth full of food, Kat inquired about Beverly's day.

Beverly's face lit up.

"Oh, Bird, it was a blessing. I enjoyed fellowship, the word of God, and the praise dancing."

"What's praise dancing?" Kat asked, helping herself to a second serving.

Beverly set her fork down. "Hmm, it's a form of dancing, but it's a way to praise and worship the Lord." Beverly sipped water to rinse her mouth before continuing. "Dancers use sign language, pantomime, and various forms of dance, like ballet, for instance, to minister or convey the message of the song. It's beautiful and edifying.

It really touched my heart. Today, when I watched, I felt I could feel the words of the song in my spirit. You gotta see it. Perhaps, you'll come with me next Sunday; my flight doesn't leave until evening."

"I don't know, Bev," Kat mumbled and looked down at her lap, searching for something that was not there.

"What's wrong?"

Kat looked up with a pained expression on her face and replied, "I'm sorry. I'm so messed up, man, I can't go in no church no more."

"That's nonsense." A gentle smile spread across Beverly's face. "Let's finish eating, and we'll talk about it."

* * *

Fifteen minutes later, sitting on the plush, black leather sofa in the living room, Beverly reached in her large tote, pulled out her Bible, and set it on the clear gemstone inspired coffee table. Grasping Kat's hand, she bowed her head. Taking cue, Kat bowed her head too. Beverly led them in prayer. At the end of the prayer, Beverly gave Kat's hand a gentle squeeze and then started flipping through her Bible. Kat excused herself and then came back with two glasses of ice water with lemon wedges. "First," Beverly began, "I want to ask you a question. Please consider carefully before answering, okay?"

Kat nodded her head earnestly.

"Despite how you feel about your personal situation, do you still believe the Bible is the infallible word of God?"

Kat's eyes darted back and forth. Perplexed, she questioned, "Infallible?"

"You know," Beverly thought for a second, "...um...inspired by God, accurate, unfailing, foolproof."

"Well, yeah. I mean. I guess." Kat hunched her shoulders. "Otherwise, I wouldn't feel so guilty."

Beverly placed the Bible on their shared laps. "You made the comment about being too bad to set foot back in church. Here in Romans, it says, 'For all have sinned and fall short of the glory of God.' I know you know this scripture."

Kat shifted to close the small gap between their inner thighs. "I've heard that scripture before, but I never focused on stuff like that.

I just enjoyed being excused from the adult service to go to children's church, and once we outgrew children's church, I daydreamed my way through adult service."

"You know you drove your mother nuts, right?" Beverly said, nudging Kat with her shoulder.

Kat chuckled. "Yeah, I know. I never paid attention to momma cuz she sounded plain crazy all the time." She circled her finger around the side of her head in the air and bugged her eyes out. "Like someone in a cult, man, whew! Plus, I was never smart about learning like you, Bev."

"Well, I don't think that is true. You might need a tailored method of learning. But that has nothing to do with you feeling like you're not good enough to come to the house of God. Look what it says here in Romans 3—10."

Kat read out loud, "'As it is written: There is none righteous, no, not one.'"

"You know this, Bird. You have no excuse for not going."

Kat asked, "If we are all sinners, then why should God care? I know the theory of we are 'made in his image,' but sometimes, I just don't get it. Like much to do about fixing what he created?" Kat hunched her shoulders again.

"Well," Beverly began. "For God…." Before she could finish, Kat chimed in, and the two girls quoted in unison, "So loved the world that he gave his only begotten son, that whoever believes in Him should not perish but have everlasting life."

"See, you know what I'm talking about. You know-that-you-know," Beverly said.

"Yes, that's why I don't go. I want to get myself together first."

"Tomorrow is not promised, Bird."

Kat smirked. "I know, Miss Save-a-Hoe."

Beverly smiled. "Girl, you ain't no hoe, just a little misdirected. That's all."

"Yea, a little misdirected," Kat repeated, her voice conveying inner reflection.

The girls continued studying in a light-hearted manner. Their love for each other evident as they sat on the sofa and respectfully communicated their most intimate thoughts and beliefs about humanity and the word of God. When they disagreed on a subject or theory, they did so diplomatically, entrusting each other to respect their individual differences. Beverly kept the study brief, not wanting to overwhelm her skeptical friend, who tried to be as attentive as possible through her drug-riddled thought process.

"When you explain things, they seem so much clearer. I enjoyed this. Dealing with mom was…just…um…you know, her relationship with Jim. They didn't act like any of this. They were always preaching at me…and the way he treats momma. He's a deacon at the church and has everyone fooled. He's mean-spirited and drinks too much beer."

"Yes, I never felt comfortable around him when we were growing up." Beverly paused and eyed Kat. "Bird, did he ever hurt you?" she asked with concern, her doe shaped eyes conveying protectiveness.

"You know the answer to that. Come on. I would've told you. You know that."

"You haven't answered me."

"No, Bev. Jim never touched me. As creepy as he is, he was just… maybe…uh…indifferent. Like I said, Momma deserves better. That's all. But in her eyes, Jim is her everything."

"Don't you see the same pattern with TL?"

"Bev, don't…please." Kat stood up, looking around as if wanting to leave.

Beverly touched her arm, motioning for her to sit back down.

"I didn't understand a lot of things back then, too, but what I do know is we have a free will to change the course of our lives. I know you don't want to rush things, but every day is not promised." Beverly paused to let the words sink in. "Honey, you can start fresh, right now. Ask Jesus to come into your life, to forgive you of your sins, and accept salvation."

Kat thought for a moment.

"I don't know. I watched so many people doing that growing up, and they are the same people I see in the nightclubs. Heck, I've even bought weed from so-called Christians."

"Yes…I know it's hard to trust, but we all have our own journey and someone else may have a different time-line than you. If you have faith and believe, I know you'll experience positive changes."

"O-Okaaay." Kat sucked air in through her teeth. "I'll do it, but you know I've done this before…when we were ten."

"Yes, but we were told to do it. Now, this is your choice."

Kat laughed. "Okay, cuz I don't want to be down in hell looking up at you in heaven."

"You so silly, come on, girl."

Beverly led the prayer of salvation—Kat repeated after her, asking forgiveness for her sins and asking Christ to have a personal relationship with her. Afterward, the best friends held a hug for an extended amount of time. "I love you, Bird," Beverly whispered with her eyes tearing up.

"I love you too, Bev." Kat wiped her own tears. "I don't know what's wrong with me."

"I call them cleansing tears. They are lightening the load."

Kat smiled wryly.

Beverly held onto Kat's hands. "I know you don't want to rush things, but we can study again."

Kat nodded her head, yes.

"If it's with you, I'd like that."

"Good. I know it is difficult dealing with your mother, but Christianity can be rewarding."

"Ok, I'll try."

Still holding the hopeful young woman's hand, Beverly led them in a closing prayer, after which, the two moved up to the rooftop with water and banana bread.

* * *

"Whew, it's hot out here. I wonder what the humidity level is." Beverly said, fanning herself.

Sitting next to her in a chaise lounge chair, Kat asked, "What made you get saved anyway? What happened in California? Remember, you promised to bring me up to speed."

"Yes. I did, didn't I?"

With her usual rough table manners, Kat sipped her water noisily and waited for Beverly to start, her ice blue eyes focused intently. Beverly put her sunglasses on and explained about her relationship with a photographer that was wonderful in the beginning but within a year began to go downhill.

Kat interrupted, "But when did you know it was time to make some changes?"

Beverly looked up at the sky and thought for a moment; the bright sun bounced off her sunglasses. "Oh, my happiness started unraveling slowly, like a gnawing inside that I couldn't put my finger on. Javier stopped being professional and lost his job. I tried helping him by subsidizing his drug dealing with start-up money. You know that ride-or-die stupid chick thing." Beverly frowned, reflecting on her lousy choice. "I don't know. When I started seeing his profits, I noticed he didn't offer to pay me back; he didn't contribute to our household, nor did he share any of it with me. I asked him what was going on. By the time his arrogant butt finished speaking, I knew I was fooling myself about the reality of our relationship."

Kat fidgeted with crumbs on her plate but listened intently.

"It was at that point I knew I needed to take several seats. I had to change my life." Beverly's mouth set in a hard line, and a furrow developed between her thick arched eyebrows.

Kat's eyes widened. "Several seats?"

The silent spider senses of both girls tingled at full blast, and they burst out in laughter, which helped lighten the serious moment. Beverly threw both palms up in an I-give-up gesture. The clanking of Kat's oversized hoop earrings sounded off when she shook her head back and forth in amusement.

Beverly continued, "I don't know. It was like an instantaneous wake-up. The wasting of money, the physical toll of the drugs and alcohol, questioning if my friends were really my friends." Beverly clicked her tongue against the roof of her mouth. "Add the spiritual and emotional emptiness. I was a mess."

Kat began nodding her head in agreement, causing the earrings to fire up another course of musical chimes.

"Bird, I felt alone, despite being around people all the time. I felt exhausted as if those same people around me were sucking the energy from me." Beverly's voice cracked as she continued, "I guess the nightclubbing, drugs and alcohol, lack of quality sleep, not eating enough; it all became too much. I felt unbalanced, and it wasn't fun anymore. I knew I would burn out If I didn't make lifestyle changes."

Hearing this, Kat felt the need to share her personal struggles, but before she could act on her emotions and blurt out her cocaine addiction secret, Beverly stood and walked over to the rooftop parapet. Kat heard her sniffling, so she joined her, protectively placing her arm around Beverly's shoulder, and drawing her close. "Aw, I didn't mean to upset you."

"It's okay," Beverly replied, wiping tears from her eyes. "I'm still healing, I guess. I thought I had laid it all at the altar, but apparently not."

Kat did not want to distress her further, partly due to her own guilt and self-condemnation, but wanted to know a little more.

"What was your drug of choice?"

Now it was Beverly's turn to look down and fumble with her fingers. "Um," she cleared her voice and looked up, "Weed. Weed and wine."

Kat could not believe it. She considered marijuana and wine lightweight, so she just gave a sympathetic nod and said, "Well, if you can quit, then there is hope for me, but you know I love my weed."

"Yes, I know, but you can't go through life in a daze."

"Keeeee!"

A misplaced broad-winged hawk screeched and hovered above, its wings floating on heated air as their eyes followed the gliding bird. The suspension of their conversation aided in an emotional reset for them both. Kat finally broke the silence when the fowl took off to find a more favorable habitat for the sake of survival.

"So, what happened to your fiancé?"

"Oh, him." Beverly frowned. "Javier couldn't accept Christianity. I wasn't serving Christ when we met, so when I changed, he wasn't cool with that. He asked for the ring back."

"What an ass!"

"Right! But that's okay. I believe Jesus has greater plans for me. I'm more than fine with the situation. I got tired of his shenanigans."

"Shenanigans?" Kat chuckled. "Where do you get these terms from?"

"Girl, he was always up to something." Beverly chuckled, too. "Lied about everything," she said lightheartedly. "I wanted his love so much, I guess I pretended his foolishness wasn't foolishness."

Looking at her friend lovingly, Kat wondered if she would ever have the strength to overcome her own demons. Kat felt like an angel and a devil were sitting on her shoulders, arguing over whether she should confide in Beverly about the depth of her struggles. In her heart, she believed she could kick drugs alone and did not want to involve anyone with her embarrassing situation. She decided not to share.

"Have you dated or slept with anyone since Javier?"

"No, like I said, I am dedicated to Christ. I cannot expect blessings with a quality man if I'm not a quality woman," Beverly offered.

The intense beam of the sun wore heavy on the pair, so the girls went back to their semi-shaded seats where Kat picked up the last piece of banana bread and stuffed it in her mouth. "Huh? I can't tell if you're messing with me or not. I know you like sex!" she said with a mouth full of bread.

Beverly put her feet up and leaned her head back on the lounge chair. "I can't argue with you on that one. To be honest, celibacy isn't easy. My mind knows the right thing, but my flesh wants something else." Beverly felt a flush of heat spread across her chest as she thought of the mysterious man from the gym.

"Oh!" Kat mouthed.

Beverly sat up and swung her feet sideways to face Kat and wrung her hands in her lap. "Ok." She sighed. "I want sex!" Beverly's hands flew to her mouth, and she continued in a hushed tone, "I'm having my first struggle since getting saved. There was a man at the gym…"

Kat interrupted and mocked, "A man at the gym."

They giggled.

"Well, girlfriend," Kat replied, still whispering, "I'll be getting you a dildo and some sex tapes for your birthday. Can you watch some porn?"

"No!" Beverly's hand flew to her mouth again.

"Aw, hell, your life is over!" Kat blurted out and then cupped her hands over her mouth, capturing the words before the heavens could hear.

"I'm sure God hears us; we are silly!" Beverly said, moving her hand away from her mouth.

The girl's high-pitched squeals woke a bird sleeping in a city-made nest in the corner of the roof, causing it to take off in flight. They continued the light-hearted conversation until about five. At that time, Kat suggested they go to the movies, thinking it was best to get Beverly out of the condo in case TL came back unexpectedly. Kat was sure she would have plenty of time to get ready for her meeting with Lexy after the movie, but it also meant her plan to take a restorative nap would not happen.

CHAPTER 8

LEXY & LILLIAN
Sunday – 7:27 p.m.

Wearing a white, summer-linen pantsuit with a white camisole and red leather closed-toe pumps, Lexy arrived at the Wood Hill Nursing Home facility for the first time and was not impressed. It was no mystery as to why her siblings avoided bringing up their aunt to her; however, it annoyed her that Lillian's new housing arrangements presented as sub-par by her standards. Lexy eyed the dirty glass doors and the suspect round handicapped door opener before hitting the oversized metal plate with the back of her hand and waited patiently for the doors to inch open.

Upon entering the facility, the nauseating smell of urine slapped her in the face, causing her to pause in subtle shock and bring her hand to her nose to stop the attack on her olfactory system. She looked around. A long corridor made of cement blocks painted white, white subway tiles, and hospital grade flooring lay before her, which gave the appearance of cleanliness, but the ammonia odor would make one think otherwise. Ineffective fluorescent lights hung from a dropped ceiling dotted with water stains, and patient room doors lined each side of the long hallway.

Lexy walked down the hall towards a nurses' station, passing a hunched figure sitting in a wheelchair. The resident's chin hung to her chest, her curved spine revealing the many miles of wear and tear on her aged body. The elderly woman lifted her stiff neck and gave a toothless smile, her cloudy eyes showing a hint of life. Lexy returned a forced smile and continued her walk towards a tall counter fashioned after a roundabout for cars. At the counter, Lexy looked down to see a stout woman in her mid-fifties with dyed, bright red hair dressed in faded medical scrubs. She waited for acknowledgment.

"May I help you?" the woman finally asked with indifference.

"I would like to see Lillian Leigh, please."

The dye job pointed down the hall and mumbled, "Room one fifteen," before returning to her work.

Irritated, Lexy held her tongue.

Outside Lillian's room, she paused and smoothed her hands over her suit. "Relax, Lexy," she whispered to herself before entering the room and quietly calling out, "Aunt Lilly?"

"Huh…what, Marlene, is that you?" answered a dry, raspy voice.

Careful to use her legal name, she replied, "No, Aunt Lilly, its Alexandria."

Lexy's eyes adjusted to the bright sunlight that invaded the room through a narrow, double-paned window. Two twin beds sat parallel to each other—positioned on each side of the window on the wall opposite the door. Two miniature nightstands sat side-by-side and butted against the bed railings to form one continuous table underneath the windows and between the beds. Two folding chairs filled the remaining space, along with a thirty-two-inch television, which sat on top of a dresser to the left of the door. Their shared bathroom was to the left of the dresser. Everything seemed crammed in the micro-sized room. Lillian's small body occupied the bed to the right of the window, and her roommate occupied the other.

"Alex…andria…?"

Coughs racked the bedridden woman's body. Lexy waited patiently for Lillian to recover from the onslaught of respiratory dysfunction.

"Took you so damn…long! Glad I'm not waiting on you to die!" Another coughing spell ensued, which ended with Lillian spitting into the tissue held in her dry, brown-skinned hand. "Where the hell you been? I've been here weeks, alone!"

Lexy realized her aunt did not remember their last fight and obviously had no grasp of a timeline for her stay at the nursing facility. The Alzheimer seemed to be getting worse. What was familiar, though, was the same biting tongue of her childhood, with the only difference being that between every other sentence, Lillian had to gasp for air or cough. Apprehensively, Lexy approached the bed, ready to deal with the only person on earth that made her nervous.

Lillian's unkempt, long silver hair lay fanned out around her head that lay on a flat pillow. The deep etching of wrinkles in her face told a story of the reckless lifestyle she once lived, which had stolen her youth and left her older than her numerical years. She wore a pink flowered gown with a pink hand-knitted shawl around her shrunken shoulders. Her eyes were cloudier than Lexy remembered.

Bending down, she kissed Lillian on the forehead, trying not to breathe in the old lady smell, and noted her forehead felt warm. "I know, Aunt Lilly. I should have come sooner, but I didn't think you wanted to see me."

Lillian did not address the statement, but instead said, "Let me see you, girl." Pointing her dry, index finger at Lexy, she moved it up and down, taking in the figure standing before her. Lillian mumbled, "Hmm, that lipstick is too red. Prostitute color."

"How are you?" Lexy asked, careful to conceal her annoyance.

"Lord, have mercy, child. Are you blind?" Lillian brought the same used tissue up to her mouth and spat in it. "Don't you see this place is hell?" she barely said before coughing ensued.

When the coughing subsided, Lexy voiced her agreement. "I thought with my subsidy to Medicaid, Tina would have found a better place. That was the whole point of helping."

"This is the thanks I get for raising three damn kids…that ain't mine…on welfare. Ungrateful mother…," Lillian's breathing came fast and labored; a long pause ensued, "…they owe me!"

I'd have taken a foster home.

"And that damn woman…," Lillian pointed an accusatory finger at her snoring roommate, "…keeps me up half the night…, Je-sus!"

Lexy noted that other than memory, Lillian's cognitive ability seemed sharp.

"Aunt Lilly, are you still having trouble with the fluid in your legs?" Lexy pulled back the covers to reveal Lillian's support hose. The right leg appeared significantly swollen compared to the left leg.

"Are you living under a rock? Stop fussing over my feet and give me some damn water!" she snapped.

Lexy took the used cups and tissue, including the one in Lillian's hand, and threw them away. After washing her hands in the public-housing looking bathroom, she went to the nurses' station to inquire where to get new cups, ice, and water. Barely looking at her, the red dye job pointed to the other corridor and said, "To the left."

Lexy's patience felt thinner.

Back in the room, she helped Lillian with the straw so her dry lips could zero in on it. As Lillian sipped, Lexy examined Lillian's features. The same small eyes and square-shaped mandibles on Lillian's face confirmed that Tina, Marlene, and Lexy were blood relatives—albeit younger versions with individual tweaks to their features. After sips of ice water and a few deep breaths, Lillian spoke with disdain, "Are you still prostituting?!"

"I'm a night club owner, Aunt Lilly. You know that," Lexy replied with self-restraint, tired of the same old argument.

"It's prostitution, dammit! That's how the good Lord will see it! You know damn well I'm right!" she said indignantly, pulling the shawl tighter around her emaciated shoulders with a tissue in hand in preparation for a coughing spell.

Lexy looked at the bitter woman and wondered how a supposedly sanctified woman of God could use the word "damn" in every other sentence. What amazed her more was Lillian's use of the Lord's name right in the same group of sentences. This was one of several examples of why Lexy did not understand Christianity. To her, most Christians were hypocrites.

The smell in the room was taking a toll on her senses. Trying not to look conspicuous, she glanced at her watch. It was seven-thirty.

"If you had enough smarts," Lillian paused and produced a gurgling sound before continuing, "you'd have made something of yourself like your sisters."

Lexy's posture went rigid.

I don't have time for this shit, she thought.

"Aunt Lilly," she said, bending over to kiss her aunt's forehead while holding her breath. "I've got to get going. I'm going to see about getting you into a better place."

Lillian eyed her suspiciously.

"A better place?" she repeated in a child-like voice; the disdain no longer detectable in her tone.

"Yes, I'll be in touch soon."

The disdain came back.

"Don't be promising me things! You hear me, girl!" she shouted the best she could for someone in her state of health. "You know you always find a way to disappoint," she continued as Lexy exited the room.

At the makeshift roundabout, Lexy asked to speak to management. Just when the dye job was going to ask several unnecessary questions, a "true" redhead came out of an open door from an adjacent area.

"Hi, I'm Rita Johnson, assistant director. What can I do for you?" She extended a hand to Lexy.

Lexy shook her hand and then used a pump of hand sanitizer that sat on the counter. Rita Johnson's Norwegian lips went tight into a hard-set line upon viewing this action. "I'm Alexandria Leigh, Lillian Leigh's niece. Do you have a moment?"

The dye job cast her eyes down and pretended she was working.

"Please, come this way." Rita extended an open palm toward her office door. Once seated behind her desk, she pulled up Lillian's electronic medical records and asked, "What can I do for you, Mrs. Leigh?"

"It's Ms.," Lexy offered. "I'm concerned about my aunt's well-being. Aunt Lilly looks unkempt and appears ill. In addition, I see and smell hygienic concerns, and security seems to be somewhat lacking here."

Taken aback by Lexy's bluntness, Rita's facial expression responded with indignation. She took a moment to look at Lillian's medical records. A smirk graced her lips. "Ms. Leigh," she said, emphasizing Ms. and addressing Lexy in an icy tone, "Wood Hill Nursing Home is state-certified; I assure you we meet all health and safety requirements."

Lexy disregarded her claims and went on with her immediate concerns. "Aunt Lilly has a diagnosis of COPD, but there appears to be something else going on. Her lungs sound wet. When did she last see a physician?"

Lexy's demeanor began to make the assistant director nervous. Something about the polished woman warned her to tone down her approach. Rita put on her glasses and scrutinized the computer screen. "Yes, I see she was admitted to our facility for Alzheimer and she…let's see…has been seen by…um…Dr. White, since her arrival…ah…a little over a month ago."

Lexy controlled an eye roll and remained composed, almost robotic. "I'm aware of the Alzheimer. That's why my sisters and I took her from her home, which was quite the challenge. I don't expect her to be a picture of health, especially since she has a history of smoking, but I do expect this facility to do due diligence regarding her care. Can you please tell me if she is still on a diuretic and is her blood pressure under control? What is being done about her breathing?"

Rita's mouth went slack. Now, she took a closer look at the woman sitting across her desk. Rita's eyes roamed over the fine stitching on Lexy's suit, the sparkling diamonds in her ears, her coiffed braids, her perfectly applied make-up, and her dignified mannerism.

"Um…," she stammered, "Let me see…" Rita looked back at the computer and continued, "Yes, she's still on furosemide and atenolol, plus a host of other medications."

"Her vital signs?"

Rita rattled off a brief record of unstable vital signs and tried to relax the caught off guard look on her face and said, "The recent strike has taken a toll on staff and…"

Lexy cocked her head and raised her eyebrows before cutting Rita off. Excuses were not what she wanted to hear. "A facility doctor needs to re-evaluate her. Until then, I'd like full vitals taken more often to determine a trend." Wanting to drum her fingers on the desk, Lexy refrained from touching the potentially germ-infested object and kept her hands folded in her lap. "Something needs to be done."

Rita's stomach churned. Was a lawsuit in the making? Could this woman be trouble? The assistant director's disposition continued to sweeten as she came to the realization that a powerful woman sat across from her.

"Oh, yes, oh, yes. We will make an appointment for Dr. Owen to see Ms. Leigh, right away. If he is not available tomorrow, I'll make sure we get her into urgent care. I will personally see to that."

Rita hated she had to suck up to the black woman, but her experience in skilled nursing dictated that she listen to her intuition and accommodate Lexy to the best of her ability.

"Is there anything else I can do for you?"

A cigarette and wine would be nice.

"After the doctor's exam, I'd like to know what the treatment plan will be. And, I heard you mention that you're understaffed, but if you could please make sure my aunt is fully bathed and groomed daily, I'd appreciate it."

"That's no problem, Ms. Leigh; we will do the best we can, given Lillian's Medicaid and financial limitations." Rita lifted her head slightly, now feeling she had the upper hand in the conversation.

"There is a supplemental payment on her account."

Rita looked at the computer again, this time noticing a large payment that she had missed upon her initial viewing of the records, her assumption that Lexy was someone important now confirmed.

"My aunt will be going to a private nursing home, but once again, if you could look after her while I make the arrangements, I'd appreciate it." Lexy stood and extended her hand to Rita. Rita felt paper transferred between their palms. "Thank you, Ms. Johnson." As Lexy walked out of the office, Rita examined the papers. Ten one-hundred-dollar bills.

BEVERLY & KAT
Sunday - 9:35 p.m.

Walking from the movie theatre at a leisure pace and enjoying relief from the daytime humid weather, Beverly and Kat strolled in silence, indulging themselves in the comfort of each other's presence. Kat wrestled with her double-sprinkled ice cream scoops, trying to stop the treat from melting past the napkin wrapped around the waffle cone. She licked with ferocious speed, getting splatters of chocolate ice cream on her face. Beverly daintily ate her single scoop of yogurt ice cream with a spoon and looked at Kat with amazement. "Bird, how do you do it?"

"Do what?" Kat replied with a puzzled look on her face and ice cream on her nose.

"Eat so much and stay thin. You eat all the wrong foods."

"I dunno." Kat hunched her bony shoulders. "Dancing for a living helps, I guess."

Beverly pointed to Kat's ice cream smudged nose. Kat wiped it with her inner wrist. "Yes, but the way you put food away, I'm surprised you're not strutting around on stage with your gut hanging out." Beverly tried looking serious but cracked a smile.

"Yeah, right." Kat pushed her stomach out, mimicking Beverly's description while walking. After the laughter died down, while licking ice cream off her thumb, Kat asked, "Did you drive?"

"No, I walked. You know how small downtown is."

"I think I would have driven," Kat said, pausing to reflect. "Yep, keeping it real, I'd have driven, even for one block," she concluded.

"What am I going to do with you?" Beverly asked, finishing her ice cream and watching Kat struggle with hers.

"Say, I have to go to the club to talk to my boss. Let's get my car, and I'll drop you off. Is that alright?"

"Sounds good to…," Beverly yawned, "…me. It's approaching my bedtime."

Kat stopped walking. "What?" she exclaimed in her baby voice. "What time do you go to bed?"

"Usually by nine or ten. I need to get rest, so I'm ready for an early shoot or my morning workout. Plus, a schedule helps me stay on track in all areas of my life." Beverly started walking again.

"Wow!" Kat exclaimed, "I usually go to sleep about four in the morning and sleep till one or two."

"Well, hopefully, we can change that. Um…say, I don't want to ruin the mood, but I was wondering…"

"Yeah?"

"Have you tried to stop drinking and smoking?"

"No."

"Why not?"

With her fingers on her lip, Kat searched for words. "Hmm, it's like when I'm clean and sober, my body and my mind hurt. Like I-I feel sad and worry about shit. I-I dunno," Kat hunched her shoulders—something she often did. "I just feel better when I'm high."

"You're not high now. Are you not happy?"

"Yeah, I'm happy. But, Bev, you can't be with me twenty-four-seven."

"I think I understand. But those side effects will get better once your body and mind heal. God can restore anything."

Kat scoffed, "I need mental meds. Something ain't right upstairs," she confessed, keeping to herself that she often thought of suicide. "You're probably right, though."

Beverly reached out and grabbed her hand. "You'll see. Things will work out."

Together, the girls continued their leisurely walk, chatting about dreams for their future until they made it to the underground parking garage. They drove back to The Bellows where they said their goodbyes. Kat promised her she would consider exercising with her the following day and then watched her best friend walk towards the hotel entrance.

As soon as Beverly disappeared through the rotating doors, Kat pulled a piece of marijuana cigar out of her purse and lit it before pulling off from the curb. The thick, foul smell filled the vehicle as Kat inhaled the gaseous particles, holding the smoke in her lungs a moment before exhaling. No sooner had she released the smoke from her lungs, the stressed addict inhaled more to repeat the cycle.

Watching a movie without being high had been excruciating. As much as she loved Beverly's company, near the end of the evening, she had gotten anxious to wrap up their time together, so she could smoke. One of her favorite songs played on the satellite radio channel, and she began to sing. Setting her cruise control, she headed to the club with the music blaring, smoking, and feeling good.

Midway through the ride, Kat hollered out, "Shit!" and shook her hand, dropping the small burning paper—now void of drugs—between her legs and furiously began searching for it before the red glow found its way to sear her exposed thigh skin, weaving in her traffic lane as she did. Once she found the ember, she threw it out the window. This reminded her that her supply was out. She had seen Taz on Friday but started smoking crack and forgot to get the weed sack from her. Now she was in need.

The thought of Taz made her nervous. Taz meant temptation, which she wanted to avoid. While driving and bobbing her head to the beat of the music, a solution came to her. Dolly, one of the dancers at the club, always had weed. Though it was only mid-grade in quality, getting it from Dolly would help her avoid Taz. Kat voiced dialed Dolly's number and left a message for her. Now, the last dilemma that needed solving was talking her way through keeping her job.

CHAPTER 9

LEXY
Sunday - 9:15 p.m.

Downtown Minneapolis exploded with liveliness due to a basketball playoff game. Fans from the Metro area descended upon Lexy's like a swarm of locusts. Despite the renowned restaurant part of the club being closed for renovations and other areas roped off, Lexy was met with a flurry of activity.

Staff was working tirelessly to keep up with the frenzied pace of the guests. Mixologist served patrons at the crowded bars. Servers, dressed in sexy fishnet stockings, black camisoles, and thigh-high, leather hooker boots, glided about with sexual grace and sensuality, and the V.I.P. staff rushed about, making fantasies come alive for clients who could afford it. Beckoning the next beauty for her moment in the money-making spotlight, soft yellow and red lights shined bright on the empty stage as the DJ announced the next erotic dancer by her stage name.

With her white linen suit standing out against the red decor of the club, Lexy sat in a leather armchair in the shark pool to get a customer's viewpoint. Surveying the stage, her eyes stopped at one of the highly polished dance poles before zeroing in on the thick, luscious red and gold drapes in the backdrop. Sitting there, Lillian's words came back to haunt her.

"Hmm, that red lipstick is too bright…Are you still prostituting?"

In all the years of being in the industry, there had been no contemplation if what she was doing was wrong. This was all she knew, and she knew it well. Now, it bothered her that she questioned her choices.

* * *

At the age of sixteen, Lexy had given up, dropped out of school, and moved out of Lillian's home due to Lillian's unjustifiable prejudice against her and the fact that there seemed to always be an ongoing shortage of food and other staples in the home. Initially, stealing and selling clothes supported her survival until gang members required her induction into their family for her to have the right to hustle on their streets, which she declined; thus, ending her effort to sell boosted clothes. A few times, she tried prostituting, but the experiences were bad. It was clear to her that she would never make a decent street-level whore. Lexy did not care for drugs because of her parents, so that was not a quick moneymaking career choice, either. Odd hustles and menial jobs sustained her until her eighteenth birthday. It was then she applied for employment at strip clubs, landing work at The Gold Mine twenty years ago.

* * *

"...Are you still prostituting?"

While contemplating Lillian's words, delicate hands cupped her eyes from behind.

"Can you do that to me again?"

The soft whisper and the rose petal scent delivered a shot of heaven to her senses. "Can you handle it, again?" she teased. Lisa came around to the front of the chair, and Lexy whistled, "Damn, I think I just came on myself!"

The tiny bi-racial beauty stood in front of Lexy dressed in a deep purple thigh-length dress that made her ultra-petite form look curvier than it was. Lisa's thick gray eyeliner and lavender eye shadow created intensity in her soft, gray eyes. Her pouty lips were colored in a glossy neutral; and her wash and wear brunette curls stood tousled on her head, framing her beige-colored face like a lion's mane. From her honey-colored hair highlights, down to her gold stilettos, Lisa looked stunning.

"Are you trying to make me go home early?" Lexy asked, not hiding the arousal in her voice.

"No. I just wanted to come by and thank you for the gift. Thank you so much!" Lisa seductively waved her arm to show off the bracelet and then took a seat across from her partner.

"You're welcome. I wanted to show you my appreciation." Lexy leaned forward and bought her hands together, as if for prayer, and bowed. Then she grabbed the arms of Lisa's chair and pulled it towards her. She gave Lisa a hug, enveloping herself in the aroma of rose cologne, shampoo scented hair, and soft skin. Lisa noticed Lexy held the embrace for a moment before releasing it.

"Leese, I'm thinking I need some unwind time. What's your schedule like?"

"When?" Lisa asked.

"Well, I'm thinking near the end of July. I was wondering if you'd like to go on a trip to the Caymans with me after I wrap up some issues with the club."

Lisa's eyes widened. "I've never been to the Caymans. I've been all over the world as an art buyer, but somehow that area of paradise has alluded me." She smiled a wide smile. "Yes, I'd love to go! Thank you!"

Lexy held up her hand. "Don't thank me yet. You need to check your schedule, and, like I said, I have some things to complete on this end. Besides, I'm the one who'll be thanking you when I see you in sun wear."

Lexy's eyes took on a smoldering look as she stared Lisa up and down. Lisa flushed and turned pink under her blush. Leaning back in her chair, Lexy checked her platinum and diamond wristwatch. There was still some time to get work done before the meeting with Kat and Vincenzo.

"Say, I've got to get rolling. What are you up to?"

"I'm on my way to the gallery on the west end. A new artist. Why? You want me to come over?" she asked hastily.

"Yes, I should be home around two if you don't mind waiting up?"

"Of course, I don't."

"You remember the code?"

"Yep, I'll let myself in."

"Ok, could you please have a bath ready? I'll get in with you. I'll call when I'm on my way."

"Okay, baby."

Lisa got up to leave. Lexy grabbed her wrist.

"Leese."

"Yeah."

"Don't forget to set the alarm."

"I will, but you know you worry too much."

"I'm serious."

"Yes, yes, I will."

Still seated, Lexy kissed the top of her hand. Watching the dainty bombshell walk away, she realized Lisa meant more to her than she cared to admit. Wanting to see Lisa regularly often pervaded her thoughts. At that moment, Lexy finalized a decision she had been wrestling with for weeks, which was to ask Lisa to move in with her.

Lexy went upstairs to her office. Before tackling the overflowing emails, she started preliminary research on nursing home facilities for Lillian. Then, most of her attention went to going through investment portfolio email alerts, reviewing background checks on new employees, and sending electronic payments for medical bills for a few of the dancers in need of help. Finally, she attacked a pile of old fashion mail, cursing under her breath that people still sent snail-mail. Glancing at the security screens on the console to her right, she saw the figures of Vincenzo's bodyguards entering the club. Watching them make their way to the bar, she lit a cigarette, making sure to keep her eyes on the monitors. It was not midnight.

The cigarette smoke circled around her head before disappearing up into the ventilation system as her small eyes stayed focused on the men. Marcus approached them with his hand extended. The men stood, and each shook hands with him, their mouths smiling and laughing at something Marcus said. Lexy could see Marcus motioning to the bartender and saying something to him. He then turned back to the three men, shook their hands again, smiled, and walked away, glancing up at Lexy via the security camera. Satisfied that Marcus had everything under control, Lexy went and got a ring sized black velvet box out of her safe and placed it in the black suit jacket pocket that she would be changing into for her meeting.

KAT
Sunday - 9:18 p.m.

Kat walked into the dimly lit nightclub and noticed guests wearing sports jerseys, which meant talented workers would make good money that night. One by one, stunning women marched out to spirited music onto the lit runway wearing various forms of provocative lingerie-styled evening wear, before entering the pool area with the sharks. No two dancers looked alike. Carefully applied makeup highlighted their come-hither looks, sensual smiles, and provocative mannerisms. Their bodies were just as varied as their faces. Some strutted with thick hips and equally thick, round bottoms while others seductively moved their model-thin frames and slim derrières. Natural breasts swung invitingly, and perky breast implants beckoned boldly to onlookers from across the room.

With the loud music blaring, the women continued dispersing throughout the club to work. With her traveling bag slung over her shoulder, Kat headed to the dressing room, scoffing to herself at the fake smiles and exaggerated sexy attitudes the women displayed to hustle the men.

The not so innocent girl knew her coworker's goals were to stroke the client's egos and be the opposite of their wives or girlfriends. The women represented fantasies. A fantasy most would never have unless they paid for it. Kat knew secret deals happened during lap dances and that undercover cops took part in those deals. She stayed clear of covert operations to keep a distance from legal problems. Dodging drug charges and avoiding loss of life from TL took up enough of her energy and time.

Kat stepped into the dancer's lounge. Looking about the large room decorated in antique white, pink, and gold, with floor to ceiling mirrors on walls not occupied by furnishings, she felt as if she had stepped into her second home. Despite sections being walled off for renovations, it was easy to see that the room's decorations were from a French vaudeville era. With beauty equipment and supplies strewn about, it was evident that the occupants had recently abandoned the backstage space.

Kat waved at a few employees who moved about straightening workstations, waiting for dancers to come in for beauty "tune-ups" between dance sets. The hairstylists and makeup artists created the goddess-like images of the dancers and kept a presence in the dressing room during all shifts.

Before heading upstairs, Kat changed out of her canary yellow ensemble and into a lime green mini skirt and matching tank top with three-inch stilettos. After placing a few red relieving drops in her eyes, spritzing cologne, and popping gum in her mouth, she went up to face the music. En route to see Lexy, a text came in from Dolly acknowledging her request, which was a good thing since she would want to smoke after the meeting. Kat spent a few moments settling her nerves before knocking on the steel-encased office door. It was ten p.m. on the dot.

Lexy opened the door and ushered Kat in. Kat took a deep breath and tried to look alert. The chain of earlier events, starting with the visit to Big Mike's, were now taking a toll on her. The loud music from the club escaped into the room temporarily and then muffled when the door shut. Lexy motioned for her to sit down while she finished a phone call. After ending the call, Lexy addressed the employee as if she were offering the exhausted girl a cup of coffee, "You look like shit. Do you need to go to treatment or something?"

Kat looked down at the desktop and mumbled, "I'm sorry. I went out and celebrated a little too much. I tried to take a nap before my shift; I slept through my alarm." The nervous picking of cuticles and biting of the lower lip began.

Lexy lit a cigarette and then followed with a minuscule sip of wine, trying to pace her drinking. Talking to the top of Kat's head, she said, "You knew you had to work. Why didn't you switch schedules with someone or put a request in for a day off beforehand?"

Lexy knew the answer to the question. An addict, is an addict, is an addict, but standard questioning was just that, standard.

Kat shifted her gaze up to Lexy's brick lipstick colored lips. Her voice quivered when she spoke. "Um, my best friend, Beverly; we hadn't seen each other in three years. I-I'm sorry. It won't happen a-again." She took both hands and wiped under her eyes.

Lexy noted the dark circles under Kat's eyes, the worn polish on her acrylics, and the thick makeup—the latter making her wonder if Kat was trying to cover up bruises on her face.

"What do you want in life?"

"Huh?"

"What do you want to do with your life?" Lexy repeated, knowing perfectly well Kat heard her the first time.

Kat looked down at a different area on the desk. "I dunno, be an actress?" she responded with a question while rounding her shoulders down as she spoke. "I feel like I'm acting when I work anyway."

Why is she asking this shit? God I'm tired, Kat thought.

"Why aren't you pursuing it?"

"I dunno. Been here working, I guess."

"Have you considered taking acting classes?"

"No."

"Kat, you can pursue anything you want. You're not limited to Lexy's. You have your whole life in front of you. Being an actor is attainable, but you must make a positive choice. Silhouettes do change. Beauty is fleeting in this industry. Either you work hard, save your money, and use this place as a stepping-stone, or otherwise, you're going to keep tricking around and going in circles. You do understand there are plenty of young girls out there that will keep this industry going well after you and I are dead."

Kat looked up and met Lexy's eyes for the first time. "You're in this lifestyle. What makes it any different for you than me?" she asked sarcastically, regretting the words as soon as they left her thin-lipped mouth. *"Shit! I' m fucked, now!"*

Lexy tapped her index finger several times on the side of her wine glass and then stopped. "The difference is that I'm not letting this lifestyle eat me up."

A trace of boredom graced Lexy's voice as if this conversation had taken place many times with other employees through the years, even if her statement was a half-truth.

"Look at you. You look like shit. Sure, anybody looking at you would say your pretty, but that's just a facade. Where is the authentic you? You are not taking care of yourself; that so-called man of yours is going to kill you before this is all over. You're a good kid with a good heart, Kat. I'd hate to see something happen to you," she said and then took a drag of her cigarette, followed by a generous sip of wine.

"No disrespect, Lexy, but it's people like you who run these places we work in. How can you be so judgmental? Because of people like me, your mortgage is paid." *Shit! I'm fired.*

Lexy stood. "Come with me."

* * *

Outside, the two women got into a limousine. Kat refrained from asking where they were going, preferring to keep to herself and concentrate on not falling asleep from the gentle sway of the vehicle. During the ride, the scenery began to change, and the economic disparity between the area they came from and the area they were going became clear. Modern buildings with clean lines and shiny windows gave way to boarded-up-in-need-of-repair graffiti-covered shells of concrete.

The fifteen-minute ride brought them to a downtown residence called The Fresh Start Center for single parenting women and their children. Kat followed Lexy into a modest building with cement flooring and a front desk enclosed in tempered glass. Behind it sat a tall, elderly security guard who smiled and buzzed them in. In silence, they walked down an empty corridor—the clicking of their high heels echoing throughout—and took an elevator ride to the third floor before walking up a stairwell to the fourth floor. Hoping the trek would soon be over, Kat was glad she did not have to work because her feet were starting to hurt.

On the fourth floor, materials and the fresh smell of paint told the story of ongoing construction. Work lamps lined the soon-to-be walls of the reception area, the entrances to the wings still had no doors, and caution tape quarantined sections of the floor. Lexy walked over to the inoperable elevator that faced the reception desk and stood in front of a plague that read: The Alexandria Leigh Wing. Her well-manicured fingers slid over the plaque. "It hasn't been easy being a philanthropist for the disadvantaged because opponents don't want money from a strip club. It sends mixed messages."

Kat stood looking forlorn, not understanding what philanthropist meant.

"This, among other things, is an example of what I've chosen to do with the money I've made as the owner of Lexy's. This is more than about my mortgage. Kat, I certainly don't feel I owe you an explanation as to how I run my life, and I don't show you this to boast. I'm just trying to reach you." Lexy paused for a moment in her own reflective thoughts. "I've never said this is the best lifestyle to live, but if you're going to work in the industry, why not use it to set the path of where you want to go? This doesn't have to be the end for you…for none of us."

Kat nodded her head yes but wished she could go home. Fatigue settled on her heavy and slow, like a wrecking ball into a high-rise.

"Why do you do it then?" Kat asked.

With her back to Kat, Lexy winced. "Because I'm successful at it, but not everyone can be me." She turned to face Kat. "Do you own in any investments or savings?"

Buying drugs and shopping came to Kat's mind as she shook her head no. This time her earrings did not sound off like chimes because she had exchanged them for oversized gold hoops.

"No, but I've been trying so I can…," she trailed off, scared to divulge too much information.

"Kat, you can't just live from day-to-day. The men of yester-years no longer exist. There is no mesmerizing a man with your vagina. Your body is not special. Women like us come a dime a dozen." She started walking back towards the stairwell door. "No one is going to marry you and save the day, and if they do, it won't last. You have to decide on a course of action." Lexy opened the door and held it for Kat to go through.

They went down to the third floor, got back on the elevator, traveling in silence. Neither woman wanted to intrude on her own thoughts. Back in the limo, Lexy continued, "I'll admit, I have not always had it easy, and I do have stories of my own; however, if I can help anyone avoid my errors, I'd like to do that." Lexy paused to light her cigarette, cracking the window a little to let the smoke out. Next, she checked her phone, indicating to Kat that her monologue had ended.

Kat sat speechless. She did not know that Lexy was this tender or caring. Thinking back on some of the nasty conversations she had joined in on about her in the locker room, despite the many times Lexy had let her off the hook when she had messed up, Kat felt guilty. Emotional instability violently swung the other way, causing tears to swell in her eyes. Kat knew her life revolved around indulgence for personal satisfaction.

Lexy ignored Kat's tears and instructed the driver to go to Currier Avenue, a few miles away. A few minutes later, the limo pulled up to a food shelf. A security guard stepped to the curb. "Evening Ms. Leigh; How are you?" the moonlighting police officer asked when she rolled the window down.

"Things are good, Curtis. How are you?"

"I'm good, but you know this neighborhood. That could change in a moment."

"You're right about that," she acknowledged.

Kat watched the interaction between Lexy and Curtis. It was different seeing Lexy out of business mode. Seeing her at the club is the only Lexy she knew.

"So, what brings you this way so late?" He asked and then quickly looked around to make sure they were in the clear for unexpected criminal activity.

"I thought I'd drop these off to you." Lexy held out two tickets to the Whiteout Ball.

"I'm honored," beamed the young man, "I'm looking forward to it. It's my birthday that day."

"Well, then make sure you get a drink on me. It will be at the main bar."

"Thank you, Lexy."

"You're welcome. Have a safe evening, Curtis."

The young man tilted his hat. "See you Wednesday."

The limo pulled off.

Kat asked, "Why Wednesday? The ball is Friday."

"I volunteer here. Wednesday is my day."

Kat looked sheepishly at Lexy and said, "I'm sorry. I had no idea you were so involved with the community. I'm really sorry."

"Look, I'll never say I'm better than anyone. It's just you've got to be confident in what you want and not let anyone, or anything, deter you from it. Yes, our job can be challenging and highly stressful; so, therefore, wouldn't you rather have an employer who didn't have you working in some fucked up situations? I know what's being said about me and how some of you girls feel, but I'd like to think I'm a better alternative than other establishments in this industry."

Kat could not help but notice that she sounded like TL but kept the thought to herself. Lexy took a drag of her cigarette and ignored her desire to get a glass of wine from the limo bar.

"This type of business will be here long after our breasts are hanging to the damn floor and we are toothless and crapping on ourselves. Hell…if we make it that long. We can't stop it, so we need to be wise about it."

As the limo cruised, Kat looked out the window and watched the downtown lights go by. The post-game activities and the warm weather created an atmosphere of merriment in the downtown area, but Kat felt blue. She wondered where everyone was going as the lights of downtown Minneapolis rolled across the blackened windows of the limousine. Looking out the window, she timidly asked, "Do I still have a job?"

"You'll need to pay your house dues from Saturday, including your tip-outs, and work tonight with full house dues."

"Work tonight? Full house dues?" Kat whined.

"Take it or leave it."

The unmoved tone in Lexy's voice made it clear it was not up for discussion.

"And please pull yourself together. I need you at the White Out looking your best."

"Need me?" Kat repeated, processing the words like a foreign language. "Um…I'm a little short," Kat said and then looked down at Lexy's Pradas.

Lexy reached in her purse and pulled out a Lexy's co-branded card. "Here," she said, holding the credit card up, requiring Kat to lean forward to retrieve it. "Your limit is five thou."

"Thank you," Kat said.

"Don't thank me. I'm only covering the dress."

Kat hesitated before asking, "So, don't you get tired of this?"

Lexy heard her but pretended she did not as she exited the car with the help of a staff member. Having scratched Kat off her list, it was time to focus on Vincenzo. She needed to shift gears.

Kat exited the limo on a mission to find Dolly. Dolly sold her what she needed; she rolled a joint and left the club to dip into the alley to smoke. Once back indoors, Kat ordered a double shot of cognac and downed it, wincing as the warm liquid burned a trail down her throat and into the pit of her stomach. A sensual R&B song blared as she downed a second drink. Next, Kat went to the dressing room, took a five-minute shower, and changed into a basketball-inspired jersey tube top and a black thong before putting on a sexy cover-up. Finally, the make-up staff applied her makeup and curled her hair. With feet hurting from the recent excursion, she ignored the pain and went to work.

CHAPTER 10

LEXY & VINCENZO
Monday - Midnight

Lexy stepped out of her office bathroom in a tailored black pantsuit, a white button-down shirt, and black pumps with her auburn braids pulled back in a severe bun. She also wore Vincenzo's favorite perfume from her Mafioso mistress days. Viewing the security monitors and seeing Vincenzo and his men rising from their bar seats, with Marcus leading the way, she went about the office checking on her hardware. She took the safety off the 9mm secured under the desk above her lap and checked the Remington hidden in the adjoining bathroom. Finally, she took the safety off the holstered Ruger on her upper body and put her jacket on.

When Marcus knocked on the door, Lexy commanded them to come in. Marcus entered, followed by a tall, burly man, an out of breath Vincenzo, and his identical twin sons. The men wore expensive black suits and had the classic greased back hairdos that were stereotypical of their professional careers. Their dated looks were dead giveaways that they were the bad guys.

Vincenzo was not aging well. His once thick, wavy black hair was now a gray comb-over, barely covering his balding head; he had gained weight through the years, and his five feet ten frame was struggling with three hundred pounds of flesh. Lexy could not believe she was once his girl. In the past, Vincenzo had a medium built and wasn't too harsh to look at. Now, the years of overindulgence in rich foods, expensive liquor and cigars, and lack of exercise, combined with too many late nights, had taken a toll on the sixty-year-old man.

He held out his pudgy arms and waited for Lexy to come around the desk to give him a hug. He embraced her, leaving the dampness of his fat cheeks against her face, causing her to silently gag from the stench of his over-saturated cologne. Discreetly, while cheek-to-cheek with her nemesis, she glanced at Marcus. He could see the discomfort on her face from his position in the room. In the meantime, Vincenzo inhaled deeply and told her how good she smelled. The release from his personal space and his not so discreet groping could not have ended fast enough for her.

Everyone in the room settled into their designated places. The twin brothers, both with rat-like eyes and the same straight, narrow noses flanked the office door. One brother—smaller than the other—sported a large cobra tattoo on the side of his neck, which appeared to be inching up towards his cheek. The third entourage member stationed himself next to the two-way mirror overlooking the club. Marcus assumed a position to the left of Lexy, near her and the entrance to the bathroom.

Everyone in the room had concealed guns. Typically, security would have frisked the attendants and taken the weapons, but this was a unique situation. Everyone could keep them out of respect for Vincenzo. Taking their firearms would have been a clear signal of a dispute before the meeting took place. Lexy hoped the respect would be mutual. It was a gamble.

The tension in the room was palpable. Vincenzo pulled out a handkerchief and wiped sweat from his brow and seated himself on the other side of the desk. Manufacturing a smile, Lexy started the meeting. "Welcome to Lexy's. How can I help you, gentlemen?"

"Bella," Vincenzo replied, his voice booming throughout the room, "how are you?!"

"I'm fine, Vin. Would you like a drink?"

"Yes, let's celebrate! We have lots to celebrate!" He dug into his pocket and pulled out a cigar.

Fat bastard.

Lexy knew he expected her to come around the desk and light the cigar. A ritual from their past. As she did, Marcus poured Vincenzo a whiskey. He was going to put the bottle back on the mini bar when Vincenzo motioned for him to pour drinks for his boys. This bothered Marcus, but he was careful not to show it and simply nodded his head in acknowledgment and went about the task. Lexy lit the cigar and then took her seat back behind her desk.

Taking his enthusiasm down, Vincenzo said, "So, you've been avoiding me, huh?" He blew cigar smoke high in the air above her head. "You don't want to do business with me?" He frowned.

Lexy relaxed the expression on her face and softened her usual monotone voice. "Of course, I'm not avoiding you, Vin. It's been crazy around here. We had a death this weekend, among other things. It has been really crazy," she repeated.

Vincenzo eyed her, searching her face to see if she was lying. He could not read her. Tension filled the room again, but, after a moment, Vincenzo burst out laughing, which caused his men to laugh on cue. The tension eased. Lexy looked at him and wished he would get to the point. It had been a long day, and she wanted to get home to Lisa.

She looked at the men lining her office walls and surmised they were weak. They were there to protect Vincenzo but sucked on their drinks and relaxed against the walls as if nothing could go wrong. Lexy clenched her jaw and felt sweat drip down her back under her jacket. "What can I do for you, Vin?" she asked, keeping her voice soft and humble.

"Things are going great at Lexy's," he said, taking on a serious tone, again. "The family has taken notice. The boys back home."

Lexy hated when he talked like an old gangster. Back home was a reference to Chicago, but Vincenzo was raised by his Italian grandmother in Essex County, Michigan, who later migrated back to the Little Italy section of Chicago when he was thirteen. His refusal to embrace proper English was his way of trying to pull off that he was an original from across the pond. It would not surprise her if he had never been to Italy at all.

"We want to offer you a great deal!" He expanded his fat arms out to gesture he had just made a grand statement.

"Vin, I appreciate whatever..."

"You can make more money, and we can help you do it," he said, as if he was doing her a favor.

So, there it was, an old fashion shakedown. Lexy wanted to laugh and spit in his face. He had to be kidding.

Do modern criminals still use manpower for this shit? Why don't they go out and commit some updated criminal activity, like identity theft or computer espionage, and leave me the fuck alone?

"I am not interested in selling; you know that."

The space between Vincenzo's eyebrows creased. "No problem. No need to sale. We will be partners. Yes, partners. Get some things done."

Lexy paused, stalling to calculate the delivery of her response. "Well…that is not something I can consider without talking to my partner," she said in her usual monotone speech pattern. The men along the wall stood straight. The static vibe in the room turned dynamic.

Leaning his large, stout body forward, as far as his stomach would allow, Vincenzo challenged, "How is this? You are the owner."

Careful to look him in the eyes, she responded, "I own ninety percent of the club," and then hunched her shoulders and sighed to convey to him her hands were tied. "Under normal circumstances, the majority control would allow me to sell; however, there is a special clause in my purchase contract, which is meant to protect me from moments like this. Unless my partner agrees, I cannot alter partnership of the club." Lexy's jaws tightened.

Vincenzo ignored her statement and reached his stout hand into his inner suit pocket, which triggered a chain reaction from everyone in the room. Marcus reached for his midsection and Lexy's hand moved toward her lap. The men flanking the door stood tall and advanced a few steps. Vincenzo held up an open, fat hand and the men behind him relaxed, as did everyone else, somewhat.

Vincenzo produced folded documents from his suit coat. He held them up, and the burly goon walked over and placed the papers in front of Lexy. The elderly man took the last swig of whiskey from his glass and then struggled to release himself from the chair. "You sign these. I will personally pick them up Friday night, me and my attorney."

Lexy did not respond; she just walked to the door and opened it. The twins left first, followed by Vincenzo, and the third man trailed behind them. Marcus exited after the group. To show respect, and to keep temporary peace, Marcus set them up in one of the ultra-lounge areas and then rejoined Lexy back in the office where he found her standing and gazing blankly out of the two-way mirror. Turning and collapsing in the chair Vincenzo had just vacated, she asked Marcus to grab drinks.

Marcus poured himself a whiskey and Lexy a glass of red wine while she lit a cigarette. The two sat in silence for a moment.

"Shit!" Marcus exclaimed, "This was only a matter of time; I can't say I'm surprised."

"I know," Lexy said in a dejected tone, pulling the hair binder off her hair and letting the micro-braids loose around her stern, square-shaped face.

Both said nothing. Muffled cat calls floated up to the office. They sat for a few seconds, listening to the sound of the thumping of the bass from the music.

"He would do this on the night of the ball," Marcus bemoaned.

Marcus poured himself another shot, which surprised Lexy because his preference was for wine. *The stress is taking a toll on him.* She almost felt sorry enough for him to offer sympathy sex, but Lisa was waiting for her.

"Well, you do own ten percent. What says you?" Her right eyebrow rose, which was a mock of what Marcus usually did.

"Hey, stop that," he smiled, amused she was acting unlike her serious self, which was a rarity. He continued, "You know it's completely up to you. I say we bounce. Bounce as high and as far as a one-way flight will take us. I don't mind an early retirement. I couldn't think of anything better than to run off with you into the sunset, an island sunset."

She looked at him with hidden pity. They would never be. The excitement between the two no longer existed for her, but she genuinely did care for him.

"I think I'm going to head home early if you don't mind. You good?"

"Yes. I'm good." He walked over to her, "You know nothing good would come of joining with them."

"I know, but we have a plan. I think things are going well. I'm pressed for time, but everything is on track. I think I can get it all together by Friday. I have a meeting with the bank this week, so I'll get the final word."

"Okay, sounds good, Baby Doll. Let me know if you need anything else from me. I've gone over all the figures with a fine-toothed comb. We are solid."

"Solid?"

"Yes, solid."

"Thank you, Marcus. I don't know what I'd do without you."

"You're welcome. Okay, I'll better get back to running our investment. I'll see you tomorrow." He kissed her forehead and left.

LISA
Monday - 1 a.m.

Ring, Ring.

"Hello," Lisa's delicate voice answered.

"Hey, I just wanted to let you know I'm on my way. Leaving the club now."

"Great! I'll start a hot bath," Lisa replied sweetly.

"Ok, Leese, I'll see you in a few."

Clad in a pink G-String and a short, pink terry cloth robe, Lisa busied herself preparing for Lexy's arrival. Upon completion, soft jazz music played through invisible speakers; the aroma of vanilla musk bath beads filled the air; multiple vanilla scented candles lined the soaking tub; a Pinot Noir sat opened to breathe; and a bowl of green and red grapes chilled in the fridge. Now, leaning over the bathroom counter, plucking a few stray eyebrow hairs, she thought she heard a noise. Her soft voice echoed through the empty house, "Lex, is that you, babe?"

There was no reply. Thinking she had mistaken the sound, she continued plucking. A few seconds later, she heard a noise again. This time, she placed the tweezers down and went to investigate, her pedicured feet gracefully crossed the bathroom floor, and she went to the end of the hallway where she descended the stairs and peered over the landing railing into the dark.

"Lex?"

The open concept rooms below were dark, but she could see the outlines of the furniture illuminated by the various skylight panels in the cathedral styled ceilings. Laughing at herself for being paranoid, she went back upstairs and resumed tweezing her eyebrows.

During the removal of her makeup, out of the corner of her eye, she saw a figure come in. "That was quick. You must have...," she began, turning towards the door. Lisa jumped back in astonishment. It startled her to see a lanky white male with slicked-back hair dressed in all black standing in the doorway. He lazily looked at her as he leaned against the door frame; she looked at him with wide eyes, words caught in her throat. Fear had her stuck and she was too scared to acknowledge the truth of the unexpected situation.

* * *

She tried to remember if she had set the alarm, but it was a moot point now. She had no way of knowing he had slithered into the garage when her car rolled in and that when the ray of the garage had been broken, and the door started lifting again from his intrusion, she assumed it was a glitch in the remote and shut the door again. It was easy for him to pick the lock to the door leading into the kitchen and wait in the shadows of the lower level, watching her open the wine and preparing the grapes. Before heading upstairs, he opened the patio and screen doors for his eventual escape.

Now, the two stood looking at each other. He had a lackadaisical gaze; her mouth hung open as her eyes filled with dread. For Lisa, time stood still, and the bathroom felt small. The air in her lungs felt heavy.

Stammering, Lisa was the first to speak, "I-I-I have cash a-and j-jewelry," she offered, her voice a low whisper to quiet the fear.

He looked at her but said nothing.

"I won't tell anyone," she whined. "Just take the things and go."

He twirled a ten-inch hunter's knife in his black leather gloved hands, his silence-bathed cocky arrogance spoke louder than words. With intensity, hooded eyes continued watching her. A grin slowly spread across his pale face, expanding a cobra tattoo on the side of his neck that inched up his cheek.

Looking at the steel blade in his hand, Lisa began inching backward until the bathtub prevented her from going any further.

He advanced towards her slowly but remained silent. The sly grin remained anchored on his gaunt face. Panic-stricken, her eyes darted around, looking for a way out of her predicament. Spotting a stone bowl filled with decorative soaps on the edge of the tub, Lisa grabbed the weighted item and hurled it at him with all her might.

Wham!

It hit the center of his forehead. His neck snapped back, and he dropped the knife.

This was the moment.

Taking off, Lisa tried to run past him but felt his hands reach out and grab her around her waist. He swung her violently into a wall. Her head hit hard, and everything went black.

Scrambling, he grabbed Lisa by the ankles and dragged her to the center of the floor and ripped open her pink housecoat, revealing her smooth, buttery skin. His excitement barely contained, he pulled one glove off with his teeth, hurriedly took his pants down, and mounted her, bringing her back to consciousness with the first thrust. He met her scream with a punch to the face and then another. Grabbing her throat, he shook his head slowly back and forth to tell her to stop resisting.

Tears streamed down her face, and she began to plead, "Oh God…please…no!"

The vice grip around her neck made the words barely audible. The assailant continued choking her, causing her eyes to bulge and her lips to go numb. Feeling her life force draining, Lisa began to frantically scratch out, raking his facial skin under her acrylic nails with each aimless contact. The violence excited him; he continued the violation. Just as Lisa went unconscious for the second time, he ejaculated. When the final release wracked his body, he slowly got off her, pulled up his pants, and picked up the glove and the knife.

Tell that to your dyke bitch!

Sensing too much time had been spent on what was supposed to have been an in-and-out job, the rapist turned and bolted out the door. Running out of the bedroom, he slammed into Lexy—pushing her into the wall as he shot down the hall. Lexy regained her footing.

Bang! A bullet whizzed past his ear. Bang!

A second bullet caught the flesh in his shoulder.

With Lexy in pursuit, he hit the stairs full speed, propelling his body down and stumbling forward while using the railings to aid his escape. Once out of the family room patio door, he ran to the back of the house and disappeared into the tree-lined darkness. When Lexy realized her efforts were futile, she turned and ran back into the house. Just as fast as she had gotten down the stairs, she reversed her route and took the stairs two at a time to get back to her bedroom.

"Leese, Leese!" she called out.

Rushing to her bedroom suite, Lexy discovered her girlfriend on the bathroom floor. She kneeled and scooped the gasping woman's small frame into her arms. Lisa's damaged vocal cords screamed in soundless agony as her mouth hung open, and her eyes began to swell shut.

Out of breath and with her lungs still stinging from the chase, Lexy tried to console her. "I got you! You're okay! I've got you, Leese! It's gonna be okay!" she passionately exclaimed, cradling the battered woman. "Come on, sweetie. I've got you!"

Lexy struggled to control her emotions. In desperation, she retrieved her phone from her pocket and voice-dialed 911 as a deluge of tears streamed down her face, which matched the salted river of despair that poured down Lisa's cheeks. Unable to speak, Lisa peered through puffy eyes for confirmation the nightmare was over. The two sat on the floor together as minutes ticked by until the sound of sirens cut through their fog of confusion and heartache. Lexy effortlessly lifted Lisa and carried her out of the bathroom and placed her on her bed.

As the sirens grew louder, Lexy hovered over Lisa and checked each breath while trying to wrap her mind around the scenario she had come home to. The situation stunk of Vincenzo. Having experienced some of his tactics firsthand, all signs pointed to him. This was a warning.

* * *

Lexy had come in through the garage entrance off the kitchen and, at once, knew something was wrong. Stifling, heavy summer air competed against cool conditioned air in the home. A warm breeze flowed in through the open kitchen sliding patio door. Lively jazz music floated down from upstairs, but the house held an eeriness that paid homage to a scene in a horror movie before insanity unleashed. Something felt wrong.

With her pistol drawn, she had advanced with guarded stealth around the lower level, checking the floor by using the glow of the streetlights coming in through the skylights. Returning to the family room and kitchen junction, she eased up the carpeted stairs and checked the two guest bedrooms and their adjoining en suite bathrooms before making it to the last open door to the left, her bedroom.

Now, she stood watching over Lisa.

"Freeze, East Lake Police!"

The command sounded like it came out warped and broken. Using the bedroom door frame as a shield, a young officer stood with his gun pointed at her.

He braced himself, ready to fire, and shakily said, "I need you to slowly take your gun out of your holster and place it on the ground! Keep your other hand in the air!"

Lexy calmly said, "Ok, easy," while putting her left arm up and slowly placing the Ruger on the floor with her right hand.

At that moment, Sgt. Watts arrived.

"What are you doing, Officer Dick?" the older man said in an even tone so as not to startle the one-year rookie. He holstered his own firearm and then pulled up on his police equipment weighted belt that had refuge under his large over-hanging stomach.

"Sarge, she has a gun!" he shouted louder than necessary and cocked his head to the floor while keeping his stance.

"Officer Dick, holster your firearm and secure the rest of this floor, now!" Sgt. Watts commanded.

Lexy stood oblivious to the two. Her stomach churned, and her legs felt weak. The sound of emergency medical technicians ascending the stairs could be heard in the background. Sgt. Watts came over to the bed and checked Lisa's pulse.

"In here guys!" he shouted. He turned to Lexy. "Ms. Leigh, do you need EMS?"

"Excuse me?" she said with a puzzled look on her face, but then registered what he said. "Um, no, Ward, I'm fine. Please, take care of Lisa," she said worriedly.

Absentmindedly, Lexy bent to retrieve her gun, but Sgt. Watts put up a weathered, age-spotted hand. "Please, leave it," he said in a gentle tone. With gloved hands, he placed the gun in a large plastic forensic bag that he pulled from his back pocket. "Please, let's step out to give them space to tend to her."

The two went into the hallway.

Scratching his round, balding head, he said, "Umm, I really hate to be so formal, Ms. Leigh."

"Huh? Please, Ward. You've always called me Lexy."

"My apologies, uh, Lexy. I need to frisk you, and I need an official statement," he said with a look on his face that conveyed discomfort.

Officer Watts and Lexy knew each other well. He visited the club often. Now, standing before her, he ran his hands along her body—something he never imagined he would do—and noticed how amazing she felt, which made him feel awkward. Afterward, he allowed her to step into one of the guest bedrooms and sit on the bed while he prepared his pen-based computer to take the incident report. He hoped whatever had gone on was justifiable. Arresting the owner of Lexy's was the last thing he wanted to do. Lexy lit a cigarette. Normally, he would have told a suspect or witness to put it out, but, in this case, he did not.

"Ms. Leigh, what happened here tonight? Your neighbors called and reported hearing what they thought was gunfire, but they weren't sure, and then we got the 911 call from this location."

"Please, Ward, call me Lexy."

He mouthed, "Okay."

"Let's see. I left the club…"

"What time was that?"

"Um, about one."

"One this morning?"

"Yes."

"Okay, go on."

"When I got here, the door was ajar. I drew my…"

"Excuse me." Sgt. Watts looked up from his hand-held computer. "Which door?"

"The patio door, off the kitchen."

"Any sign of forced entry?"

"Uh, I don't know."

"Okay, then what happened?"

"I, ah, drew my gun and went upstairs. That's when I found...," she trailed off.

"What did you find?"

"Um, someone knocked me into the wall. I fired." Lexy sighed. "Can I see Leese now?"

"Please, Ms. Leigh. I mean, Lexy. I need you to finish your statement," he said apologetically.

"Of course," she replied wearily and rubbed her temples.

"I'll need your permit to carry, please."

"I'll have to get it out of my purse, which is downstairs on the floor, near the garage door."

"Okay, um, we will deal with that. So, did you know the intruder?"

"Ah...well...it was dark, so I didn't get a good look at him. I chased him, but he ran out the patio door."

"Did you notice anything missing?"

Lexy looked at the officer in bewilderment. "Missing? Everything happened fast. I don't know, Ward," she said, then shook her head and rested her elbows on her knees before dropping her head into her hands and running her hands over her head, flattening her loose braids in the process. "I called you guys and then sat with Leese."

Reading her body language and hearing the stress in her voice, Sgt. Watts shouted out, "Say, Riley, where you guys taking her?"

"This is a level one. We're headed in," the medic yelled back from the room.

With compassion, Sgt. Watts said, "Lexy, they're bypassing East Lake and taking her to the trauma center. You know, county. Let me finish this, and we'll have you on your way."

Lights from emergency vehicles continued to light up the block while Sgt. Watts completed the incident report, and more personnel arrived on the scene. The commotion in the oversized home continued well into the wee hours. East Lake neighbors peered out windows and stood at mailboxes. Situations of this nature were taken seriously in the upscale Caucasian suburban city.

"Ms., I mean, Lexy, at this point, you cannot leave the state. Formality, you know. If you remember anything, please don't hesitate to call." He gave her another apologetic look and handed her his card with the incident number on it. Quietly he added, "See you Friday," and pulled up his equipment laden belt.

Lexy automatically went into business mode, despite the circumstances. "Of course, Ward, I look forward to seeing you. It's been a while since you've been down. I was beginning to think you were tired of us," she said.

"Ah, you know how it is, family life and stuff. That's all. But right now, the family is out of town," he said and winked.

"Okay, I'll see you soon," she replied and then produced a manufactured smile.

"You betcha. I hope things work out here," he said and gave her one last "I'm sorry" look.

After speaking with Sgt. Watts, forensic personnel dusted Lexy's hands for firearm residue and poured throughout her home, taking note of even the most insignificant items. Word within the small police department traveled fast, so she endured a second interview from Detective Hall, another faithful client of the club. He was more rigorous than Sgt. Watts, but she understood why. It was a man thing, more than a detective thing. Normally, their paths crossed in her club, but now, as the lead detective, she was on his turf and he displayed professional dominance. Lexy did not care about Detective Hall's ego. Someone had broken into her home, assaulted her guest, and threatened her well-being, which justified the shooting.

Marcus showed up to offer support, but more importantly, to discuss their next move. Once cleared by the police, Lexy and Marcus walked to his car—parked further down the street because the emergency vehicles blocked the cul-de-sac—and she filled him in on the details of the evening. They discussed making Lexy's home more secure and the plans to deal with Lisa's rape, the media, and Vincenzo. The two turned and reversed their path to walk back to her car parked in the garage. Concerned, Marcus watched a police officer maneuver his squad car out of Lexy's path. He wished there was a better way for him to take control of things but knew he had best follow through with her wishes on all matters discussed.

CHAPTER 11

Lexy
Monday - Sunrise

As Lexy drove to the hospital, she clenched and unclenched her jaws repeatedly while coming to terms with what had happened. She deduced it was time to call in outside help, something she seldom did. The Twin Cities were not large metro areas; therefore, there were a limited number of powerful people. Lexy was one of those people, and she could usher in both legal and illegal help from the other few. Things had gotten personal and she could not ignore that.

* * *

As the sun rose, morning mist evaporated from the dew on the grass of the hospital grounds. Lexy's eyes ached, but other than that, adrenaline still coursed through her body. Once she obtained Lisa's room number and registered with security, she headed to the third floor. A tired-looking nurse verified Lisa's location and directed her down the hall. As she approached the door, she heard voices on the other side. She stopped and smoothed her hair before knocking lightly. A man's voice instructed her to come in.

Lexy stepped into the room to the scene of Lisa laying in a hospital bed with her Caucasian mother standing next to her, holding her hand, and her African American father on the other side of the bed, facing the door. Lisa's father glared at Lexy; her mother followed with a disapproving look. Mentally, Lexy dismissed them both and began advancing towards the bed.

"You are not welcomed here!" Lisa's father shouted.

Lisa's mother shot her husband a look. "James, this is a hospital."

Lisa's soft, curly hair was pulled into a lightly secured ponytail on top of her head—evidence of her mother's nurturing care—and oxygen flowed into her nostrils through plastic tubing. Lisa turned her swollen and bruised face towards her mother and then to her father. "It's ok, mom, dad. I'm fine," she hoarsely stated and raised her hand, which had been used to secure an I.V., to touch her father's arm.

"You don't have to do this!" Her father's hostile stare stayed locked on its target as her mother stood with a pained expression on her face.

"Please, dad." The small woman whispered.

As Lisa's father walked towards the door, he continued to glare at Lexy. He did not take his eyes off her until he had no choice but to turn to walk out. "We'll be right outside," he said, looking back at Lexy with hatred.

Lexy paid no attention to them. Her concern was for Lisa. Looking at her tiny body in the bed, she felt responsible for what happened. There was so much she wanted to say but did not know where to begin. Quietly, she made the final approach to the bedside. Pulling up a chair, she sat down and began stroking the natural waves in the bedridden girl's hair. "Leese, baby, I'm so sorry. I'm so sorry this happened to you." Looking into Lisa's swollen eyes, she wished she were lying in that bed.

"Lex, I'm so glad you came," she whispered. "He could have killed me."

Lexy's heart sank at the sound of Lisa's inflamed vocal cords. She laid her head on the upper part of the bed railing, not wanting her girlfriend to see the lost look on her face. Lisa reached out and placed a hand—with broken acrylics—on Lexy's leg. Caught up in her own thoughts, Lexy spoke without thinking, "Fuckin' Vincenzo!"

"Vincenzo, what does he have to do…?"

"I will make this right, Leese," Lexy said, without realizing what was happening.

"This? What do you mean, this?" With eyes focused on the top of Lexy's head, Lisa's expression interchanged between a question and an accusation as the spoken words registered. "Is this all because of you?"

Lexy jerked her head up, now realizing the implication and pleaded, "It's not what you think, Leese!" and reached out to take her hand.

Lisa recoiled, pushing back into the comfort of the bed, her body aching in the process. "I-I can't do this, Lex, I can't." Tears found their way down her swollen, bruised cheeks.

"Leese, no, baby, I'll make things right!" Lexy pleaded and tried to soothe her with gentle hushes.

Lisa pushed her away with what strength she had, wincing in pain with the motion. Barely able to get the words out, she continued, "I can't live like this. You people are too risky; I tried. I should have listened to my parents."

Lisa's words stung like a punch in the gut.

Confused, Lexy stood up. "You people?" she repeated.

"I should have never given my time to someone like you. Your lifestyle and all the other bullshit that comes with it." Lisa reached up and placed her hand lightly to her neck and winced. "What? I die over you?"

Despite Lisa's quiet, strained voice, the expression on her face said it all. Her attitude was fierce from the "We told you so" talk she had just gotten from her parents.

"W-why…why…why did this ha-p-pen?" Lisa stammered and began to cry.

Lisa never heard the reply. Lexy walked out the door. Lisa's sobbing became fainter and fainter. Likewise, she did not notice the scowl on Lisa's father's face when she strode by working hard to push back the crushing feeling of rejection and guilt while moving on weak legs and willing herself not to collapse in the hallway. Her cell phone buzzed incessantly in her pocket, but her disjointed emotions did not register the activity.

While waiting at the elevator, she tapped the fingers of her right hand at an accelerated pace against her pant leg, her thoughts swinging between the feelings of condemnation for her part in Lisa's rape and indignance at the reference of "you people." She did not hear the footsteps upon her until it was too late.

Intuitively, Lexy swung around and came face to face with Lisa's father invading her personal space, his mouth inches from hers with an expression of barely controlled hostility on his light-tan face. He spoke through clenched teeth and pointed his index finger close to her lips, "Stay away from my daughter! You hear me!"

Lexy stood motionless, sizing up the sturdy black man. Her muscles tensed. "You better back the fuck off!" she replied loudly.

Without warning, the angry man shoved her shoulders, slamming her into the wall between the elevators. Nostrils flaring and eyes narrowing like Satan's messenger, he spoke in a low voice with heated breath directly in her face, spitting as he did. "Listen, stupid bitch, my daughter was never into women until you came along! Stay away from her! You hear me! Stay! Away! From! Her!"

Lexy did not speak. Without fanfare, she maneuvered her Ruger LCP from her holster and eased it up between them, pressing the gun under his chin.

His expression changed.

"Now, take your motherfuckin' hands off me!" she hissed like a snake spitting venom, "Or, I'ma blow your motherfuckin' head off!"

Just as she said the words, a woman stepped off one of the elevators. He released her shoulders, staggered backward, and turned around before making his way back down the hall. He passed a man with freckles and strawberry blonde hair. Lisa's father looked away from the man to avoid eye contact. The man did the same. In the meantime, the hospital staff met him partway as they came in his direction to investigate the outburst. He pretended he did not know what was going on and made his way back to his daughter's room. The woman eyed Lexy with caution. Lexy regained her balance off the wall, hit the elevator button, and glanced up at the camera in the hallway before stepping in the elevator and keeping a watchful eye. At the lobby, she headed outside, taking note of the activity at the security booth, hoping personnel had not seen the situation with Lisa's father on the cameras. Once outside, she lit a cigarette and made a phone call.

"Yes, I need her secure, but don't make it obvious. Yeah, that's important. She can't know your company is protecting her. It might scare her…yeah, uh-huh, twenty-four hours. Yes, at all costs. I understand. I'll take care of it."

Next, Lexy checked the messages and texts left for her while she was with Lisa. Going back towards the hospital entrance, she reached into her pocket, pulled out the velvet box with a diamond ring in it, dropped it in a trash bin next to the door, and headed to the emergency room. Lillian had been brought in by the paramedics for shortness of breath. Despite her exhaustion, it was important to be there for her sisters.

* * *

A little after eight a.m., Lillian was stabilized and admitted to a private room with a bleak prognosis. The sisters went to a family waiting area to discuss Lillian, make business calls, and check emails. Between conversations with Tina and Marlene, and phone calls with Marcus, Lexy internally ruminated about the surmounting pressure in her life: Lisa's rape, Vincenzo, the shooting and pending police investigation, the upcoming meeting at the bank, the club renovations, Friday's ball, Sandy's overdose, Sandy's powerful family, and now Lillian.

Stress was nothing new to the woman with nine lives, but now it felt like looming devastation. To stave off the pain of living and adjust her thinking, Lexy instinctively began locking down her emotions. Tina and Marlene, accustomed to her flat demeanor, did not ask what was wrong, but instead assumed it was because of Lillian's illness. No longer able to sustain herself physically or mentally, Lexy gave her sisters reassuring hugs and supporting words before leaving the hospital.

* * *

Sitting in her car, Lexy hit the steering with balled up hands. "Ugh!" she shouted with a heart filled with anger.

What have I done to anyone?

With her mouth set in a hard-pressed line, Lexy pushed her body back into the leather seat with force and then lunged forward, hitting the steering wheel, again, struggling to hold back tears. Then, just as quickly as she had gotten angry, she went numb. She drove a few short blocks to the Ambassador Suites Hotel. From her hotel window, she could see the hospital. Before shutting the curtains to keep out the Monday morning sun, she texted Marcus to let him know she had made it to her destination, opened a bottle of red wine from the executive suite refrigerator, and stepped onto the balcony to smoke a cigarette.

After a shower, she took two Benadryl tablets, chugging them down with wine like a sailor on a weekend pass, and then laid across the bed wrapped in a towel. When the sleep aid and the wine mixed in her system, heaviness engulfed her body, and her strained eyes closed. Slowly, Lexy faded into a deep, dark sleep, the last images in her mind were of her cradling Lisa's violated body and looking at her pummeled face. Upon waking at sunset, the sullen woman took two more sleeping tablets and drank the rest of the bottle of wine, causing her to drift back into another bout of nightmare-filled darkness.

CHAPTER 12

MARIA
Monday 4 - 12:10 p.m.

In a low-income St. Paul neighborhood known as Frogtown, Maria paced frantically back and forth across the worn, wooden living room floor of a first level, small, two-bedroom duplex she shared with her grandmother and her older sister, Estelle. Her thick, black hair whipped around each time she reached a wall and u-turned to go in the opposite direction. The fascinating temptress from Jordan's party was no longer present. In her place, a fatigued young woman, without make-up and with frizzy hair, marched about. The beginning of dark circles formed under her eyes, and her skin looked pale, almost sallow, instead of the porcelain glow from the previous evening. Her clothes were simple. She wore a pair of cut-off jeans and a white tank top; her naturally large breasts strained against the thin material.

The tiny, sparsely-furnished living quarters housed a plain couch covered in brown fabric with two laundry baskets on it, a matching wing-backed chair positioned in front of a picture window, and a displaced wooden thrift store coffee table that sat lodged between the couch and the chair from when the pacing woman shoved it out of the way. The walls were bare except for a large oil painting of Jesus with outstretched hands, which hung over the couch.

In the adjacent room, the formal dining room, Maria's frail grandmother lay in a hospital bed. The stench of sickness permeated the air. Medical waste and supplies lay scattered throughout the room, along with Catholic prayer candles. The kitchen, accessed through a narrow door to the rear of the dining room, fared no better.

Dirty dishes had piled up in the sink and the trash can was full, which contributed to the not-so-nice smell. The elder Gonzalez lay in her bed oblivious to the untidiness of the home or the questionable actions of her granddaughter. Narcotics maintained the terminally ill woman in a comatose state as she waited for the pull of death.

Both livid and worried, Maria looked at her phone and sighed. Since Jordan's party, TL had not responded to her numerous texts or calls, thus placing her in the position to debate whether to be concerned or irate. Anxiety got the best of her, so she concluded that he had abandoned her. Also, fear gripped her over her upcoming audition at Lexy's, and she desperately wanted his reassurance. Just as her frantic fingers started dialing his number to leave another rambling message, Maria heard footsteps on the front porch. Barefooted, she bounded to the door and flung it open. Estelle stood on the porch with groceries in her arms. "Oh, it's you," Maria said disappointedly.

Estelle stepped inside. She noted the condition of the rooms and wished her double shift had not prevented her from cleaning last night. Setting the groceries down, she advanced into the dining room to check on her grandmother. Seeing that she was fine, she returned to the living room and confronted her sister. "¿Cual es tu problema?" (What's your problem?)

Maria swung around.

"¿Estás bien?" (Are you okay?) Estelle inquired.

Maria lashed out, "Speak English! We live in America, you know! Shouldn't you be at work?"

Her pacing resumed.

Estelle did not respond. She took the groceries to the kitchen. Next, she walked back through the dining room and down the hallway leading to the bedrooms. In Maria's room, she took a medication bottle out of the nightstand drawer and headed back to the living room. Catching Maria on her pacing route coming back towards the dining room, she asked, "¿ha estado tomando su medicación?" (Have you been taking your medication?)

"If you don't speak English, I won't talk to you!" Maria shouted.

Estelle glanced at her grandmother and back at Maria. "Well?"

"Of course, I am!" Maria shouted, disregarding Estelle's look that said, "Keep your voice down for Nana."

Not believing her, Estelle asked, "Okay, if you are, what is this?" and showed Maria the medicine bottle in her hand, her face frowning in exasperation. "Look at the date on it. It's full."

Maria glared at her. Fussing in Spanish, and saying a few unladylike phrases, she marched into the dining room and grabbed a medicine vial near her purse. Spinning around, she threw it across the room at Estelle. The bottle hit Estelle and bounced off her medical scrubs.

"You have my spare prescription!" Maria lashed out.

Estelle looked embarrassed and set the container down before crossing the small distance between them. "I'm sorry," she said and tried to hug the enraged girl.

Maria pushed her away and went to the living room picture window. Staring out, she watched African American children playing kickball along trash-strewn Edmund Avenue, delaying their game each time a car came down the pothole-filled street.

Estelle tried to fix things. "It just looks like you haven't had sleep. This place is a mess, and you're so angry…um…anxious…I…"

Still fuming, Maria sarcastically interrupted, "Yea, fix it by shoving anxiety medicine down my throat."

Estelle joined her at the window and lovingly said, "You know I love you. This medication is for a time like this when you get a little anxious. I just want to make sure you're alright."

Despite her irritation with her sister, Maria needed to hear the words of concern. Anxiety filled her, and against her will, her mind kept racing and conjuring up terrible scenarios. With two sleepless nights under her belt, all issues seemed magnified and caring for her grandmother was becoming increasingly difficult. In addition, Estelle often worked overtime or double shifts, which did not allow Maria much time to spend with TL. Maria's confused mind told her she would die if she did not see him. He was her world. He made her feel important and desired. Without him, she felt no validation.

Maria slumped down into the wing-backed chair and turned her large, gold-flecked brown eyes up to Estelle, who had begun rubbing her back like she did when they were children. "What has gotten you so upset?" Estelle said, brushing stray, long hairs out of the disturbed girl's face.

With a childlike demeanor, Maria confessed, "Nothing sleep won't cure. I'm sorry things look so unorganized. I've had such a busy weekend, plus caring for Nana gets a little overwhelming, sometimes."

"I can relate," Estelle agreed. "I-I was overwhelmed, too, before you came. I appreciate you being here."

"I'm glad to be here, too," Maria said with honesty. "Everything is fine," she finished with a lie before casting her eyes downward.

Estelle looked down at the long lashes on Maria's eyelids and hoped she was telling the truth. It would be difficult for her to care for both Maria and her Grandmother if Maria could not cope with things. Estell pondered whether her sister needed to speak to a professional about her feelings but dismissed the idea, wanting to believe the script offered to her from Maria was the truth.

"You know I'm here for you. We are a team. Let me know if you wanna talk, okay?"

"Si," Maria said flatly, her expression lackluster.

Estelle eyed her and added, "Maybe we should get a medical aid to come in and watch Nana. You and I can both take a break and spend some quality time together. I think we need it."

Maria did not reply. Estelle would not understand how much she wanted to please TL and forge a future with him. She was waiting for the right time, preferably when money was coming in, to explain things, but, even then, she knew money from the sinful act of dancing at Lexy's would not sway the staunch Catholic. When the time came, it would be a battle, but it would be worth fighting if it meant being with TL.

Estelle pulled her cell phone out of her scrub pocket and gasped. "Oh, I'm going to be late. I gotta get going. Please, put the groceries up for me and get the house straight before Nana sees it," Estelle stroked her hair one last time, "and think about what I said, okay?" Not waiting for a reply, she kissed Maria on the top of the head and ran out the door.

As Estelle left, Maria's cell phone trilled, displaying TL's number. Maria's heart leaped with joy. TL spent the next ten minutes soothing Maria's emotions. He fed her classic lies; she did not notice. His voice made her high like an illegal drug. She felt high off the promise that he was not abandoning her and the confirmation he would make sweet love to her again. By the time they got off the phone, her only mission was to tend to her grandmother, including giving her a dose of morphine to keep her comfortable and placid. Next, she tended to the home, starting with picking up the medicine bottle she had thrown at Estelle. Maria began moving about the dining room cleaning and humming.

Unfortunately, Estelle had been right about her assessment of Maria's instability. The pill bottle Maria threw belonged to her grandmother. Maria felt she did not need the anxiety medication and had stopped taking it weeks ago. The euphoric feelings she felt being with TL had convinced her she did not need meds. As far as Maria was concerned, she was fine. Tugging her shorts down below her pelvic line, she ran her fingers over the new TL$ tattoo on her voluptuous hip.

BEV & KAT
Monday - 4 p.m.

Beverly arrived at the Jeté School of Dance on Grand Avenue, located across the street from the Café Grand bakery. She was excited to take a drop-in ballet class and spend time with Kat. The small, well-established school had been a staple in the community for the past twenty years and helped produced quality dancers from throughout the Metro area.

After making her way down steep cement steps, to access the lower school level, Beverly walked along a narrow hall lined with framed photos of former and existing students in various dance positions while hearing the familiar cadence of the dance world echoing off wooden floors. As she advanced, a feeling of nostalgia washed over her. Breathing in the familiar and comforting smells of the mustiness of the old building, like a child enjoying the scents of a distant memory of a day at the fair, her journey continued towards the sound of the count of an unseen instructor's voice, towards remembrances of past dreams. "One, and two, and three, and four…"

Stepping into the adult dance studio, she surveyed the room. Various women stretched, chatted, or busied themselves on electronic devices as they waited for the class to begin. Beverly spotted Kat in the front of the class and headed to the far side of the room to join her. The girls hugged but refrained from boisterous banter. They maintained a more serious demeanor due to the disciplined environment. In hushed tones, Beverly commented, "Bird, it seems like just yesterday we were here."

"I know," Kat gushed, "I can't wait to do some real dancing."

"Well, my limber friend, I'm conditioned to run and lift weights, so I'll admit my flexibility has a lot to be desired." Beverly twisted her fingers to denote stiffness. "I'm glad I've been taking a few classes here and there. Otherwise, I wouldn't have the nerve to come here."

"I'm hoping it's like riding a bike. I kept coming after you left, but this last year not so much," Kat admitted.

"You'll be fine. You are a natural," Beverly encouraged.

Throughout the class, the unofficial twins would occasionally look at each other in one of the many mirrors. Kat would wink or smirk, causing Beverly to stifle a smile. Their discreet antics did not cause the girls to falter in their moves. They were naturals and followed the instructor with ease. Kat, indeed, was the more flexible dancer and moved about with the agility and the grace of a gazelle although her smoking had impacted her breathing. Beverly exhibited great technique, which translated into precise, powerful movements. A few of the seasoned dancers, who had worked up to the advanced level during the years of Beverly and Kat's absence, looked at the girls out of the corner of their eyes with jealousy. To them, there was nothing worse than a beautiful girl with exceptional dance skills, let alone two. Following the class, a few dancers complimented them, and the instructor told them how good it was to see them. In unison, and linked arm-to-arm, with spirit, they quoted the school's motto, "Dance, someone is watching!" Then, they collapsed into laughter.

After class, the girls walked across the street to a smoothie shop next to the Café Grand. Settling in a booth, they chatted about how good it was to dance together again and complimented one another, each trying to outdo the other. Then they walked down Grand Avenue occasionally admiring goods in the windows of boutiques shops that lined the historic street. They came upon a pet store and gazed at kittens romping in the front window pet pen. "Oh, let's go in, Bev. They're so cute."

Within minutes, the girls were standing in front of the enclosure with a staff member. Kat cuddled a tiny black kitten in her hand, showering it with kisses on its small head. The kitten's weak meows came at a fast pace, wondering where the warmth of the other kittens had gone. Beverly could see how much Kat loved the kitten and offered to buy it for her.

Kat tried to place the ball of fur down but realized its tiny claws clung to lose hair tendrils framing her face. "Aw, that would be nice, but cost isn't the problem. TL can't be around cats," she said and continued working to untangle herself from the now playful kitten.

Beverly looked at her inquisitively. "Allergic?"

Kat giggled. "You might say that," she responded, keeping to herself that TL would not be around a pussy he was not sleeping with.

The two girls left the shop and walked in silence back towards the dance school. Kat reflected on the fact that she could not have something as simple as a pet because of TL, but he could have all the women he wanted. The thought depressed her. There were so many things she wanted to do, to experience. Life seemed like a rut. She glanced over at Beverly and noticed a glow about her.

Could Christianity work?

Beverly caught Kat looking at her from the corner of her eye. "What's wrong?" she asked.

"Oh, nothing, I was thinking, thinking of life. There is so much I want to experience and do. I think I'm going to get a cat."

"I thought you said TL can't be around cats."

Kat smirked. "Yes, true. But who says I'll be with TL when I get it?"

"I see. I see," Beverly mused. "I don't mind having another cat around. Jetta would like that."

"Bev."

"Yes."

"I love you."

"I love you too, Bird."

* * *

Well, look at this! Ain't this some shit!

TL sat in his parked car in a lot across the street from where Kat and Beverly were walking, waiting for one of his girls to come out of the corner store. He could not believe his luck when he saw them. He had identified the woman from the gym. TL settled into the leather seat and crafted a chess move based on the newfound information. Through slanted eyes, he focused on her. There was something familiar. He searched his memory and flashed on Kat's social media account and Beverly's picture on Kat's phone as a contact photo, both of which, at the time, he viewed with passing glances as just another insignificant person.

So, you're Beverly.

TL licked his thick lips. "Game on."

KAT
Monday - Evening

After departing from Beverly, Kat drove along a deserted, winding two-lane gravel road with the sun descending westbound along with her vehicle. Still dressed in dance wear and an over-sized white T-shirt, which hung and revealed a bony white shoulder and exposed her slender, lanky legs—she muttered under her breath, cursing Dakota County for constructing a rural road that looked like a scene from a slasher movie. There were no lights, rocks hit against her Range Rover, and the setting sun caused the trees and foliage to take on an eerie glow.

Why would anyone live out here?

In the distance behind her, a car's headlights headed in her direction.

"Aw, fuck!" Glancing down at her oversized purse and then back in the rear view mirror, she consoled herself, "Ok Kat, you're good… you're good…you got this." Bringing the white four-wheel-drive to a stop, she exclaimed, "What the hell! Why put a light here?!"

Looking at the bizarrely placed traffic signal, she decided not to mess with the alcohol in her purse and focus on getting to her destination in the country outskirts of the city of Burnsville. Taking a deep breath, she relaxed a little and tapped her over-due-for-amanicure acrylics on the steering wheel and glanced in the rear-view mirror. "Oh, shit!"

To her horror, she realized the car that had been gaining on her was a police cruiser. Now, parked behind her at the stoplight, with an open container of alcohol and drug paraphernalia in her purse, her heart beat at an ominous pace. When the traffic signal turned green, she sat frozen and wide-eyed. Her stomach churned when the lights on the patrol car lit up. Slowly and carefully, so as not to roll the vehicle down into the ditch off the dirt shoulder road, Kat moved over to the side, ready to accept the fate of jail. To her astonishment, the cruiser's motor roared, and the police car surged forward, maneuvered around her, and sped off into the night with sirens blaring, its strobe lights creating a disco scene against the blackened country road. Sighing with relief, she pulled back onto the road, wondering if the police car was a warning and if it was best to turn around and go home.

* * *

Twenty minutes later, Kat sat in a kitchen on a bar stool, next to a cheap folding table, in the company of four African American men of various ages. The table displayed all the things necessary for serious gambling. In an adjacent family room, consisting of a hodge-podge of mismatched furnishings, a handful of people lounged about drinking liquor, smoking cigarettes, and engaging in drug use while talking over low-volume R&B music. The colorful characters at the wobbly table bantered loudly as they drank and smoked. A man named Junior slapped a card on the well-used table, causing it to almost give way. "Take that, mothafucka! You ain't got shit, bitch!"

A twenty-something man named Snake countered, "Yeah! I got ya bitch ass, niggah!"

Junior yelled, "Niggah, you ain't never had no bitches, with your punk ass! TK! TK, you hear this shit! That niggah ain't got no card skills, and he sure ain't got no bitches!"

With a cigarette parked between his dry lips, TK spoke gruffly, "I can't hear ya, Junior, I gotta hit y'all niggahs with these pips," and pounded his cards down on the table, after which he raked the pile of not-so-new bills in his direction.

"Naw, niggah! You owe me from last night," Snake declared, rising to his feet.

"Man, sit ya broke ass down!" Junior growled.

The room got quiet.

Snake grabbed a nearby lighter as if that was the reason he stood and sheepishly sat back down before rebounding with an off-the-cuff insult directed to the fourth player at the table, Chop Shop, who, at this point, sat quietly nursing his drink because he lost a considerable amount of money on the hand.

While the home was more social than the basement of Big Mike's, the ravages of drug use were equally apparent. The dirty floors and soiled, matted carpet, black-ashen ashtrays, over-flowing trash cans, and the stale smell of smoke, foul body odor, and alcohol were all evidence that the once beautiful home was now a miniature Sodom and Gomorrah.

The upstairs rooms, with sex-stained mattresses and unsanitary bathrooms, kept with the same destructive living theme of the lower level, a den of destruction. A dense smoke haze hung in the air, which Kat usually abhorred, but several shots of vodka had given her a well-balanced buzz, which helped her tolerate the fog of death.

Now, with the prayer of salvation and her earnest pledge to change her way of life forgotten, Kat sat next to a gray-haired Junior, whose years of harsh living did not wear well on him. His yellowing eyes told a story of a liver tired of the daily barrage of spirits and other poisons he put in his body. Fumes of alcohol emitted out of his mouth when he spoke, which confirmed his inner decay matched his dry and wrinkled deteriorating outer appearance. This, and his semi-permanent intoxicated slur, did not bother Kat. Junior was fun. He made her laugh, despite his rough look and menacing mannerism.

Not being much of a card player, she enjoyed posting near the action to watch while getting high. A steady infusion of vodka helped her keep a social disposition and avoid the jitters or paranoia that often went with her drug of choice.

With cursing and laughter ringing out around her, Kat thought about the incident at the stoplight and shuddered. The cop rolling up behind her, as well as a few other unexpected pullovers, could have gone badly. It had been mere luck that a cloud of marijuana smoke had not rolled out of her car when she had lowered her window for the approaching officers, seeing that she was accustomed to smoking whenever she drove. Lately, dodging the law seemed to be a reoccurring theme. While in thought, Kat felt a hand rub against her back and looked over her shoulder to see Teddy Boy standing behind her, grinning as if he won money. "Shit, woman, when you gonna let me hit that? Get some of that good lovin'!"

Teddy Boy, an old hustler from Minneapolis, via Chicago, compliments of Gary, Indiana, came around to her side, smiling so wide it looked as if his face hurt. With a receding hairline, his graying, matted dreadlocks hung to his shoulders as he stood his small, boy-like frame with confidence. He looked at everyone with dark, beady, deep-set eyes. Wearing black jeans, with his hands on his boyish hips and his bird chest puffed out, displaying a large gold chain hanging over an ironed white T-shirt, he licked his tongue out in a perverted gesture and winked, running his kid-sized hands along his slim, coffee-colored chin, which was sparsely covered with graying hair.

Junior let out a boisterous laugh and slurred above the conversation and music in the rooms, "Ah, Nigga, she don't want ya washed-up ass!" and then, with a flick of his wrist, slapped the table with his card. "Get off me, fools!" he exclaimed, glaring at competitors around the table. Everyone around the table broke out in laughter.

Teddy Boy responded to Junior by pulling out a plastic bag from his front jean pocket, making sure his stance highlighted his athletic shoes. "You sure 'bout that, niggah?" he shot back, exposing a bag of pills and cocaine, thrusting his hand in Junior's direction and exclaimed, "I don't play, no sir'ee. I quit school cuz I didn't wanna go out to recess! I be taken care of bizness," Teddy Boy bragged.

The room exploded into another round of boisterous foolishness.

"Aw, niggah…you can take care of me; I'll suck-ya-dick!" Junior reciprocated, locking in on Teddy Boy's hand, causing the snickering to continue from the men around the table. Kat laughed, too, glad the attention was no longer on her.

"You both can shut the hell up! Come on, TB. Whatcha got?" TK asked, pulling money from the stack next to his cards.

Teddy Boy pulled a chair to the table and began selling drugs for cash and credit, momentarily feeling like the most important person in the house, which stroked his inflated ego and gave the tiny man a bigger feeling than his stature conveyed.

Kat spent her remaining money and shared her drugs with others, which helped her feel like she had better control of her situation by not depending on anyone to sponsor her high. In the end, though, sharing still did not stave off the drug-fueled request for sex.

Once her drugs and alcohol were gone, the cigarette smoke started making Kat ill. Die-hard players still gambled; however, the game had long since changed to dominoes, and the faces at the table had changed, too, based on the influx and the departure of new people to the home. With the music low and the house in a silent uproar, Kat said her goodbyes and left at midnight, which generated a few subtle responses as she let herself out with empty pockets and the awareness that the perceived fun just experienced seemed a waste of time. Having the stress of blowing her high for a sixty-mile drive home while avoiding the police and getting herself together before an encounter with TL did not seem worth it. Misery settled upon her.

* * *

Fifty minutes later, Kat made it safely to a gas station off highway I-94 and Lexington Avenue to grab cigar rolling papers. Knowing the stop presented a risk to cross the path of law enforcement and hoping she did not look high, she hurried in the store. Once back outside, she groaned. Teddy Boy's 1972 black Cadillac Eldorado convertible—white walls included—sat parked next to her vehicle. "Damn," she mouthed.

"Hey, sweet thing! I'd know those long legs anywhere!" he shouted.

Kat looked around nervously, wishing he would not be so loud and continued towards the driver's side of his car. "Hey, you," she said, bending down and leaning her long frame into his window. "Whatcha know?"

"You good?" he asked.

Kat bit her lower lip and looked up over her shoulder at the camera positioned on the wall of the convenient store. "Let me go in and hit the ATM," she said, giving in to the rationale that this was a moment of convenience, dismissing the self-deprecating thoughts from earlier and the emotional stress that had filled her mind during her ride home.

Teddy Boy winked at her.

A few minutes later, Kat sat in the Cadillac. Glancing at Teddy Boy's open beer container in the center console between them, she said, "You know you have to be careful with that. It's hot over here."

"Aw, fuck 'em!" Teddy Boy shouted with authority and slapped his bony chest to show off. "This is my motherfuckin' hood. I'm not worried about these mothafuckas!" he proclaimed.

Kat felt on edge. Sitting in the car with glossy eyes, faded lipstick, and reeking of cigarette smoke, she hesitated for a moment before exchanging a hundred dollars for crack. Teddy Boy was about to say something when light penetrated the car, beaming first at his face and then on the beer in the center console. A Caucasian police officer stood at his window.

In one discreet, swift movement, Kat slipped the crack rocks in her bra and then straightened the oversized t-shirt dress on her upper torso. An African American police officer walked up to her side, pulled the door open, and asked her to step out with his free hand resting on his holster. His partner motioned for Teddy Boy to exit the car, too.

Animatedly, Teddy Boy exclaimed, "Aw, man, it's just a beer. You guys know me!"

The officer handcuffed Teddy Boy and placed him in the back seat of his squad car as a black, marked SUV pulled up. The cop that detained Kat addressed the approaching supervisor, "We're good here. Open container; he's a regular." The stern-looking officer acknowledged him and left the scene. Kat stood biting her lower lip, hoping the tight leotard would hold the drugs secure in her bra against her barely-there breast.

"What are you doing here?" the officer asked.

Despite her fear, with a voice as soft as melted butter, she replied, "We were just talking," and offered up an exotic dancer's smile.

"Do you know this man?" he asked, seeming more relaxed than his counterpart, who rummaged through the Cadillac while Teddy Boy looked helplessly from the back seat of the patrol car.

"Yes, I do," Kat replied in a whispery voice while holding one arm under her breast and across her rib cage to prevent the drugs from falling to the ground. Innocently, she stroked her neck and rolled her hand seductively across her shoulder with the other hand, causing the t-shirt cover-up to slide partially off her shoulder and expose her delicate skin.

The officer shouted, "Are you sure about that? Looks like something else going on here," as he began looking under the front bumper of the Cadillac.

Standing in the early morning muggy heat, sweat dripped off Kat's brow. The strobe lights from the police cars began to make her feel dizzy. Scared, she remained silent.

"What's his name then?" the nicer officer challenged.

"Teddy Lee," Kat answered quickly and then produced another smile.

He smiled back and asked for her identification. Then he told her to wait and walked a few feet over to his car to run her license. Coming back, he said, "Okay, you're good," and handed back the license. "You're free to go."

Feeling frazzled, Kat climbed into her vehicle and pulled off as Teddy Boy watched her drive away. Breathing fast, she touched her chest and felt the items still in place. The feelings of fear and anxiety began to dissipate the more distance she put between herself and the strobe lights of the police vehicles. Now, she felt relieved she was not going to jail and grateful she had not swallowed the drugs or ditched them on the ground. With the narrow escape over, more than ever, Kat wanted a drink.

While driving, she dug in her purse and pulled out a blunt, thankful the officer had not searched the bag. Now, focused on smoking to calm her nerves, the rational thought to be concerned about the encounters with the police no longer felt relevant. The events no longer felt real. As the weed washed over her, her emotions lifted. Then, Beverly came to mind and her emotions crashed.

Why am I so screwed up?

Kat wanted to cry, but her heart felt numb. With blurry eyes and struggling to stay in her lane, Kat barreled down the highway to find somewhere to smoke her drugs.

CHAPTER 13

LEXY
Tuesday – 4:59 a.m.

Oh, shit! Where am I?

Lexy awoke from her nightmare with a jolt. Her breath came in short, rapid pants as she sat in the middle of the wet bedding in the king-size hotel bed, appearing as if a deluge of water had rained upon her. Sweat dripped down her forehead, her bra and panties clung to her sinewy body, and a river of salted fluid trickled down between the valley of her firm cleavage. The nightmares were consistent but varied, often a twisted version of a tragedy that had occurred in her life. This time, an episode of one of the rapes she endured with added visuals of Lisa's disfigured face, the two devastating events melding together in one horrific motion picture. Stress triggered her nightmares, but the businesswoman never acknowledged the thorn in her side; therefore, disturbing dreams remained a consistent part of her life.

It took a moment for her faculties to clear, but the unwelcome memory of Lisa's rape, the shooting, and the hospital visits tumbled fast to her consciousness. Slowly she inched out of bed, achy, tight muscles carrying her to the bathroom. Getting back in bed deemed easier.

Like a child trying to soothe herself, Lexy sat in a dry spot with legs bent, arms folded across her knees, and her forehead resting on her forearms. Her braids hung down, creating a curtain around her rounded posture. Her head hurt, but her heart ached more. She wanted to cry but refused to let the tears flow. The world seemed darker than usual. She listened as hotel staff shuffled in the hallway. The sound of Tuesday morning traffic, blended with the hallway noise, reminded Lexy that life continued regardless of her pain.

Lexy sat motionless for some time before making her way to the shower. The hot water helped revitalize tired muscles and provided an outlet for the retirement of her self-imposed pity party. She tucked Alexandria's reckless emotions over Lisa neatly away in the abyss of her sub-consciousness. The tenacious woman dressed and readied herself to leave the hotel. There were monumental things to do, and time was not on her side. Getting back to a regular routine to reset her life became a priority. Maintaining a schedule, even that of a nightclub owner, was essential to staying balanced and sane. Opting to go to the gym versus using her home equipment, she got in her car and headed towards East Lake, calling Marcus on the way to see if he wanted to meet her there. Having just arrived at the facility, Marcus agreed to join her in the cardio area.

* * *

Lexy peddled slowly next to Marcus on a stationary bike.

"So, how do you feel?" Marcus asked.

"About what?"

Marcus stopped pedaling and looked over at her. "Baby Doll, don't pretend you're not being affected by all that's going on."

"I'm fine, Marcus," Lexy said and gripped the handlebars tighter, keeping her pace steady.

On a treadmill in front of them, an attractive thirty-something woman of Indian descent, with warm brown skin, large exotic eyes, a nose ring, and a jet-black, waist-length ponytail periodically glanced back at them. Marcus noticed with silent, personal hope.

"It's okay to express your emotions. Keeping them bottled up is not good," he concluded.

The woman looked back at them, again, before stopping her treadmill and walking over to the pair with a slight sway of her flat, wide hips.

"Hi, excuse me for interrupting," she said in a thick South Asian accent, "you're Ms. Lexy, right?"

"Yes," Lexy replied courteously, careful to present a business persona.

Feeling invisible, Marcus interjected, "We are not hiring right now, but you are more than welcome to put an application in online."

With obvious irritation, the woman responded, "No, I am not in need of a job," and looked at Marcus dismissively. Turning her attention back to Lexy, she said, "I just wanted to introduce myself and say hello."

"Hello…ah…?"

"Aadhya, Aadhya Raja." Aadhya smiled and tilted her head, causing the diamonds in her pierced cheek dimples to catch light and sparkle before extending her henna tattooed hand for Lexy to shake.

"Nice to meet you, Ms. Raja."

Marcus noted Aadhya held on to Lexy's hand a little longer than culturally expected though Lexy did not notice. Relieved when Lexy politely ended the exchange, Marcus followed her to the free weight area, hating the thought of lifting, but appreciative for the moment to have her focused on his presence and their agenda. Careful not to bring up the elephant in their space, Lisa, he faced her as she sat on the end of a flat bench performing overhead shoulder presses.

"You know," he began while admiring her shoulders, "St. Bart's doesn't sound so bad right now. Couldn't you see us there?"

Musing over his choice of the words, "See us there," she did not answer. After her set, she set the weights down and looked up at him. "Marcus, you do know the decisions I make impacts more than just you and me, right?"

Exchanging places, he pretended to focus on the task of working out and waited for her to continue.

"The girls rely on a steady paycheck and a safe work environment; we provide quality services to our clients, which in turn supports both of us. And the community needs us…the funds that go back… it's not that simple to just walk away."

Marcus set the weights down without finishing the reps and gave her a stern look. "You can't fix or save everybody! You know that, right!" Realizing he had raised his voice, he looked around to make sure he had not drawn attention their way.

Lexy answered him with a blank expression and a tone of indifference, "You have your opinion, and I have mine. I'm sure our course of action will work, but if you're not on board, you're welcome to cash out. It's up to you."

Marcus thought, *why do you have to be so cold? For once, put down the tough act and listened to reason.*

He hid his hurt feelings, stood up, and kissed her on her cheek, tasting her salty sweat in the process. "I think I'm going to hit the dry sauna. You wanna join me in a few?"

Without looking at him, she replied, "No, you go ahead. I'ma finish up here and then take a kick boxing class."

Marcus walked away with the dual feelings of sadness and annoyance. It was wearing on him to continue to experience the stress of the business and the lack of love in his own life. He felt he was watching his vitality and happiness tick away as gray hairs piled up on his head. He knew she would never love him like she once did, but he could not imagine life without her. Sometimes Marcus felt like the girl in the relationship. Her tepid responses always seem to leave him feeling emasculated, yet he knew he was her backbone.

* * *

Later, in the locker room with a towel around his waist, Marcus assessed himself in a mirror. He frowned at his hairy, gray-speckled chest, the folds of his man breasts, and his waistline appearing larger than he remembered. He sucked his stomach in and turned sideways to view his profile. Hearing a scoff, he looked from his peripheral. A muscular, young jock shook his head, smirking at Marcus' actions. Marcus felt embarrassed. He put his shower shoes on and headed to the sauna with a newspaper folded under his arm. A photo of Lexy covered the front page.

KAT
Tuesday – Late Morning.

Kat awoke feeling rested. Stretching her elongated body caused her large feet to stick out from under the emerald green Egyptian sheets. She extended her slender arms above her head, touching the black leather-button upholstered headboard of the XXL bed. Gazing tenderly over at TL, she noted his soft breaths. Even in sleep, he looked refined, his ebony complexion smooth, and his bone structure strong. The temptation to run her fingers along his full lips presented itself, but she did not for fear of provoking a barrage of insults from him for disturbing his sleep.

* * *

Reflecting on the previous night's activities with Teddy Boy and the police, Kat felt satisfied with the final choice she made to call an acquaintance named Old Man—a Caucasian, frail senior in his mid-seventies with spats of gray, woolly hair on a balding head who suffered from ailing respiratory health and walked with a slight limp. Medical challenges did not detour the ex-con from drinking and smoking in excess because he was making up for the fifteen years in prison on a manslaughter charge. In a government housing unit, in an older section of downtown St. Paul, she had listened to the blues, drank whiskey, and shared the drugs bought from Teddy Boy while enjoying Old Man's embellished stories of his adventurous youth. During her visit, no one stopped by; therefore, the environment remained peaceful. Blurry eyed and stumbling, Kat had left at 4 a.m., not realizing the dangerous condition she presented to other motorists. Her only concern was getting home before TL, which she did.

* * *

Now, TL stirred next to her as she slipped out of bed and went into the bathroom to prepare a shower. Her spirit felt good; life felt good, and the thought of moving to California no longer prevailed. Not hearing him come in the bathroom, she continued prepping the water, sticking her hand in to check the temperature. He exposed his presence by placing a firm hand on her thin, flat waist and cupping her just-hit-puberty sized breast with the other large hand. "Pony, I need a ride," he said in a deep, sexy morning voice.

Encouraged by the use of her nickname, which was an indication of his good mood and an inspiration for her optimism, his bright attitude reinforced the decision not to leave him. She replied delicately, "Okay, Babe."

TL pulled her lanky torso into his hard body and nuzzled her neck with his thick lips.

Her mouth went slack.

"Oh, hold on," she whispered and tried to peel his hands from her body to lead him into the shower.

His hands stayed glued.

With her back to him, he guided her to step into the steamy, stand-alone glass enclosure, their bodies glued together as he mimicked each of her steps. She smiled as they advanced, feeling like the teenager that met him three years ago. Once inside, they stood under the rainfall shower head like an exotic couple of a throwback velvet poster from the seventies; their bodies pressed together tenderly, displaying a moment of masculine strength and delicate beauty in black and white.

TL swept Kat's long, thin hair to the side and began tenderly sucking her neck, causing moans to escape her slightly parted lips as the water trailed down his well-formed back. He tipped her face sideways towards him, seeking out her lips, nibbling on them while slowly turning her around. "You're beautiful," he whispered, now face to face with her, the water streaming down their faces and creating a romantic backdrop of a couple caught in a gentle rain.

Initially, he kissed her softly, but then began to rule her mouth with tantalizing darts of his tongue, followed by reinforced sucking of her lips. Kat returned the passionate kisses, but her thin lips were no match for his. Surrendering, the needy woman gave in to the desires of her heart and her body. It had been some time since the pair had made love, and she was more than ready. Pulling away from the comfort of his dominance, Kat whined in a childish voice, "Babe, are we alright?"

"One-hundred," he responded with throaty vocals and then pressed his oversized member on her to confirm his response.

Kat did not pursue the subject further, not wanting to ruin the moment, and continued enjoying the lavish attention directed upon her, which was now on one of her ears, as pleasurable shocks went through her body. Standing four inches taller, he tilted her face up and looked down at her angelic, heart-shaped face and into her wide-lidded, needy eyes. "It's you and me, no doubt," he said.

That was his catchphrase for "I love you."

"I love you!" she replied in a heated frenzy.

He kissed her lips, and her heart swelled like a river receiving rain from a tropical storm, the thought of leaving him unthinkable. He took the tip of two of his long fingers and guided her by her shoulder to turn to face the opposite glass wall. Then, barely touching her neck, he signaled for her to bend forward. Once bent over, he slowly entered her partway. Their man and woman parts throbbed in unison. Thrusting forward, he entered her fully, smiling when she let out a loud gasp.

"What do you need, Pony?"

"I need you!" she exclaimed desperately.

He began to make love to her. Pleasant sensations rippled through her body, causing another round of soulful moans to involuntarily escape her lips. As he relaxed his firm grip on her waist, she began to match his rhythmic strokes, her wet hair fanning down her back, which turned him on more. His goal was to have her climax first before enjoying his own, which she did, thus reminding him why Kat was number one.

TL wanted to wash and leave the glass enclosure when they finished; however, he decided, in the best interest of their partnership, to cuddle with her for a moment. His time would be brief because he was sexually satisfied and had other things to do. Hanging around with Kat was not one of them. They finished in the shower by Kat soaping and washing him up. After the sex in the shower, Kat felt exhausted but restrained herself from getting back in bed. A full day of preparing for the ball lay before her.

* * *

Later that morning, Kat drove her white SUV out of her underground garage, blasting hip-hop music. Wearing a short one-piece romper, which highlighted her giraffe-like legs, a pair of white canvas athletic shoes, and an overabundance of accessories and makeup, she donned her aviator-style sunglasses to ward off the glare of the sun. Kat waited impatiently for pedestrians to cross on the downtown sidewalk that traversed her path. After pulling into 5th street traffic, and having only made it around the corner, she returned to the condominium to retrieve the getaway money she had stashed. Leaving TL was no longer a consideration. Living in the moment was her focus.

* * *

Wrapped in a white towel with scented oils wafting through the room and spa music playing, Kat could not help but think that she was forgetting something. Something important. From the position on her stomach, she pulled up the calendar on her phone to check the date.

"Oh, shit!"

"Am I pressing too hard?" the alarmed massage therapist asked.

"Oh, no, no. Uh, you're fine." Kat pushed a speed dial contact on her cell phone.

"Hello," a weary voice as soft as hers answered.

"Hi, Momma."

Silence filled the connection.

"Happy birthday, Momma," Kat said, trying to sound as if she spoke to her mother daily.

"Thank you," her mother stiffly replied.

Silence.

"How is your day going?" Kat blurted out.

The shorter version of Kat spoke rigidly, "I'm at work. You caught me on a break."

"That's too bad you have to work on your day," Kat replied lightheartedly, trying to ignore the stoic demeanor on the other end of the phone. "Say, you wanna meet for dinner? Beverly is in town."

Without a smile in her voice, Joanne replied, "For Pete's sake, Katherine, you call me as an afterthought. I betcha didn't know it was my birthday."

"Of course, I did. Why'd you think I'm calling?"

The biting of the lower lip began. Kat shrugged the masseuse off and sat up while motioning the bewildered girl away to dismiss her from the room.

"What do you want, Katherine?"

Kat gripped the cell phone tighter, drew in a deep breath, and exhaled sharply. "I want to see you. It's been…"

"It's been two months, two months since I've seen or heard from you. Do you know when that was?"

Kat gathered the cotton blanket around her nude body and tried not to think about the hospital bedside preaching that took place during their last encounter.

"Momma, don't."

"When I was working a double in the ER, and I had to watch you come in by the medics. Are you still with him?"

Kat sighed.

"Why do we have to do this? It's your birthday."

"Where did I go wrong, Katherine? Did I not raise you to be respectful, to live right, to be a decent human being, huh?" Joanne's voice rose. "Your lifestyle is going to kill you! I watch people like you come into the ER. It never ends well, don't ya know!"

"People like me?" Kat's facial expression set into a frown. "Momma, do you want to go eat or not?"

"Are you still smoking that stuff?"

Kat stood up.

"Are you still with your so-called husband?" she shot back, falling into the natural rhythm of their dysfunctional communication style.

"I'm not the one with the pimp or smoking dope!"

Kat felt bewildered, not understanding why things were falling apart.

"Momma, do you love me?"

"What? Katherine, my love is not the question here. You need to get your life together. Jesus Christ can forgive you," she continued, signifying an impending sermon. "You can't go about life being a whore."

Kat hung up on Joanne. Hanging her head, tears welled in her eyes as she wished for a different conversation with Joanne. She wanted her mother to ask her how she was, if she was ok, or if she needed anything. The little girl in her wanted her mother's unconditional love, no matter what she had done wrong. Kat longed to sit with her mother and laugh and talk over dinner the way she and Beverly had. Communicating with her mother made her feel dirty, cheap, and worthless.

Tears that hung on the lower rim of her eyes found their way down her cheeks as she squeezed her eyes shut. Kat had no idea how to quell the feeling of pain and loneliness erupting from within. The feeling of isolation, of being misunderstood, overwhelmed her. All she wanted was to have her mother back, the mother she had before her stepfather and extreme Christianity invaded their lives. The optimism and happiness of the morning seemed a lost memory as if the time in the shower and the sunny errand day had not taken place. Suicidal thoughts began to slip into a narrow crack within her psyche.

As if on cue, Kat's phone rang. She forced herself not to answer. It went to voice mail. The phone rang again. The same caller. This time, Kat relented and answered.

"Hey, you, what's up?" Taz's slow voice drawled.

Kat turned on the fake charm.

"Hey, you. Nottin'. 'Bout to go shopping for a dress. You going to the ball?"

"Naw, that shit ain't for me. Too many uppity mothafuckas. So, what's up?"

Kat hated the cat and mouse dialogue Taz used as her not-so-transparent drug selling tactic, especially when Kat did not initiate the call.

"I'm good. I gotta go shopping."

"Ok. I'm just saying, shit on fire, baby. I got you."

"I'll call you if I need you."

Kat got dressed and left the room to pay the confused woman at the front desk, paying full price for the partial massage and purchasing a gift card, too. In the car, she lit a marijuana joint to shut Taz's call out of her mind, but it did not work, so she drove to her mother's home in St. Paul and placed the enveloped gift card in the mailbox and left her mother a text to let her know to check for the birthday gift. Then she called Taz back. Occupied with the new mission, the anger at her mother dissipated. Something more important had her attention—masking her pain with drugs and alcohol.

BEVERLY & TL
Tuesday Afternoon

A slight, warm breeze sent city paper debris swirling past Beverly's sandals. Her white cotton, A-line skirt fluttered around her knees as she contemplated which way to go after exiting a rail car in downtown Minneapolis. With her straight brown hair pulled up in a top bun and her face makeup-less, she looked down at the directions on her phone while exaggeratedly pouting her plump lips, thus displaying her confusion. The directions were wrong; clearly, she would not make it to the photo shoot on time. As she contemplated whether to walk, order a ride, or try getting back on the rail car, someone in a black Cadillac shouted in her direction. "You look like a lady in distress," a deep voice yelled from the vehicle stopped in traffic.

Annoyed drivers—already impeded by mid-morning traffic congestion—honked impatiently at the Cadillac. Beverly glanced over at the lowered passenger window. She gasped under her breath when she saw the handsome, ebony-colored man from the gym leaning over to peer up at her. Words parked in her throat; she looked at him with wide doe-like eyes.

"Can I be of assistance?" he shouted over the traffic, flashing picture-perfect teeth.

"Ah, no, thank you," she answered, regaining her composure. "I'm fine."

"Yes, indeed you are," he stated under his breath.

Not sure of her next course of action, Beverly stood perplexed, looking at her phone.

He continued his pursuit from the car.

"I don't bite!"

Trying to dismiss him, the stressed model continued walking and looking at her phone but then looked up to shout, "I'm late, so if you'll excuse me, please!" She continued walking while keeping an eye on him from the corner of her eye.

TL's vehicle continued to advance with her, which further slowed traffic. Drivers on time constraints honked their horns, but he ignored them until he found a place to illegally park. In a few long strides, he caught up with her. "It's obvious you need help. I can see it all over your face. Why don't you let a gentleman help?" He looked down at her, his height making the tall woman seem short. "My name is Terrell, and you are?" TL said charmingly, using his middle name so technically not lying about who he was.

"No. No, really. I don't need help." Flustered, and not knowing what to think or do, Beverly walked faster towards no destination.

Up ahead, two bike patrol officers straddled their bikes at an intersection crosswalk. Hoping they would be a deterrent to the good-looking possible psychopath at her side, she continued in their direction. As the couple approached the men, TL hollered out, "My brothers in blue!"

The men nodded and smiled at TL, extending their gloved hands to him when he and Beverly made it to the intersection corner together. The officers addressed Beverly politely, as if she were with him, which caused her to look at him with renewed interest. Her eyes and ears took in the friendly rapport between the three men, noting how personable TL was as he interacted with them.

Before Beverly could ask for directions, the men received a call, which left her standing alone with the tall, well-dressed man. He was the temptation her spirit struggled with, but time was an issue, and she did need help. Feeling a bit more at ease, she decided to let him assist her, which proved to be a good decision. She made it to the shoot on time.

Standing in front of the warehouse shooting location, Beverly expressed her gratitude, "I can't thank you enough, Terrell. Thank you!" Her genuine appreciation gushed forth as she clasped her hands together in front of her chest.

"I can think of a way." TL winked.

Beverly's smile faded. "I'm not that kind of girl, Terrell."

TL contrived a hurt look on his face. "I was referring to taking you to lunch. That's all."

"Oh! I'm so sorry. I'm sorry. I-I didn't mean to offend you!"

He looked at her with gentle eyes and reached out to grab her slim hands, engulfing them with his own. He took a step closer. "Then say yes to fix my bruised ego." He smiled at her with slanted eyes.

A warm feeling swirled inside Beverly, making her feel like a teenager.

"Okay," she sighed, smiling innocently. "I should be done around one, but…um…this could go on 'til two or three. I wouldn't want to hold you up."

"For you, I'd wait." He applied a caring pressure to her hands before releasing them and holding out one of his. "Your phone, please."

"My phone?"

"Yes, so I can put my number in it. I wouldn't want you to give me a fake number."

Without questioning his passive-aggressive request, and not wanting to be late, Beverly handed it over. He placed his name and number in her contact list and then dialed his number from her phone before handing it back to her.

"Call me when you're done."

"Okay, I will."

TL placed two long fingers to his thick lips and blew a kiss at her. Completely unaware of the roll-of-the-dice cast, Beverly blushed before turning and floating inside the building.

CHAPTER 14

LEXY
Tuesday - Mid Afternoon

Lexy stood next to Lillian's hospital bed wearing a form-fitted, mid-calf, jade green dress with black patent leather pumps and simple teardrop pearl earrings. With flawless neutral-colored make-up and her multitude of micro-braids pulled into a ponytail at the base of her strong neck, she stood looking down at the medically defeated matriarch, who no longer spat sarcasm or mean-spirited insults. The ill woman's center-parted silver plaits gave her the appearance of a Native American, and the deep etching of her wrinkles showcased the effects of her reckless lifestyle from previous years, which late-life sobriety and Christianity could never erase.

For most of her life, Lexy had willed for Lillian's early death. Now, what seemed like an eternity later, here it was, but it did not give the satisfaction she had hoped for. Lexy shifted from side to side in her high-fashioned pumps. The stark coolness of the hospital room with the sounds of medical devices whirling, clicking, and beeping around her and low lighting caused a feeling of isolation.

Lexy headed for the door, hoping to feed her craving for a cigarette when she thought she heard a moan, but the sounds of the equipment made it hard to discern. She turned around to find Lillian's tiny, aged eyes locked on her. She walked back across the floor, which reeked with the odor of a dirty mop head and bleach. She approached the bedside.

"I'm...," Lillian struggled to talk through the oxygen mask.

Gently touching her hand, Lexy quietly said, "I'll find a nurse."

Lillian reached a dry hand out and grabbed Lexy's wrist. "Sorry," she whispered.

Lexy stood forlorn at the side of the bed. Dampness formed under her armpits. Something did not seem right.

"Rest, Aunt Lilly, I'll get the nurse."

Lillian tried pulling the oxygen mask down, sending her debilitated body into a coughing fit.

Lexy took her free hand and gave Lillian a tissue to spit in before repositioning the mask. "Sorry, for what?" she asked, expecting a rude statement to follow, despite Lillian's fragile state.

"You look…," Lillian tried to smile beneath the mask.

Why is she smiling?

"For…give me, pl…ease?" she asked, her hand still resting on top of Lexy's wrist.

"Of course," Lexy reassured her, assuming the question was for the treatment Lillian subjected her to throughout her miserable childhood.

"We…," Lillian gazed steadily at Lexy, which made Lexy feel even more uncomfortable than she felt earlier.

Dampness continued forming under the quality lining of her silk dress.

What are you up to, Auntie?

"I did good…didn't I?" Lillian whispered.

"Uh, yes."

Lillian mumbled incoherently but eventually formulated words. "Will…you?" Lillian asked, looking longingly at Lexy, "…forgive?"

"Yes, I am grateful to you. Thank you for raising us."

She was not sure if she meant it, but it seemed the right thing to say.

"You're…s-strong."

The sound of the beep from the heart monitor slowed down, triggering an alarm. Lillian closed her eyes.

"Aunt Lilly!"

The older woman's hand loosened around her wrist. The heart monitor went to a single continuous line, the slow beeps gave way to a singular tone. Knowing the truth of the moment, Lexy turned to go find someone.

Responding to the alarm, hospital staff flooded into the room, followed by Marlene and Tina—who had just arrived. A nurse politely but sternly ushered the three women into a waiting area. A half-hour later, a physician entered and addressed the worried women. The news of Lillian's death, due to complications of pneumonia, evoked a variety of responses from her nieces. Marlene let out a wail and collapsed onto the floor. Tears streamed down Tina's face and onto her quivering lips, but she had no time to react to her own emotions as she rushed to Marlene's side. On the other hand, the information had no impact on Lexy. Lexy stood in front of the physician feeling numb.

"Thank you," she said, trying to dismiss him with a short nod of her head.

With a look of fatigue on his face, the doctor handed her a bereavement packet and said, "Perhaps, this will help."

Looking at him with furrowed brows and then down at the pamphlet placed in her hand, Lexy returned her gaze to the physician's face as his mouth moved to explain the hospital procedures for the handling of Lillian's death. Meanwhile, Tina's cries intermingled with Marlene's wails as the two women clung to one another. When the doctor finished with his spiel, Lexy took on the role of the eldest and tried her best to comfort her grief-stricken family members.

After what she thought was the appropriate amount of time, she feigned the need to be alone. This was far from the truth. Walking to her vehicle, she pondered the scenario in the hospital room. Her concern was not about Lillian's death but about Lillian's life. Something was wrong, but she just did not know what. Instinctively, she headed to Marlene's home.

* * *

In Marlene's Summit Avenue Victorian home, Lexy made her way to the attic to look through Lillian's stored belongings. With strict orders from Lillian to leave her property alone, a lifetime of poverty-filled boxes and plastic bags sat in a corner collecting dust. Wiping the top of one of the boxes with her handkerchief, she watched dust particles float in the air, swirling through the rays of sunlight that beamed through the round attic window. Rummaging in the box, Lexy came across a photo album—the edges of the pages yellowed from time and covered with disintegrating plastic page protectors. She smoked a cigarette, breaking Marlene's no smoking rule as she flipped through the fragile, vinyl picture holder viewing photos of a smiling, younger Lillian.

To see her aunt beaming was a rarity, especially considering Lillian's abrasive demeanor and sarcastic personality. It was foreign to see her eyes shining innocently through the faded photos. Lexy thought of how the family often joked that Lexy got her tendency not to smile from Lillian. Lillian looked beautiful in her sexy but classy outfits. She wondered why she had never seen the pictures before but realized her frosty relationship with Lillian never allowed her to learn the older woman's younger history.

Each flip of the worn pages revealed a variety of social settings, with different groups of people and changes of seasons. Despite the varying scenarios, there was one constant, an extremely tall African American male with a broad face, a flat nose, flared nostrils, and wide lips. The older man sat next to her aunt in many of the pictures, usually with a protective arm around her waist or shoulder. From the look of the hairdos and fashions, it appeared the photos were taken in the late sixties or early seventies.

Midway through the book, the photos stopped. Lexy took a drag of her cigarette and placed the photo album back in the box. Before continuing her investigation, she set the cigarette in an ashtray found among Lillian's items, unzipped her garment, and peeled the Jacki Onassis styled dress down to her waist so she could get relief from the attic heat. Reaching her French manicured hand back into the same box, she retrieved what appeared to be a diary, noting the pink cover seemed a stark contrast from Lillian's nasty personality. Barely able to read the scribbled, faded handwriting, Lexy began invading the writer's privacy as the images of the entries played in her head.

Dear Diary: *Sep 3 Started school. Can't wait to leave this fucken house!!!*

Dear Diary: *Oct 31 Momma such a bitch! Can't do nottin. Can't wait 'til I graduate. She treats me like a baby!*

Dear Diary: *Dec 20 Went to a party with Diane.*

Dear Diary: *Dec 31 Stuck with kids! Not fair! Diane has a new boyfriend.*

Dear Diary: *Jan 7 No boyfriend yet. Diane went back to kid's daddy. He is a junkie. Momma keeps saying he ok. She says that cuz he buys her drink.*

Dear Diary: *Mar 15 I don't write much. Need to do better. School hard cuz so much shit at home!*

Dear Diary: *June 10 I'm excited about technical college!!*

Dear Diary: *August 31 I hate everybody!!!!*

Harsh random ink marks and holes on the pages followed the last entry. Lexy flipped through the rest of the pages but found nothing.

This didn't help. Everyone knows about mom and dad's heroin addiction.

Lexy gained no new knowledge going through her aunt's personal belonging, other than confirmation that Lillian was a miserable person. It was no secret her family suffered from ingrained dysfunction. They all worked tirelessly to overcome early life emotional turmoil. The damage was not as apparent on Tina and Marlene, but, nevertheless, Lillian's unforgiving attitude and psychological instability haunted all of them equally. She always seemed to be on a personal mission to bankrupt everyone's spirit, to have them all join her in her misery.

Lexy hunted through the rest of the belongings but found nothing of interest. After pulling up her dress, she left the suffocating attic, called Marcus to share the news of Lillian's death, and told him she would not be at the club until after the funeral, which she planned to have on Thursday, if possible, but would continue to handle club business remotely.

After a few more phone calls, she sat in Marlene's living room to wait for the women to arrive from the hospital and thought about her mother. Lillian had not allowed the girls to speak Diane's name in her presence. They had obeyed out of fear of sending Lillian into a rage. Now, with Lillian gone and having read the diary entries, Lexy could not get Diane's name out of her mind. She contemplated whether it was time to find her mother to get questions answered.

* * *

Lexy had seen her mother only a few times in her life. These were times when Diane came home under the pretense that she was going to straighten up her life but usually sought money from relatives and then disappeared. Tina and Marlene had better memories of Diane and a closer bond, but Lexy was an infant when she ran off, so she felt disconnected from the absent birth giver. When Diane showed up at the club five years ago, Lexy told the staff to say she was not there. She had watched on the security cameras as the disheveled and nutritionally challenged stranger walk away.

* * *

Lexy's thoughts went to Lisa. She wished she could call to check on her, share the news of Lillian's death, and ask her opinion about whether to look for Diane. The clenching of her jaw began. Her desire to be in control settled the battle, causing her to dismiss the notion of contacting Lisa, thus avoiding rejection. Instead, the stern woman called her private investigator. It was time to track down her mother.

Beverly and TL
Tuesday - Early Evening

Beverly kept her word and called TL after the photo shoot. During their lunch, conversation flowed with ease between the two so much so that halfway through the meal, they both realized Beverly had not divulged her name. When she did, he gave the opinion that her legal name sounded wise, but Bambi came to mind when he looked at her because her eyes resembled that of a baby doe, and they were the prettiest windows-to-the-soul he had seen in a long time. The young woman blushed, as any girl would in the company of an attentive, well-mannered suitor.

After the late lunch, he talked her into going with him to an art gallery in uptown Minneapolis. At the exhibit, they lingered at various paintings and sculptures entitled "To Love." At times, the pair suspended small talk and moved about the gallery in silence, guided by TL's hand in the small of Beverly's back. Initially, she felt uncomfortable and embarrassed, making her wonder if she made a mistake going with the stranger because the stone art resembled men and women engaged in compromising sexual positions.

Her embarrassment about the lewd art diminished and curiosity provoked stimulating conversation between the two about the subject of love versus sex. TL had an answer for every angle of the conversation. They lost themselves in the erotic statues and paintings, in each other's company, and in the soft whispers of new love as the hours waned on and the sun slid further west. The day transitioned into early evening by the time they completed their second tour around the small two-tiered building.

"It's about that time. Are you hungry?" he asked.

"We just ate a few hours ago," she said and giggled like a schoolgirl with a crush. "Besides, I can't take up any more of your time. I'm sure you have more important things to do."

He persisted. "Do you have plans?"

"Um, no," she answered with a smile, feeling butterflies in her stomach.

"Well, by the time we get back to The Paul, clean up and change into evening wear, I'm sure you will be hungry."

TL's take-charge manner impressed Beverly. He was unlike her irresponsible and unorganized ex-fiancé back in California.

"Sure, I'd like that," she said with the hope of true love ringing in her response.

TL took Beverly by the hand and led her out of the gallery. Beverly felt both a rush of excitement and a trace of trepidation as they got into the Cadillac. There was an awkward silence in the car as they made their way through downtown Minneapolis. Glancing over at him, she wondered who the good-looking, self-assured, and knowledgeable man was. The desire to fill the void in the car became overwhelming, so she tried to engage him with deeper conversation than the superficial ones they had at lunch.

"So, are your parents alive?" she asked, turning in the passenger seat to look at him.

The sun shone on his strong facial features before it temporarily disappeared behind a skyscraper and reappeared from a space between the downtown buildings to illuminate his face, once more.

TL spoke in a subdued tone. "My mother is, but we ain't cool like that. My father is dead."

His earpiece alerted him of an incoming call before Beverly could reply. While waiting for him to finish the call, she admired the rich wood grain and the supple texture of the leather seats. His call gave her a moment to question her decision to spend time with a stranger and contemplated whether to cancel the dinner plans to spend quiet time in her room in prayer instead. Then, taking into consideration his interaction with the bike cops, his commitment to physical fitness, his love for the arts, not to mention he neither smoked nor drank alcohol and behaved like a perfect gentleman, she dismissed her thoughts as unwarranted paranoia.

When the call ended, TL explained that the government took him from his mother because of her drug addiction, thus causing him to grow up in foster care and that his father, who he barely knew, was murdered by a girl his father had been dating.

"Oh, I'm so sorry." Beverly placed her hand on top of his and stroked it sympathetically.

TL chuckled. "You didn't cause my misfortune, and God carried me through."

"You believe in Jesus?" Beverly asked, a hint of excitement gracing her tone.

"Of course, I do," he answered and then slid his hand from under hers and placed his on top. He lowered his naturally deep voice an octave and said, "Jesus bought us together, Bambi."

Beverly's heart melted.

* * *

The truth was TL grew up in a whorehouse in Los Angeles, where he had many prostitute mothers to raise him. His pimp father would come by occasionally, and when he did, TL strived to gain the hustler's attention, but it never worked. He was invisible to his father; therefore, he relied on studying the bigger-than-God man from a distance, mimicking all that he saw in the dysfunctional life of the sex trade business.

The upside of his childhood, he had plenty of half brothers and sisters, children born to other women in his father's stable of prostitutes, to play with. When TL turned ten, his father was poisoned by one of his women. Currently, TL's mother was living in Los Angeles. She had retired from the game to live a clean and sober life. TL never shared these truths to anyone and played up the foster care system scenario to gain sympathy from unsuspecting targets.

* * *

The tedious work of stalking his newest prospect had paid off. When the unsuspecting girl exited the rail car, TL intercepted her. Luckily, Beverly had left her rental car at the hotel to avoid the hassle of downtown parking and to revisit Minneapolis in a more intimate manner. He knew the potential risk of Beverly telling Kat about meeting him, aka Terrell, but to a hustler like him, it would be a minor detail to handle at that time. The only thing that mattered was that the set up for Beverly had begun.

KAT
Tuesday - 7:00 p.m.

During Kat's drive to get to drugs, the thought of forgetting her mother's birthday resurfaced. Recalling the uncomfortable conversation with Joanne only agitated her more.

"…watch you being wheeled in by the paramedics. Are you still with him? …huh…Are you still smoking that stuff? …I'm not the one with the pimp…Momma, do you love me? …Your lifestyle is going to kill you…"

The desire to drink liquor and smoke cocaine continued hitting her like a blacksmith's hammer on an anvil, a high impact force causing a different personality to surface. The dual personalities interchanged with lighting speed, familiar but difficult to manage. Kat tried to improve her mood by rationalizing the purchase of the gift card as a measure to redeem herself from being a lousy daughter. It worked temporarily, however, her unstable emotions prevailed, bringing her spirits down and making her wish she could talk to someone.

Anxious and puffing her cheeks, Kat let out a long breath and then pulled her bottom lip into her mouth, securing it in with her top teeth, then took another breath and forced the air out through her narrow, minutely crooked nose. Knowing the right thing to do was to turn around, she passed the Dale Street exit, letting her unhealthy desires prevent her from taking the opportunity to exit the freeway. The next option—Lexington Avenue—loomed ahead, and she thought of Beverly. With the jerk of the wheel, Kat dangerously switched lanes and left the freeway, speeding ahead and leaving behind road rage from the driver she cut off. With resolve, she maneuvered her way over the bridge and began positioning herself to shift into the left lane to go back eastbound—away from Minneapolis and away from the darkness of an ill-gotten decision.

Backed-up traffic met her at the light, halting her progress to enter the freeway ramp, so she eased over into the right lane to head towards Selby Avenue. While fumbling to light a joint, she missed the turn, causing her to continue southbound towards Summit Avenue, an alternate route to head away from Minneapolis.

Kat made the left onto historic Summit Avenue and rode down the immaculately trimmed avenue lined with Victorian mansions. The sun shone bright, highlighting the exquisiteness of the early twentieth century homes lining the stately street. Her mood shifted to a better place, and she realized the beauty of the bright day felt better than sitting in a dark, morbid room drinking and smoking; thus, further confirming the right choice to stay on a drug-free course had been made. While passing nationally registered historic residences, churches, and the law college, she noticed crowds of people dispersed along the street. Hundreds of individuals lined both sides. Kat turned her music down.

Crowds of protesters occupied three blocks and campaigned unapologetically. They stepped off curbs and purposely took their time using the stop sign crosswalks to impede the flow of traffic. Careful not to run over pedestrians and bicyclers, Kat squinted through marijuana-glazed eyes, trying to read the bold, brightly colored posters; "Torn from the Womb," "Pro-Life," "You Are

Forgiven," "Jesus Loves You," "Don't Kill Our Future," "Come and Be Healed," "Abortion Kills," "Repent."

With their faces twisted in passion and desire for their cause of moral justice for unborn fetuses, the conscientious objectors' shouts and screams permeated through her rolled-up windows. It was obvious one of the churches along the corridor sponsored the event, but not clear as to which one—not that this mattered to Kat. The only thing that concerned her was that the activity unleashed stuffed, unwanted emotions that came flooding back from her heart like a slow-motion nightmare.

* * *

Kat took the protest personally. Seeing the protesters brought back memories of when she announced to TL that she was pregnant. They had been together for several months, and when she told him of the baby, the news did not go over well. It was the first time he revealed his true character. He demanded that she get it "taken care of". Kat cried and pleaded her case to no avail. When TL and Kat had gotten to her abortion appointment, protesters were there, leaving a narrow pathway for them to enter the clinic.

Using choice words, TL menacingly had told them to get out of his way, challenging any pro-life partisan who tried to block their path. None did. TL's heartless coercion also confirmed her mother's assessment of him, something she would never admit to Joanne. The abortion was physically painful and emotionally crippling; it was one of the loneliest times of her life, and the ordeal had left her scarred. The two never discussed the loss of the baby, nor did she confide in anyone, not even Beverly.

* * *

From Kat's perspective, the protesting Christians were judgmental, bringing up the past, and enacting choice shaming as a call-to-action to bully her into repenting for her past mistake. They also reminded her of her verbally abusive churchgoing, drunken stepdad, and her holier-than-thou mother. Pain from an abyss crashed on Kat like a wall of bricks falling on her head. The renewed thoughts of losing the baby, the thoughts of TL forcing her to abort, and the hordes of people lining the sidewalks snapped at her psyche.

"Fuck you all! Fuck you all!" she screamed from the top of her lungs, trying to keep her eyes on the road but turning her head to yell at the protesters.

Kat struggled not to plow her SUV into the protesters as the signs went up and down in the air with ferocity. Gut instinct told her to call Beverly for help, but instead, she called Taz.

"Waddup," Taz drawled through congested lungs.

Kat hesitated and then said, "I'll call you right back," choking back tears as she spoke.

"Bet," Taz replied.

"Call Beverly," Kat spoke into her phone.

Beverly picked up the call on the first ring.

"Hey!"

"Uh…Hey."

"What's up? You sound weird. You okay?"

"Y-Yeah…um, I'm okay. Are you busy?"

"Ah, I'm having dinner with a new friend. What's going on?"

"Nothing. I just wanted to tell you I love you," Kat replied.

"I love you too, Bird. What's wrong?"

Kat turned on fake happiness. "Can't a girl tell her girl she's loved?"

An alert for an incoming call caught Kat's attention. "Oh, it's my boss. I gotta take it."

"Okay. I love you," Beverly repeated with concern.

"Okee-dokee," Kat said, keeping the smile in her voice.

Anxiously, Kat answered the incoming call, "Hey, T!"

"Waddup? Thought you was calling me back?"

"I'm still on my way."

"Bet. And stop talking so sexy, girl, damn."

Kat turned on the charm, "Alright, boo. I'm on my way."

"See, you messen with me. TL bedda watch it. Come on, sexy. I'm waidden on you."

"I'm on my way, T."

Kat made a left turn on Dale Street and headed back to the freeway to take the westbound entry ramp towards escapism.

CHAPTER 15

KAT

Sixty minutes later, Kat sat in her vehicle in a gravel parking spot behind Big Mike's place off the alley. A group of young, shirtless, tattooed African American men, with jeans hanging and exposing their undergarments, congregated around a rotting picnic table in the backyard of the duplex next door, drinking beer while a white, underweight Pit Bull roamed about the grassless yard rooting for food. The men, wearing dreadlocks and various braided or twisted hairstyles, kept an eye on her, making her aware they watched her every move. Tired of waiting for her phone to ring, Kat placed a call.

"Where are you?"

"Shut the fuck up!" Taz yelled above loud, explicit rap music to the occupants in her car.

"What?" Kat asked in bewilderment.

"Naw, man, not you! These mothafuckas here!" Taz yelled—a rare moment of her speaking fast and loud. "Waddup?"

Kat frowned. "Waddup? Where 'ya at?"

"Be 'bout five!"

Kat whined, "T, twenty minutes ago, you said five minutes. I could've gone to the liquor store by now."

"Shut the fuck up! I ain't play'n. Watcha say?"

"I said, I could have gone to the liquor store!" Kat yelled, causing renewed glances from the intimidating group of young men.

"Bet! Do dat! Be there 'bout time ya get back!" Taz assured her while pulling up to a home twenty minutes away to make a drug delivery.

Backing out of the space, Kat wondered if TL was right about the need for her to carrying a gun. With her pre-get-high-headache throbbing and holding her urine becoming a full-time job, Kat slipped her aviator glasses from the top of her head and headed to the liquor store around the corner on Plymouth Avenue.

At a corner-lot package store, Kat looked about with concern. The parking lot bustled with weekend type activity, atypical for a Tuesday night. The number of peopling milling about did not match the number of cars in the lot. This troubled her. For safety reasons, she left her purse tucked under the front driver's seat, took her identification and cash, and a small can of pepper spray.

As she walked across the pothole-filled asphalt, hoping the old security cameras pointing towards the parking lot and doors worked, two destitute looking men begged her for cigarettes, and a woman pleaded for money to feed her children. Brushing them off politely, she tried to put what she thought was a little toughness in her walk, but it only made her stand out more in the poverty-ridden North Minneapolis neighborhood. Vulnerability hung on her like a sunburn in a desert.

Inside the shamble of a building, the store buzzed with an atmosphere of impatience. Just inside the door, a burly police officer sat partially on a tall stool, one foot up on the footrest and the other foot on the floor, with his gun hanging visibly on his side. Kat smiled and handed him her identification, which he looked at and then shoved back at her and shifted his focus to the next person waiting to come in. Kat joined the irritable patrons, her height standing out above the customers as they jockeyed to insert themselves into a valid line to reach one of the three salesclerks. After buying vodka, she stopped at a fast-food restaurant to use the restroom, which left her with the same uneasy feeling she felt at the liquor store and whose restroom was no cleaner than Big Mike's bathroom. Kat walked quickly to the safety of her vehicle, relieved to get away from the open exposure of the hustling grind of the ghetto.

* * *

Back in the gravel parking spot, Kat sipped vodka and checked her social media account, ignoring the stares of the young men from the yard next door, when she heard the distinctive, obnoxious sound of Taz's jalopy. Taz pulled up and stepped out of the heap wearing expensive red designer athletic shoes, her customary uniform of jean shorts, and a sweat-stained white T-shirt—her rundown car had no air conditioning—a red bandanna tucked in her obese pant waist, and a boy's crisp-to-the-scalp haircut.

"Waddup, girl?" she smoothly said to Kat, and then threw up a tattooed arm to acknowledge the men.

"Up to shit," Kat replied, anxiously waiting by her vehicle, wishing the group would hurry along.

Jackie, dressed in the same clothes from Sunday, which no longer looked fresh and appeared to have served as pajamas, too, and Big Mike, in short-sleeved soiled mechanic coveralls, got out of the car. They all disappeared into the house, down the basement stairs, and into the back room. Once inside the familiar hot-box, Taz informed Kat she sold out and was waiting for a supplier to stop by.

"What?" Kat exclaimed, towering over a seated Taz, looking at her in disbelief through squinted eyes, the anger of the difficult decision, the long wait, and the disappointment erupting all at once. "I told you I was coming! Hell, I could've shopped for my dress if you weren't ready!"

Taz did not let Kat's outburst affect her laid back disposition, especially since Kat's whispery voice came off soft and annoyed, rather than loud and angry.

"First come, first serve. You know the game," Taz informed, lighting a marijuana cigar from her designated spot on the couch.

Kat debated leaving but decided to stay. She took a seat in the same spot she had occupied on Sunday and lit the rest of her own marijuana cigar. "Fuck, man!" she muttered out loud and then took an oversized gulp of vodka. The harsh spirit seared her throat on its journey down, causing her to cringe when the acrid drink hit her stomach.

"Aw hell, girl, I got someone coming in a sec. You gonna be aw-ite."

In the meantime, Jackie and Big Mike pulled out paraphernalia and crack. Kat looked at Jackie.

"Kat, I don't have much," she responded, her gravel voice sounding like she needed a drink of water. Jackie nodded her bony skull in Big Mike's direction.

Seeing Jacki's head motion, Big Mike hurried and threw a large piece of rock cocaine on his apparatus, smoked it fast, and blew a large cloud of smoke over everyone's head.

Kat's large lidded eyes opened wide with disbelief, and her over-tweezed eyebrows lifted on her forehead. With low volume disapproval, she said, "Big Mike, that's fucked up. You know I shared the last time I was here." Her face flushed red with anger.

"W-What?" he asked before sinking low in his chair and leaning his still-in-need-of-a-haircut head against the moldy basement wall to settle into a drug-induced trance.

Jackie pinched off a small piece and handed it to Kat. It was not enough, but she thanked her and smoked the crumb. It made her want more. In the meantime, Taz read a text message out loud to announce that her supplier was on his way.

Kat looked around the room she had been in many times. Nothing had changed. The dirt, dust, and yellowed walls looked worse than ever. The table-top fan sat in the same place, blowing the same dirty air. More trash lay strewn about than on the last visit. Shaking her foot back and forth, Kat glanced up at the towel-covered window. The angle of the light told her the sun was starting its descent. She had not bought her gown and the internal debate about leaving started again. In the midst of contemplation, Big Mike spoke, interrupting the personal conversation in her head. "How ya been?" he mumbled.

"Um…good," she replied, hating the small talk and annoyed that he was trying to speak to her after what he had just done.

Big Mike eyed Kat's long, slender legs jockeying for comfort in the tight space between the couch and the creative table.

"Uh…Uh…you know, Kat, I got more if you wanna hook me up." He hungrily looked at her and placed his hand on his crotch and rubbed. His mouth hung open in a grotesque display of sexual arousal.

"Asshole," Jackie muttered, seething at her boyfriend with hatred.

Kat's eyes trailed down from Big Mike's sunburned face, to his dirt-filled fingernails and tried not to crinkle her off-centered nose at his sweaty, greasy coveralls and dirt covered work boots. The thought of having sex with him disgusted her and made her think of choice words to say to him, but she refused by responding, "I'm good," careful not to insult the rude host, thus losing a place to sit and smoke. Turning her attention to Taz, she said, "Say, Taz, I thought you said your peeps were 'bout to pull up."

"No doubt, no doubt. They com'n," Taz lazily replied.

Big Mike and Jackie watched Kat bring her traveling container to her mouth. Feeling the heat of their stares, she asked, "You guys got something to drink out of?"

They both looked around at the debris on the glass-covered crate and each chose a used, dirty plastic cup without regard to what was in them or who drank from them last. Kat filled each cup halfway and then sat back to wait.

RAZOR
Tuesday – 8:01 p.m.

Many irons in the fire of Lexy's life tugged at her heart and mind, but nothing compared to the heartbreak she felt over Lisa's rape. The thought of suing the nursing home had crossed her mind, but that had been placed at the bottom of her things-to-do list. The private investigator tasked with finding her mother had just begun his work—an objective that was more of a personal puzzle-solver but had no bearing on the day-to-day quality of her life. And then there was Marcus. His emotions for her hung on him like a poorly fitted shirt. It nagged at her that after all their history together and his years of loyalty to her, she could not muster the feelings to match his.

Moreover, lately, her conscience tended to reevaluate her part in objectifying women. Negative thoughts of second-guessing her life were becoming more intrusive as the weeks went on, something she never had wrestled with before. Despite the many anvils hanging over her head, Lexy knew the situation with Vincenzo's son required an immediate response, even if dealt with vigilante-style.

* * *

After staying with Marlene and Tina for a respectable amount of time, Lexy excused herself to go home. Back in her personal sanctuary, she prepared herself for an important meeting. Stepping out of the shower, the fog of the steam hovered in every inch of the bathroom, making it difficult to dry off. Wrapped in a towel, she went into her room to allow the en suite to vent. After exchanging the towel for a black thong and strapless bra set, she lathered herself with a hundred-dollar bottle of scented lotion, pausing to run her fingers over barely visible scars on her arms and other parts of her body, thankful her adult skin helped to diminish the tragic marks of her childhood.

When the bathroom cooled off, she returned with a glass of red wine, a bowl of strawberries, and pieces of dark chocolate, popping the sweet treats in her mouth before savoring a sip of the crimson-colored liquid while examining her reflection in the oversized vanity mirror.

Examining the structure of her facial bones and the integrity of her skin, she slid her hand across her forehead and along the contours of her face before angling her body to view her backside. Frowning, her vision took in the subtle signs of the unavoidable process of aging.

Shit, the clock is ticking.

Turning around, she appreciated her defined abdomen but looked disagreeably at her softening obliques. No one else detected her perceived physical flaws, but according to her standards, they were glaringly obvious.

Refocusing her energy, she applied her make-up with the ease of an artist and then released the micro-braid bun on the top of her head, shaking her head to let the high-quality extensions fall to frame her angular face and then fluffed them with her hands to create volume. Dressing to impress, she opted for a sleeveless, black chiffon mid-thigh dress, a pair of gold four-inch stilettos, a five-carat diamond strung choker, diamond hoop earrings, and a canary yellow satin clutch purse. Satisfied that she looked red carpet ready, Lexy headed out to enact street justice.

* * *

Fifty minutes later, Lexy reached the City of Bloomington. Sitting in the parking lot, the determined woman checked her makeup, re-fluffed her braids, and stalled for time before heading to a top-floor apartment in a well-kept three-story building. When the door to the expensive unit opened, a light-complexioned Latino man in his mid-thirties with a shaved oval head and a disproportioned masculine jaw that protruded like that of a primate stood before her. His wide-set, light-brown cat shaped eyes could have had a gentle look if it were not for the three tear-drop tattoos under his right eye and a scar running from the left corner of his mouth up to his left eye, both physical alterations conveying his mindset.

Carlos Rivera, aka Razor, mockingly bowed his short, muscular frame. Averting his mischievous eyes up to Lexy as he did, the closely shaven, goateed gang member took her hand and kissed it. Upon straightening up, he smiled an off-center smile, exposing platinum upper teeth—replacements for originals lost during one of many confrontations with the law or rival gang members during his youth.

Lexy walked through the door and caught the scent of his cologne wafting through the air. Razor smelled good. Still holding her hand, he guided her further into the narrow hallway, shutting the door behind them with unintended force. Ruggedly handsome, what Razor lacked in height he made up for with his solid Bulldog physique, quick wit, fearlessness, and over-the-top confidence. He stood before her dressed in black pants, a black silk short-sleeved pullover shirt that fought to hold his bulging biceps, and black leather dress shoes. He wore gold chains of varying thickness around his thick neck, which gave his modern clothes the vibe of an eighties rap video.

Delusional grandiosity and violent outbursts plagued the man, and his use of drugs and alcohol did not help matters. Razor easily and regularly secured women, but he did not keep them long. If they were lucky, they found out how deranged he was and escaped a relationship of brutality. Friends from his youth bestowed the nickname "Razor" on him because of his preference for using knives over guns—not that he did not use guns—thus, giving validity to his alias.

Razor looked Lexy up and down and then whistled. "Tú eres bien sexy." (You are sexy.)

Lexy smiled and replied, “Gracias, Papi.” (Thank you, Papi.)

“¿Hablas español?” he asked with a raised eyebrow. (You speak Spanish?)

“Muy poco.” (Very little)

Razor ushered her to a gray leather couch in the living room before going over to a mirrored wet bar. Lexy looked around. The living room was clean but basic. The decor consisted of simple gray leather furniture, white marble tables, and gold and white accessories. The residence did not look lived in.

“Do you mind?” Lexy held up a pearl-encrusted cigarette case.

“Tengo algo que puedes poner en tu boca, Mami,” (I’ve got something you can put in your mouth) he mumbled under his breath as he poured drinks. “No,” he said, a little louder, grabbing a cigarette for himself off the bar and placing it between his lips before picking up the drinks and walking over to offer her one.

Lexy graciously accepted without telling him she preferred red wine instead of the fine cognac he gave her. He turned on an air purifier and then took a seat in a chair next to the couch. Razor lit his cigarette without offering to light hers, revealing the moment of being a gentleman at the door was just that, a moment. Lexy took a seat on the end of the couch near his chair.

“You wanna smoke a blunt?” he asked.

“No, thank you. Weed makes me sleepy.”

“Sí, sí, I prefer the coco myself. I keep the THC around for others.”

Taking a sip of liquor and a deep inhale of her cigarette, she waited for Razor to start the conversation. In the interim, she pondered why he did not go by his legal name because Razor sounded immature.

“Mami, it’s taken a while for you to get at me. ¿Si?” he said, looking at her seriously, no longer grinning.

“I appreciate you seeing me on such short notice,” Lexy said, keeping her voice delicate, her eyes soft.

He held his glass up, beckoning for her to toast. “To new la familial!”

Their glasses clinked. Razor downed his drink while Lexy took a sip, watching him over the rim of her glass. He made another trip to the bar, this time returning with the bottle.

“So, what is it you need?”

Lexy explained her dilemma, pausing at times to measure Razor's reaction. During the meeting, Razor occasionally muttered in Spanish under his breath. She picked up a few words and deciphered there was no love lost between Vincenzo's organization and Razor's. She reached into her clutch and pulled out two two-inch stacks of hundred-dollar bills. Lexy also took out photographs from her hidden surveillance system—something she had not shared with the police—and pushed the items across the smoked glass table towards him. He barely looked in the direction of the items; instead, he focused his eyes on her firm legs. A bulge formed in his groin area.

"Do you need anything else?" she asked.

He picked up the photographs and looked at the man with the cobra tattoo on his neck, then muttered in Spanish.

"No problema. You want two for one? The other one?"

"No, just this one. Just this one."

"No hay problema," he said and licked his lips while focusing on her legs. Razor stood up and offered an outstretched hand to her. "I got you, Mami."

"This means a lot to me, Razor."

"I gotcha, Mami."

Forcing a smile, Lexy downed her drink, grabbed the bottle, and took his thick hand, following him to the bedroom to complete their contract.

For an hour, Lexy gave Razor A-list treatment. Braless, clad in her G-string and a pair of fishnet thigh-highs she had stashed in her clutch, she massaged his body with an edible coconut oil. She showered his knife and bullet-scarred torso with tantalizing licks and bites in between rubs, during which she pretended to enjoy. Once she lavished his back, he turned over and received the same pleasure on the front of his body. Upon reaching his manhood, she rolled a condom on him with her mouth. He moaned and grabbed her head between his hands and guided it up and down on his short, thick penis, his biceps flexing with each motion. His tempo picked up but then he stopped her, pulled her up against his chest, and tried to kiss her. Her head tilt caused his lips to graze her cheek.

Shit, I must get this over with, Lexy thought.

Having waited for years for the opportunity, Razor could no longer hold his desire. In a strong, smooth motion, he flipped her over on her back and entered her. An animal grunt escaped his lips; he felt he had entered heaven. Her inner garden felt tight, moist, and deliciously warm. Lexy, in turn, gasped, not expecting the fullness of the head of his penis to feel good. She inched her way toward the headboard to ease the intensity of the primal coupling. Effortlessly, he eased forward with her, preventing a gap from forming between their dancing bodies, holding her with his arms locked around her back like a dog locked in heat.

Lexy internally rejected his passion, but with each stroke, something began to change. Unexpectedly, the rigidness of her body relaxed. Stifled moans stayed in her tightly closed mouth, but the dam broke, and she gave in, releasing the last four days of turmoil upon Razor, forgetting, momentarily, he was the bad boy she had been holding at arms-length for years but, now, a welcoming force of rebellious nature. Razor, intimidating and full of unyielding raw lust, lost himself in his woman crush. He stroked while wielding unchecked kisses on her neck.

With their copulation no longer feeling like a job, she began aggressively matching the passion of the Latino hard body on her. Instinctively, she embraced him fully while orgasms rippled through her body without warning, which encouraged him more. He began passionately shouting in Spanish, and his thrusts became stronger.

This brought Lexy back to reality. She felt the brutality of the true man above her, so she began to encourage him on with explicit sexual talk. She was ready to end the session. His explosive release left him seeing stars. Razor collapsed on top of her. Patiently, she waited with the heaviness of his body upon her while listening to his rapid breathing. “Mi amor,” he said, breathing warm air into her ear. With wobbly legs, he backed off her and stood by the edge of the bed, looking down at her in amazement.

CHAPTER 16

KAT
Tuesday - 9:47 p.m.

The decision to hang out in Minneapolis was not going well. Kat had nursed her drink and watched time tick from five to twenty to forty minutes, during which time she intermittently checked with Taz on the whereabouts of her supplier. When, for the tenth time, Taz informed her they were just around the corner, someone knocked hard on the back door. Kat straightened her posture with anticipation, Jackie stopped talking, and Big Mike left the room in haste, hoping whoever was stopping by needed a place to smoke. He came back with Teddy Boy.

In Teddy Boy's usual in-your-face manner, he spoke loudly and dominated the conversation in the room with inflated stories of himself while attentive, drug-hungry eyes stayed focused on him. Wanting to outshine Taz, he stroked the sparse hairs on his weak chin and then paused, as if in thought, before telling Kat to follow him up the street because he had what she needed.

"Aw, Nigga, how you gonna come in here taking folks?" Taz sat up from her deep embedded position on the couch, the thought of losing money eliciting movement from her obese body for the first time since she sat down.

"If it don't make money, it don't make sense," he replied, grinning from ear to ear, revealing thirty-year-old gold teeth that made his mouth appear odorous. "I can't help it if you ain't got your shit together!" he continued, brushing dreadlocks off his shoulder in a feminine manner.

Taz eyed him and slowly said, "Niggah, you gonna get fucked up out here."

"Don't hate. Don't hate," Teddy Boy replied, still grinning and helping Kat to her feet.

With a delicate slur, Kat defended her action, "T, I've been waiting for over an hour. I'll hit you next time, okay?" She bent down and gave Taz a hug, trying not to transfer Taz's sweat to her romper and hoping the embrace would pacify the drug dealer enough to mend any perceived slight.

Taz slumped back into the depression in the couch and lazily replied, "Bet."

Kat said her goodbyes, leaving Big Mike and Jackie fuming as they watched a free high walk out the door.

* * *

Kat walked into a small, one level craftsman house. Teddy Boy turned on a lamp, which cast a dim light on a living room with dark crown-molding, flowered couches, simple wood tables, and porcelain-based lamps with white shades. The poorly chosen decorations continued with an over-abundance of candle sconces and brass butterflies lining the walls. The thick, tan carpet held a musty odor, but other than that, the room appeared tidy.

Teddy Boy instructed Kat to have a seat and disappeared down a hallway off the adjoining dining room. Perching herself on the edge of the couch, her eyes moved around the room, taking in the built-in dining cabinetry and the many aged photos taken in various nightclub settings. Kat sat for about ten minutes and began to wonder what was taking Teddy Boy so long. Feeling anxious, she refrained from calling out to him because she was not sure what the situation was in the house. Her street instincts told her to hold tight and stay quiet.

Sliding into the room like a ghost on water, Teddy Boy startled her when he said, "I got you, girl!"

Having changed, he now wore a full-length black bathrobe and loafer slippers, which exposed his bony ankles. The robe, secured at his narrow waist with a tie, revealed his small chest through the upper folds of the garment.

Alarmed, Kat stood up. "What's going on?!"

"Whoa," he held up his hands, "calm down, Legs. I'm done for the night. Store closing after we handle this business. Can't a man get comfortable in his own crib?" He grinned and reached in his robe pocket, pulling out a handful of plastic bags, each stenciled in red with the letters *POW*. "Chill out, woman." He chuckled and placed the tiny bags on the table. "Take your pick."

Kat sighed. Looking apologetically at him, she said, "I'm sorry. It's been a long night."

Teddy Boy lowered his animation. "Mos def. No harm."

The exchange took place, and Kat turned to leave.

"Don't you want to take a hit?" he smoothly asked to the back of her blonde head.

Kat hesitated at the door and turned around and said, "What about your girl, your kids?"

"Aw, they ou'da town for some family shit."

"Uh…you sure?"

"Mos def." He beckoned her back with his hand.

"Man, would be nice. I-I mean if that's okay?" she confirmed.

Teddy Boy piped back up. With an over-the-top motion, he clapped his hands together. "What's understood need not be explained. Sure, Legs, you know we cool like that!"

Kat's face lit up. "Okay, let me go grab my drink."

"Cool, just come back in; no need to knock."

Within seconds, she was back in the living room, not taking note that Teddy Boy had altered the setting by turning on romantic R&B music. He lit candles, explaining they helped with smoke, and sat next to her with a powder cocaine covered mirror. Kat finally took a drag of the drug she had been seeking for most of the night. Easing back into the couch, she sat and let the fluttery feeling engulf her. The feeling did not last, which annoyed her. After all the fuss it took to get what she wanted, the drug was not strong enough.

"Whazup, Legs?"

"Nothing, I-I'm just tired. I'ma go. Thanks, TB."

"Aw, baby, let me help wake you up." Teddy Boy stood and retrieved more bags from his housecoat pocket. This time, the labels read "STARS." He reached up and placed his hand on her shoulder and squeezed. "Here. Try this."

Kat looked at his open hand. "What's this?" she asked, her inner eyebrows dipping towards the center of her forehead in suspicion.

"It's my V.I.P. stock."

Kat looked at him, confused. "So, you're selling me bullshit? That's fucked up, Teddy Boy. If you had this, why'd you give me that other shit?"

"Aw, Legs, you ain't even letting me take care of you. I'm trying to bless you, baby. Two for one. You can use the other stuff to roll in your weed. I know you like to make Mack joints."

Kat eyed him for a moment and then started laughing. With a voice that cut through the air like baby powder, she said, "Damn, Teddy Boy, why you fucken' with me?"

"I'ma take care of ya, Legs. No worries."

Kat relaxed and smiled.

"Yeah, like how you took care of me the other night. Our asses almost went to jail."

"Shit, woman! I did go to jail! But the man can't keep me down!" Teddy boy hit his chest with his classic King Kong motion, grinning his wide split-your-face grin.

They both laughed, and Teddy Boy handed over the other brand. Indeed, the potency of the replacement batch delivered a punch. As she exhaled the white smoke out of her mouth, her body slowly melted back into the flowered couch, helping here escape from the drudgery of daily existence, no longer dealing with life on life's terms. For a suspended moment, TL did not matter. Lexy did not matter. Her mother did not matter. The abortion protesters did not matter, and her guilt of hiding her truth from Beverly did not matter. Most of all, her pledge to God to change her life did not matter.

Teddy Boy watched her, waiting for his moment to continue the hero role. When Kat sat back up, she began talking, sipping vodka from her to-go-cup, and enjoying the ambiance provided. Teddy Boy remained unusually quiet and attentive as Kat discussed issues of her heart. The two sat for hours, listening to music while Teddy Boy provided an outlet for Kat to dump her problems on—compliments of the vodka—as he snorted powder cocaine. One a.m. crept upon them in no time.

"I'm going to get going. I didn't realize it was so late." Kat stood up and swayed.

Teddy Boy jumped up and grabbed her by the elbow. "I don't think you should drive, Legs."

With red eyes and a forlorn look on her face, Kat steadied herself. Pulling her elbow out of Teddy Boy's hand and stammered, "I'm-I'ma be alright."

"I got more dope. Why don't you do a little dance for me, Legs," he said, walking with Kat and advancing to stand between her and the front door."

"I'm good. I gotta go," she said and swayed again.

He did not move.

"Come on, Teddy Boy, quit playing; I gotta go," Kat slurred.

"Who said I'm playing?" He held his stance.

The temperature in the room got hot. Kat looked down at the small man through drug hazed eyes and wondered what was wrong with him. No sooner had the thought gone forth; she noticed his right arm hung relaxed along his side, and his tiny man-hand held a 9mm gun pointed toward the floor. He looked up at her with cocaine clinging around his nostrils and glazed eyes.

Kat whined, "Come on, Teddy Boy. Don't do this."

"Do what?! You always prancing around me. I know you want this good dick!"

"What the hell you are talking about?" Kat looked at him in disbelief. "You know I'm with TL."

Kat's voice remained soft, still not grasping the severity of the situation, assuming Teddy Boy was just being Teddy Boy and expected him to start laughing at any moment.

"Don't play stupid, bitch!"

The force of his words cut through her altered mental state like a bucket of water on a campfire, bringing reality forefront. Her emotions flipped, and the vodka now became instant courage.

"Fuck, man. I ain't got time for this shit! Wait till I tell TL!" she screamed and attempted to get past him, but he shoved her back, knocking her to the floor.

Kat jumped to her feet and instinctively swung at the advancing man. The blow caught its mark, landing solidly on his nose, catching them both by surprise. Blood erupted from his cocaine-loaded vessel. He grabbed his nose with the gun still in hand, trying to hold back the outpour of bodily fluids. With a racing heart, Kat sprung around him and out the front door, distancing herself from the sound of him cursing at her back.

After two or three blocks of excessive speed, she slowed down. It was not until she was on the freeway entrance ramp that the municipal lights revealed the splattered blood on her white romper. Everything had happened fast, so she tried to recall the events to make sure she was not in the wrong.

Placing a finger, with a broken acrylic nail, in her mouth, she sucked on it to try to reduce the pain, knowing the threat to Teddy Boy was fanfare. Telling TL about the incident meant telling on herself. It meant risking a beating for being at his place and doing drugs. Staying away from Teddy Boy was her best recourse but would also cut off one of her suppliers. Remembering that she still had drugs and vodka in her purse, Kat hit the accelerator and sped down the freeway, reasoning that the drama that had just unfolded was a justifiable reason to find a new spot to smoke.

RAZOR
Tuesday - 10:10 p.m.

Razor sat naked on the edge of the bed with his forearms on his knees, leaning forward and smoking an e-cigarette while Lexy washed up in the master suite bathroom. When she came out, she looked at him and noted how strong his short, squat frame was and how brutish he looked.

He glanced up at her with an intimidating stare. In a husky tone, he spoke Spanish. Despite not knowing what he said, shivers ran through her body. It bothered her that, for a moment, she released herself to the man with primitive characteristics who caused her to have a well needed and satisfying orgasm, which she had not expected. This was not good. Getting personal with the dangerous Puerto Rican could prove fatal.

With eyes intensely locked on her, he followed her movements as she ran her manicured fingers through her bed head braids, rearranging them back into a coiffed lion's mane. His preoccupation with her made her uncomfortable, so she tried lightening up the mood by asking him questions about the e-cig he was smoking. He laughed, exposing his platinum upper teeth that did not match the yellowed lower ones, and told her it was vaporized THC oil, but that it could work for her as a vape pen, which revealed he had lied when he said he didn't smoke marijuana.

After a few minutes of light talk, he wrapped a towel around his waist and walked her to the front door. He then told her to hold on and went back to the living room, returning with the money she had given him.

"Razor, please, I can't," she said with a look of concern on her face, keeping her hands close to her body to refuse the money. "I don't want to be in debt. I know how these things go."

"No, Mami, no debt. We square," he said, pushing the money towards her. "We good. Consider things taken care of." He flashed a crooked smile and looked at her with a boyish charm, far from the killer she had just sat across from and conducted business with.

Not wanting to disrespect the notorious gang member, the money exchanged hands. Her inner alarms went off, but her hands felt tied because the streets worked like this. In the future, Razor could be a thorn in her side, but getting things done now took priority. Regardless, there was a side of her that was not surprised by his actions and suspected he might return the money. Lexy walked out of the condominium with the fifty thousand back in her purse, and her jaws unclenched.

CHAPTER 17

LEXY & DETECTIVE HALL
Wednesday - 9 a.m.

Lexy stood erect in a whitewashed East Lake Police interrogation room wearing a midnight blue pantsuit and ankle-high black leather boots. Her clothing gave her a subtle but militant look and presented a stark contrast to the sterile backdrop of the small, bright room. While looking out an exterior window, and wondering why the interview room had a window, she heard the door open behind her.

Detective Hall came in, placed a small laptop on the square table, and hung his suit coat on the cushioned office chair next to the door and said, "Ms. Leigh, thank you for coming in. Please, have a seat. Can I get you anything? Water? A pop? We have bagels and cream cheese if you'd like."

Lexy dismissed his fake pleasantries and took a seat across from the average-looking white man, knowing their conversation could have taken place by phone. "What can I do for you, detective? Have you found the rapist?"

"Technically, we have not, but someone else has."

"Meaning?"

"Well, it seems everything has checked out with your story."

"My story?" she squinted in disapproval, forcing wrinkles at the outer corners of her small eyes.

"Let's see." He placed thick glasses on and tapped the computer screen in front of him. "It's all here; your alibi verified: the forced exit that tore the patio screen; the suspect's footprints on your carpet; the trajectory of the bullets pulled out of the walls; blood spatter pattern from your firearm discharge. Uh-huh, your firearm permit…ah, let's see. Let's see…oh, yes, Ms. Foster's account of the incident, the paramedic report, and hospital records all support your statement, but there is one question."

Lexy cocked her head and looked at the detective with a flat facial expression and waited.

"Minneapolis PD is investigating that homicide," he said as if she knew.

With boredom, she asked, "What does this have to do with me, detective?"

"It turns out, the blood found at your home, the skin retrieved from under Ms. Foster's nails, and the specimen from the rape test kit all match the profile of the deceased from the Minneapolis case, as well as the bullet wound pattern to his shoulder and his footprints." He discreetly checked her body language but kept direct eye contact as he spoke. "It will take several weeks to get the DNA analysis to confirm, but we're sure they'll match.

Lexy showed no reaction. They sat looking at each other.

"You know, the streets are talking that you don't mess with The Queen."

"What are you implying?"

He slapped his hand on the table in a quiet but forceful manner. "Come on, who are you kidding?" His tone of voice teetered on the edge of unprofessional.

Lexy continued looking at him.

There was a knock on the door; an officer came in and informed Detective Hall he had a phone call. He asked Lexy if he could have a moment, since her presence was voluntary and excused himself from the room. Instead of taking a call, he joined a fellow detective in another room and watched Lexy on a monitor.

They waited for a few minutes to examine her actions. Lexy sat in the chair, drumming her fingers on the table with impatience; she cracked her neck, and then checked her phone. Finally, she stood, went to the window, and gazed out. Detective Hall rejoined her in the room.

"Would you like something to drink?" he asked for a second time and waited for an answer that did not come before closing the door.

With mild irritation in her voice, Lexy spoke with authority, "Detective, what do you want?"

"I want to know if you were involved with the homicide?"

"What?" She frowned. "There are plenty of homicides in the Twin Cities. Who died?"

The obvious game continued.

"You don't know?"

"No."

"One Vincenzo Abela, Jr.; twin of Vincenzo Abela, II, nicknames of Junior and Vinny, respectively; sons of one Vincenzo Abela, Sr."

"No."

"No?"

"No, detective."

"Lexy."

"I'd prefer you call me Ms. Leigh during these formal proceedings."

He sighed. "Why, of course."

She stood up; he stood up.

"Detective Hall, if you're going to charge me with something, I'd like to call my attorney. If not, I'm leaving. I do have a full calendar. If this is your official notification that the person who assaulted Lisa has been found and is no longer a threat, I appreciate the work of East Lake PD. Lisa and I are both grateful for your service."

Detective Hall's expression softened. He knew the truth but had no proof; and, in this situation, he doubted the truth would ever be revealed.

"No, you're free to go. But do know, I feel you know more than you're admitting."

Lexy proceeded to leave, her mind disengaged from the adjourned meeting, but, at the door, she turned around. "The streets? The Queen? Really?" She scoffed. "See you at the ball, detective."

* * *

On the drive to the homeless shelter, Lexy wondered if she made a mistake trusting Razor. Since the night she saw him, they had not talked. Word of the twin's death reached her—Junior's body turned up in the Mississippi river with a slit throat—which sounded like a classic Razor move, but Junior had his share of enemies, and anyone with a bruised ego could have taken him out. The odds were that it was Razor. Lexy hit the accelerator and sped down the freeway. After working in the food line, she would need to attend a meeting at her bank and then stop by the funeral home to pay for Lillian's memorial service. There seemed to be not enough hours in a day for her to effectively manage life.

Pulling up to the shelter, a groan escaped her lips. Media personnel lined the sidewalk. When she got out of her car, reporters shouted her name, clamoring for attention. They gathered around her, shouting questions about Sandy's death, Lisa's assault, and tried addressing rumors of the sale of the club. One aggressive reporter jumped in her path.

"What do you have to say about your role in objectifying women, Ms. Leigh?" a female reporter asked and shoved a microphone towards Lexy's face; her camera person zooming the lenses in tight.

A security guard and fellow volunteers intervened, stepping between Lexy and the zealous woman to provide an unobstructed path forward for their respected friend. With a straightforward gaze, the sought-after business owner went into the building with cameras and microphones recording her every move.

BEVERLY & TL
Wednesday – 10 a.m.

Wearing a pink, cotton A-framed dress and sandals, Beverly walked into the Bellows hotel lobby. To her disappointment, TL was not there. She looked around, hoping he had not stood her up. When he strolled through the main doors, she smiled.

"Bambi, you look beautiful."

"Thank you. But compared to you, I feel under-dressed," Beverly said as she admired his beige, linen summer suit.

"You're perfect. I'm sure you can wear a potato sack and make it look good. For what we're doing, you're dressed fine."

Beverly laughed timidly. She wasn't sure why, but she felt like a teenager in his presence. He took her hand. The two headed out the hotel door.

* * *

When TL and Beverly arrived at the Mississippi River, they began their walk along the man made path that followed the flow of the water. Beverly marveled at the expansion of the riverfront. The new City Walk Development Project had replaced the once-abandoned water-front properties with newly constructed communities that consisted of row homes, condos, and amenities such as banking, convenience stores, and coffee shops, to name a few. Beverly did not want to come across as a bore, so she kept the air free of silence by commenting on everything before them.

As he listened to her, TL thought, *Damn, this bitch talks too much.*

"What do you think, Terrell? Should this project have been made more accessible to low-income residents?"

"No, I don't. I believe in capitalism. That's what America is built on."

Beverly's smile faded.

"That's disappointing to hear. Especially since America was built on the backs of slaves. We never got our 40 acres and a mule."

"And, if all that had not happened, I would not be here with such an intelligent Nubian Queen."

"You're trying to change the subject, Terrell."

"Bambi, we can't change the past, but we can move forward to do better for today. If the white man wanna build condos, led'em. I prefer to give back through community programs developed with the agenda of empowering people to create their own destiny. Not wait around for subsidized housing. Our people need to get out of the hands-out mindset."

Beverly reflected for a moment before replying, "I can see that point of view."

TL took them to a picnic area where they found a shaded area and set their blanket and food out. TL studied Beverly while she ate. His eyes locked on her lips, causing Beverly to blush.

"Bambi. I feel calm and relaxed around you. I could watch you all day. We could spend the rest of our lives doing this."

Beverly played along.

"This," Beverly said, and swept her hand like a car showroom model, "would be difficult. You know, the California thing."

"Work takes me West."

TL noted Beverly's exposed knee. He reached over and pulled the hemline down in a protective manner.

"So, fashion commodities, huh?" she said, trying not to linger on the feel of his hand.

"Yes, think textiles. Bulk," he replied as he stroked her skin below the hemline.

"So, we are in the same industry," she said, struggling to control the pending crack in her voice.

"Yes. In a sense."

"Where is your office?"

TL did not answer. He took his index finger and trailed the white stitching on the pink dress.

"Terrell?"

"Yeah?" his finger stopped exploring. He moved closer to Beverly and took her hand. "My office is wherever you are. You and I, my queen, could be a power-couple."

Sitting close to him, she became aroused by his sexual innuendos. Beverly felt dizzy with desire. TL leaned in. She thought it was the moment, but instead, he picked a stray hair off her exposed shoulder.

"I'd love to invest in you," he said, flashing a smile.

"You would," she responded light-heartedly, slightly relieved that she mistook his intentions.

TL leaned towards Beverly, again, and said, "With the right support, I know you'll be successful."

Beverly felt a magnetic pull from his well-placed words. They both understood what would come next. Her posture relaxed. Without a thought, she welcomed his mouth. His lips touched hers. Her lips parted. She let him in. The kiss was soft. Beverly wanted a deeper kiss, but he stopped and offered small pecks on her cheeks. He lingered with each one. Beverly felt like they were the only two in the park until two children ran close by and interrupted the magical moment.

"Terrell, I…," she began.

TL placed a finger on her lips to silence her. "Let's enjoy this moment, Bambi." He then donned his sunglasses, stretched out his legs, and laid his head in her lap. He smiled up at her before taking her hands and placing them on his chest. They sat in silence, listening to birds chirping. Beverly sat basking in the contentment of her heart. They enjoyed their time together until TL stated he had a meeting to attend and stood to extend a hand to help her stand up.

As they gathered their belongings, they heard someone shout in their direction, "Hey, Baby!" A striking brunette, dressed in a deep red, form-fitting business skirt and a white, sleeveless ruffled blouse with black stilettos daintily made her way across the grass. Setting aside her struggle with her heels on the grass, she looked like a model out of the pages of a Vogue magazine. Her blunted bob haircut gave her the appearance of a CEO on a lunch break. Carefully, she made her way towards the couple.

"Do you know her?" Beverly asked.

TL held up a hand to indicate to Beverly to stay put and said, "No. I don't. But I'll see what's going on."

TL moved with purpose to maintain the distance between Beverly and the woman. When he reached her, and out of earshot of Beverly, he said to the professional-looking woman, "Don't you see I'm in a meeting?"

"Daddy, I'm sorry. I just finished seeing my doctor client, and I saw your car. Just dropped by to see you," the refined woman said, speaking as proper as she looked.

TL pointed towards the street leading to the main road. The woman looked too. TL dropped his arm and told her, "Diamond, I'll swing by tonight. Go, do your thing, moneymaker. Okay?"

"Yes, Daddy. I'll see you later."

When TL got back to Beverly's side, she asked, "Is everything alright?"

"Yes. She mistook me for someone else. But it's cool. I provided her some directions. Her GPS had her lost."

"I can relate to that," Beverly said. "That's how I met you."

The two gathered the rest of the picnic supplies, and then TL dropped Beverly back off at her hotel, promising they would get together again, soon. Beverly was elated and could not wait to tell Kat about her new friend.

* * *

TL turned the deadbolt to the apartment door. Cookie heard the click of the lock and felt her stomach bottom out. Despite being in her own home, she felt vulnerable. Her mouth went dry, and she had the urge to have a bowel movement. A loose one. Tightening her sphincter muscles, she held her breath as TL walked into the bedroom. He said nothing as he began to undress. Cookie sat quietly, trying to read his mood. He lay naked on the bed with the remote in his hand, flipping through channels. Cookie stood to go to the bathroom.

"Sit ya ass down."

"But, I…."

"Bitch, I didn't ask you shit. Sit your punk ass down!"

Cookie walked towards the bed.

"No! Sit your ass down in the corner and face the wall since you think you all smart and shit!"

Cookie obeyed. She sat in the corner for hours while TL took a nap. When he woke, he handcuffed her to the radiator.

"Please, Baby! I promise I won't fuck up again!"

TL bent down and grabbed a hand full of weave, twisting the fake hair that was sewn into her braids, "You make one sound, and I'll kill your bitch ass!"

Naked and achy from sitting for hours in her own urine, Cookie looked at him with her tear-stained face and shook her head yes.

"Bitch, let me see you run off now," TL said as he walked out the door, leaving Cookie to stay locked to the radiator naked, except for her TL$ tattoo.

MARCUS
Thursday - 5:30 a.m.

The alarm on Marcus' phone cut through the silence of the air-conditioned room. Still sleepy, he pushed the covers back, exposing his graying chest hair and white boxer shorts before pulling a blackout mask off his face. He blindly grabbed at the cell phone, indiscriminately tapping at the blur of buttons to dismiss the alarm.

Before he could gather his thoughts, the phone in his hand rang, causing him to jump. It was the kitchen club manager calling for authorization to bring in an extra prep chef. No sooner had he hung up, a journalist called asking for an exclusive, which left him wondering how she got his personal number and questioning her professionalism for the early morning call. After putting on his glasses, he replied to a dancer's late-night text, asking if her cousin from Atlanta could work the ball. He replied, "No." Still sitting in bed, he grabbed the remote and turned the television on.

"Shit!"

Surrounded by news personnel, Lexy's image dominated the screen as she pushed her way into a homeless shelter.

"In entertainment news, the owner of Lexy's Gentleman club has been turning heads, but not in a way that one would think. The influential socialite is involved in a homicide investigation…"

Marcus sighed.

"…and the club has yet another legal suit filed against it; the current one involving an overdose of an employee, which has the conservative right questioning the licensing of the business while proponents point to the many charities and community developments the owner of the establishment contributes to. Tune in tonight at five. Our panel will discuss the moral and ethical issues surrounding charities accepting donations from controversial venues such as strip clubs and weapon organizations.

This is not the free press we need.

Shaking his head, Marcus climbed out of bed, hoping no new drama would unfold during the final preparations for tomorrow's event. He felt relieved he did not have to be front and center at Lillian's home going service later that morning; however, at a moment's notice, he would go to Lexy's side, if needed.

Before heading to work, Marcus stopped at the gym. He spent twenty minutes on a stationary bike—not a second longer—and then headed to the dry sauna, his favorite place to be. After reading the main sections of a discarded newspaper, he showered and shaved in the locker room. Despite Lexy's proclamation of casual attire days during construction week, the next-in-command stayed true to himself and dressed professionally each day. He left the gym in a tailored dark blue suit.

* * *

By 8:30 a.m., Marcus arrived at a bustling work environment. Assistant managers hustled about to manage the organized chaos for the final twenty-four hours of preparation for the big day. Downtown police representatives sat waiting on him while sipping on-duty "broken oaths" at one of the newly constructed bars. This did not bother Marcus; he understood the dark side of the entertainment industry and the murkier side of human nature. Sometimes, it was best to mind one's own business. This was one of those times. He nodded in the men's direction and held up a finger to acknowledge them. The police officers held up their alcohol-filled glasses and then went back to enjoying the complimentary drinks.

Marcus checked on the other three beverage stations. All four of the massive, ornate bars had been replaced with clear acrylic pieces of art that were designed to resemble smooth blocks of ice. That morning, electricians were installing special lights inside the cavities of the perceived ice so the bars could glow and, in the shelves, to back light the displayed spirits. Except for Lexy's and Marcus' offices, all the work in the establishment was complete, including the new exterior art deco styled *Lexy's* sign above the front door.

In his main level office, Marcus checked emails, made a few calls, and then radioed the floor manager to have the in-house security team, the contracted security representatives, and the police liaison escorted to the conference suite. The group reviewed the details of their security measures. After the meeting, the quiet, stately man returned to his office to work on the accounting. Looking around, he felt gratitude that Lexy left the original design of his cherry wood decor untouched. He did not care for the white used in the new color palette in the setting he spent most of his life in; he preferred the familiarity of the classic design of his office.

A knock on the door interrupted his accounting task. An exasperated floor manager asked for help at the front door. Marcus looked at the security monitor to see an unhappy Vincenzo, flanked by three men, glaring up at the camera in the foyer. Marcus instructed the nervous employee to escort Vincenzo to a V.I.P. suite.

Marcus retrieved his revolver from a safe and tucked it in his pant waist before securing the single button on his suit coat. He thought about calling Lexy but did not want to distract her from Lillian's funeral, so he decided to meet the aging gangster alone. When Marcus entered the private suite, he dismissed the electrician working on the surveillance system. Vincenzo, sitting in a black leather armchair, tried to stand, but his weight made it difficult. His entourage came rushing to his side, but he waved them back and heaved his large body out of the chair.

Marcus extended his hand to the winded man. "Vin, please excuse the mess. As you can see, we are finishing things up here. Um, Lexy will not be in until tomorrow. That's when we're scheduled to meet, right?"

Locking his damp, fat hand with Marcus' and sending whiskey fumes into his face, Vincenzo replied, "Thursday, Friday, it's all the same, yeah?"

Marcus looked puzzled. "What can I do for you?" he asked, still standing as Vincenzo stuffed his massive body back into the chair. With concern, Marcus glanced at a briefcase one of the men held.

Vincenzo did not speak but looked around admiringly. Finally, he said, "This is nice," and pulled a cigar out of an inner suit pocket and lit it.

Marcus cleared his throat. "Uh…say…there is no smoking outside of the cigar lounge, Vin." He retrieved a glass from the mini-bar and added water to it before offering it to Vincenzo.

An uncomfortable silence followed.

Vincenzo stared at Marcus but then nodded to one of his men to put the cigar in the improvised ashtray. "Yes…hmm…best to protect my new investment. Yes?"

"What can I do for you?" Marcus asked, showing his poker face, his nervousness sliding into irritation over the fact that Vincenzo was infringing upon his limited time.

"Just the notarized documents," Vincenzo said with a smirk. He picked up his whiskey and took a drink. "Ah, good stuff." He wiped the corner of his mouth with the back of his hand, feeling no need to pull out his handkerchief because Lexy was not in the room. "So, you own ten percent, eh?" he said louder than necessary.

Marcus raised a peppered black and gray eyebrow. "It seems."

"We talk then." Vincenzo motioned for Marcus to sit across from him in the matching chair. Mockingly, Vincenzo said, "You don't favor me much, eh?"

"I've never said that," Marcus lied as he took a seat.

"It's, how do you say? Written on your face, eh?"

"I have not been fond of what you have put Lexy through in the past, but, as of now, I have no complaints."

"Yes." Vincenzo nodded in agreement. "Things happened; that is the past." He tried leaning forward to retrieve his cigar but stopped short, realizing he had placed it in the glass of water.

"Are you trying to hurt her? Is this necessary?"

"This is business," Vincenzo offered and reflected for a moment. "You know, you're going to have to choose. You know the right thing to do, eh?"

"And that is?" Marcus asked, unable to control his eyebrow.

"Talk to la Bella signora; I can't guarantee her safety this time." Vincenzo lifted a fat hand in the air. The man holding the briefcase came forward. It landed with a thud on the table between them. "In the meantime, I buy you in."

The minion opened the case. Marcus kept a neutral demeanor and slowly reached in his pocket for a handkerchief to wipe the lenses of his glasses. Internally, he panicked. Stacks of bills filled the leather-lined carrier. It did not take the accountant long to calculate it held a half million, which, he knew, in the end, would end up back in the Mafia's pocket and not in his.

Shaking his head and wondering why the old man used the type of attaché case that carried the stigma of a crook, Marcus held up both hands like a suspect under arrest and spoke matter of fact, "I can't take this, Vin."

Typical Vincenzo style, he exploded. Pointing a pudgy finger towards Marcus, causing Marcus to flinch, he shouted. "So, you going to wear a skirt for the rest of your life?! Get some palle!" (balls).

"I-I-I can't take this," Marcus stuttered.

Before he knew what was happening, Marcus felt the cold steel of a gun nozzle at the back of his head. Despite strapping himself with his own gun, he did not have the street sense to predict when to pull it. It did him no use tucked under his coat jacket. Marcus swallowed hard. His eyes darted about as if looking for an escape route. A wave of nausea swept through his stomach and sweat formed under his armpits as he sat suppressing his body language.

A heaviness registered on the old man's face. "Now, I have to go plan a funeral. Tomorrow, business, eh." Vincenzo engaged in a small fight with the chair before standing and heading towards the suite's double doors. Stopping, he turned and waved his hand. "Tomorrow!" he said with a booming voice, the melancholy of a few seconds ago no longer detectable.

The weapon remained at Marcus' head until the other men left the room. The last man eased backward and out the door, keeping his eyes and his aim on Marcus the entire time. Marcus let out a deep breath and wiped his forehead with the handkerchief in his hand. The briefcase lay open on the table. Closing it, he contemplated what to do. He needed time to think. Preoccupied with the impromptu meeting, he did not realize the technician had been removing the old security cameras—not installing new ones. The new cameras were already up and running and had recorded everything.

CHAPTER 18

BEVERLY
Thursday - 9 a.m.

Beverly's morning started off-script. For the first time in months, her routine strayed from its usual disciplined approach. After sleeping in, her workout got swapped for a quick stretch in bed, and her prayer and scripture reading was conducted like a high school student rushing through a research paper. Daydreaming about Terrell consumed most of her energy while she lounged in the hotel's luxury bed, eating doughnut holes and drinking whole milk, two items she had deprived herself of since refocusing on her modeling career.

Excited to meet Kat to go shopping, Beverly decided she would refrain from giving too much information about her date, in fear of Kat questioning the Christian advice on men she gave her, or at least until she confirmed Terrell's level of dedication to Christ. While urging herself to leave the coziness of her bed, her phone chimed.

"Hello, Sister Beverly!" Sister Sarah's soothing, southern accented voice flowed through the connection.

"Hi, Sister Sarah, how are you?"

"I'm blessed! And you?"

Beverly sat up with eyes shining bright. "I'm doing great!"

Beverly brought her mentor up to date on her vacation. Her speech pattern became fast and animated as she gushed about the wonderful experience with Terrell and how intelligent, witty, and professionally accomplished he was. Her update ended with news of her scheduled meeting with Kat to shop for a ball gown.

"Are you attending this ball?"

"No, ma'am. I don't believe God would approve. Don't you agree?"

"I agree. Our Savior would not like you in a strip club or any club that serves alcohol and everything else that comes with those type of places. God has not called you to minister at this stage. You're still a babe in Christ." Sister Sarah continued in a motherly tone, "But, you know, you must be mindful of how easy our flesh can be a thorn in our side and how cunning the principals of darkness can be. Ephesians 6:10-18 comes to mind.

Beverly rolled her eyes.

I know the scripture, Sister Sarah.

"The scripture instructs us to be mindful of wearing the full armor of God."

"Um…Sister Sarah," Beverly interjected, "Do you believe I am weak?"

Sister Sarah noted Beverly's defensiveness.

Irritated, but maintaining a respectful tone, Beverly continued, "This is not about the ball. Are you referring to Terrell?"

"Sweetheart, Satan comes like a thief in the night. You have to stay prayed up and mindful of His cunning ways."

"I understand, but do you think I'm too naïve to discern if I'm placing myself in harm's way? I know I came to you with a concern earlier, but if you met him, you would see he is a good man."

"I'm not saying your naïve, baby. It's just that some people have their own agenda. You are special, Sister. You deserve a righteous man after God's heart."

Sitting on the edge of the bed, Beverly grabbed a piece of the blanket and balled it up in her hand, squeezing and relaxing the bamboo-green material in her grip. "I understand, but he isn't like anyone I've ever met."

"This may be true," Sister Sarah said, keeping her voice even and gentle. "I'm not judging you. I just want you to be careful. Sometimes, things are not what they seem. Did the two of you discuss the Lord during your time together?"

The assault on the blanket stopped, and Beverly smiled. "Yes, we did."

"Is he a believer?"

"Yes."

"What kind of believer?"

Beverly's smile faded. A hot spot formed on the back of her neck. "He is a Christian."

"I see. Well, if you are prayed up about this, please proceed with caution. It is easy to focus on feelings and lose sight of serving Christ. Be careful."

After assuring Sister Sarah that she would be mindful and stay prayed up, the two women prayed together. Sister Sarah made Beverly the direct object of the prayer. Beverly hung up, feeling annoyed at her prayer partner, and wished Sister Sarah had not called. For the first time in their mentor-mentee relationship, Beverly felt resentment towards Sister Sarah.

MARIA
Thursday - 9 a.m.

Maria hummed a Spanish song as she dressed, happy that she convinced Estelle to omit both the vigil service and liturgy for their grandmother and to move directly to the Rite of Committal. Estelle, who wanted to give her grandmother a proper Catholic burial, listened to reason that family from Albuquerque could not afford to come and that her grandmother had outlived her friends, so it made sense to have an abbreviated Catholic service for the few parishioners and the handful of medical personnel that were attending. Maria was glad the service would be quick. It was not that she did not love her grandmother; rather, she was excited to pursue a new life with TL.

Standing in front of a cheap, rectangular door mirror, which leaned against a cracked wall in her cramped bedroom, Maria checked her appearance one last time. Running her hand over the black material of her dress and across her flat stomach, she could not wait to buy a pregnancy test to confirm what she suspected. Maria had been retrieving TL's used condoms and using needleless syringes to insert his semen into her vagina. Other times, she managed to discreetly poke holes in the condoms or smear ejaculated semen from off her body and into her lady parts. Now, her menstrual was late, and she was overjoyed with the thought that she was carrying TL's baby.

Maria placed her hair in a high, tight bun, added large, gold hoop earrings, and put on a pair of black pumps before going to her closet and pulling out her white gown. Holding it up to her body, she twirled around the room with it, hearing imaginary music in her head and giggling with anticipation. TL preferred her in red, and the thought of wearing white for the ball was refreshing. Maria felt on top of the world. He had paid for the funeral service and given her money to shop. After placing the dress back, she carefully applied the cherry lipstick TL told her to wear. Now, it was time to bury her grandmother, bury the past, and move on to her future.

LEXY
Thursday – 10:20 a.m.

The visitation and burial of Lillian Leigh took place on a slightly overcast, humid mid-morning. Lillian's former church used the lack of membership as an excuse not to hold services for the mean-spirited deceased, which may have had more to do with Lillian telling half the congregation what she thought of them before taking her leave years ago; therefore, the would-be mourners filed slowly into a bungalow sized funeral parlor in a St. Paul neighborhood on a corner lot.

Some friends came to show their respect, while others showed up to gloat. Despite standing room only, the atmosphere in the small venue was quite festive. Lillian's body lay in a white silk-lined black casket in a pink dress with her long gray hair professionally coiffed, a stark contrast from the two untamed braids she had worn for the last two decades of her life.

Lexy stood in a small foyer dressed in a masculine black pantsuit with her braids pulled into a loose neck bun. She greeted mourners as they came through the door, nodding and smiling at them on cue. Tina sat with her legs crossed in the first seat of the first row on a wooden bench near the casket. Wearing a black sheath dress, she daintily dabbed her tears with a handkerchief as attendees filed past the casket and stopped to extend their condolences to her. On the contrary, Marlene, in a black, formal jumpsuit, coped by fluttering around making sure everyone was comfortable at the memorial soiree that smelled of mothballs and cheap cologne.

An ineffective air conditioning unit struggled to cool the foyer and main room. Some attendees had to take off suit coats or constantly wipe sweat off their brows. Over-dressed elderly women from the church suffered the most in their peacock-feathered hats and layered polyester dresses. The ladies fanned themselves excessively with funeral home cardboard advertisements as each competed to look better than the other. Lillian would have been proud of the discomfort everyone endured on her account.

Lexy continued her job of greeting guests, not noticing a tall figure entering the foyer—standing heads above the rest of the mourners despite his stooped posture. He wore an ill-fitting suit that hung loosely on his bent frame. He was an elderly man with a square head, a broad flat nose, oversized dry black and pink lips, and an unshaved face. Lumbering up to her with big feet that seemed to struggle with each step, he took his hat off, revealing a large bald spot on top of his head.

Lexy squinted. He looked familiar, but she could not place who he was or where she had seen him. Absentmindedly, they exchanged polite words for the occasion, and then he turned to resume his pilgrimage. Watching him shuffle away, it dawned on her. The attic. The photos. Her eyes followed him around the room as he painstakingly made his way to the casket in the brown suit that looked as though it fit him well at one time but now hung on his frame like an afterthought.

"Where have you been?" she whispered.

"Dear?"

Lexy shifted her focus to Mrs. Rose, who stood in front of her. "Pardon me?"

"I was saying it's sure a lovely day to send Sister Lilly home, isn't it?"

"Yes, ma'am," Lexy replied, trying to look engaged while keeping an eye on the man who passed the casket with hat in hand. Having no patience to search for a seat, he started his journey towards the exit. "Ah…ah…Mrs. Rose, thank you for coming." She held the woman's hand briefly and then let it go to follow the man out the door, leaving the bewildered senior standing at the guest book.

"Excuse me, excuse me!" Lexy called out as the feeble man made his way down the steps holding the metal handrail. Lexy advanced past him, reached the bottom of the steps first, and helped him the rest of the way down. "I'm sorry to bother you…uh, you knew Aunt Lilly?"

He cleared his throat. "Why, yes," he answered, looking at her with clouded eyes. "We were quite close at one time." Remembering something good, he smiled slowly, showing a set of false teeth. "You must be Alexandria."

"I am. And you are?"

"James Thomas."

"Do you have to leave, Mr. Thomas?" she asked, examining the weariness of his eyes and deep wrinkles in his face.

"There is no room for an old man like me. I can't stand long."

"Please, come sit with me and my sisters, please!" she insisted.

"I couldn't impose." He made a step to go around her.

"Nonsense," she replied in a soft but firm tone, taking hold of his elbow and steering him back up the steps. Back inside, Tina and Marlene looked at Lexy when she arrived at their seats with the older man in tow and then looked at each other. She offered him a seat beside her, causing the row of people to have to shift over.

During the service, speakers said what was expected of them. Lillian was a good woman, which could be debated; you could count on her when you needed her, which was usually at a cost; and she loved God, if he did not piss her off. No one strayed from the script of proper etiquette memorial protocol. Periodically, Tina and Marlene stole glances at Lexy and the stranger, which Lexy ignored.

To close the wake part of the service, a church member sang a soulful rendition of "Precious Lord," which brought tears to many eyes, but Lexy sat stiff and unmoved. When the song ended, images of Lillian began to appear on the wall over the casket and above the flowers. They were images of Lillian at various stages of her life, including pictures with Tina, Marlene, and Lexy, mere children, all under the age of five.

There were photos of Lillian with the small girls at church, at the zoo, or at an ice cream shop. In some pictures, the siblings wore matching white cotton dresses. In others, they wore different outfits with the same striped or floral patterns. In most photos, the three girls shared the same plaited hairdos. Lexy had not seen the images before. Marlene squeezed her hand and Lexy felt a lump rise in her throat.

Where did these come from? I don't remember them.

A tear slid down her face; she wiped it away impatiently. The photos and the ad-libbed portion of the song seem to go on forever. Lexy couldn't leave, so she sat waiting and wrestling with uncomfortable emotions. She wished it would end. When the song and photos finally concluded, the funeral director asked everyone to be patient, so the family could leave first.

Outside, Mr. Thomas looked confused when Lexy attempted to usher him in the limo. He declined and pulled back. Lexy entered the vehicle and then rolled the window down. "Thank you for coming."

"Thank you for having me."

When the limo started, he reached down and patted her hand that rested on the door. "Your mother would have been proud of the service."

"You mean my aunt," she corrected as the vehicle crept away from the curb.

Lexy pushed back into her seat and noticed Tina looked nervous. Their eyes locked. Unfamiliar silence saturated the compartment. Marlene sat ignorant to the unspoken communication. Lexy searched Tina's eyes before Tina turned and looked out the tinted window.

The epiphany hit her like the percussion of a mass explosion; the silent revelation shattered the airwaves. Lexy felt the caving in of her chest. Her manicured hand went to her throat, and she tried to catch her breath. The neurons in her brain connected. It all made sense. It was there all the time, so obvious.

Images flashed: the girls all looked alike, but Marlene and Tina resembled each other more in height and body type; the resemblance of her and Lillian, which was explained off as strong family genes, and the difference in treatment, both Lillian's disdain at her and Tina's over-protectiveness. And there was Lillian's attempted death bed confession.

Tina turned to address Lexy. "You don't understand," she began and started to close the distance between them in the limo.

Lexy threw her arm up to fend off the approach, stopping Tina in her tracks. "How could you? How could you?" she hissed through clenched teeth.

"Lex, I still don't know. You've gotta believe me." Tina hung her head down to hide the panic-stricken expression on her face.

Lexy exploded.

"Stop your fucking lying! How dare you!" she yelled.

Startled by Lexy's outburst, Marlene asked with alarm, "What's going on, you guys?!"

The usually calm woman's anger continued to rise like a hurricane gaining momentum, infuriated at her sister for not trusting her enough to share her doubts and equally upset that she had spent many years in unnecessary emotional turmoil.

The funeral car procession crept along Dale Street towards Elmhurst Cemetery, slow enough for her to jump out and storm off, but avoiding scandalous headlines took priority. For now, she was stuck in a moment of family dysfunction with no escape.

"Please, what's going on?" Marlene begged.

Tina, cut from the same family cloth, found her own resolve and looked up at Lexy with renewed strength. "I tried to protect you… us!"

"By lying to me!" Lexy shouted, her small eyes widening.

"It wasn't just about you! It's was about all of us! I was trying to take care of us!" Tina shouted back.

Marlene grabbed Tina's arm. "You guys are scaring me," Marlene whined, "What's going on, Teen?!"

Tina let out a long sigh. Her posture weakened as the air left her lungs. Lexy and Marlene waited for her to speak. With resounding sadness, Tina spoke to no one in particular, "I-It's all so fucked up. I-I-I don't know where to start."

The dam broke, and salty fluid streamed unchecked down Tina's face. Lexy folded her arms and sat back, regaining her composure, internally processing her range of emotions, and listening as Tina tried to explain, through body-wracking sobs, Lillian's derailed attempt to attend school and her unwanted pregnancy.

"Ok. So." Lexy shrugged her shoulders forcefully and scowled. "Teenagers get pregnant all the time. That's nothing new. What does this have to do with Aunt Lilly denying me?"

"Well, Diane…um…I mean mom and grandma worked things out, I-I think. Lex, you gotta believe me," Tina stuttered. "I'm-I'm not even sure. I'm going off a childhood memory."

With horror registered on her face, Marlene listened intently.

Letting her arms fall from their folded position across her chest, Lexy leaned forward and pushed her balled up fists into the black leather seat. "What does that have to do with Aunt Lilly passing me off as her niece and mom feeling guilty about what?" she snapped, the thought of referring to Lillian as mom and Dianne as her aunt never crossing her mind.

Marlene shook her head back and forth and wailed, "No, no, no, no, no, no!"

In unison, Lexy and Tina shouted, "Shut up, Marlene!"

Marlene tempered her emotions and cried quietly while rocking to console herself, not sure what would happen next. Lexy reached a shaking hand into the bar compartment and retrieved cognac. She threw the shot back and then lit a slender cigar and cracked the window. Through tight eyes and a tighter set mouth, she waited for Tina to finish.

In a deflated voice, the eldest continued, "I-I suspected s-something was wrong, but I was so young." Tina paused to fill her lungs with air through her nose and then eased the air out of her mouth. "I remembered seeing Aunt Lilly gaining weight, and then she went away. After you and Aunt Lilly came home, I kept asking if you were Aunt Lilly's baby. I was told you were my new sister; I was told to take care of you." Tina slumped back into the seat; her shoulders rolled forward, and her gaze shifted to the floor; she whispered, "That's what I've done all these years. Mom and Aunt Lilly were never around. We were left with grandma…I don't know…th-things were so blurred. I d-did my best to take care of us," she stuttered.

Lexy sat seething with anger. Feeling the frost of bitterness seep through her veins, she responded, "So, basically, the bitch didn't want me, huh? Wow. And you. You've had how many years to share your suspicions?"

Tina looked sheepishly. Marlene stared on in shock.

"Obviously, somewhere along the line, you figured things out. What happened? I want the truth."

This time it was the non-drinker who poured three shots of cognac from the limo bar. Tina handed them to the others. The three somber women took the liquor without the usual teasing by Lexy and Marlene at Tina's expense because the latter could get drunk off a half cup of champagne. The tinted limo continued in the procession along Dale Street. The only thing missing was rain. Lexy broke the resonating silence with what could be construed as inappropriate calmness. "Go on."

"I remember when grandma died, Aunt Lilly came back. You weren't the only one she was angry with. Mom never helped with us, and I watched Aunt Lilly get bitter with each passing year."

"Meaning?" Lexy asked.

"I don't know. Maybe cuz of us. You know, Aunt Lilly not going back to school. The dancing." Tina stopped talking and refilled the shot glasses before continuing. "Aunt Lilly…well…she did what you did. That's why she hated you dancing."

"Oh, Teen," Marlene grabbed Tina's hand. "Why didn't you tell us!"

While necessary, the details did not impress Lexy.

"Wow," Lexy said with disdain. "So, when did you find out? Find out I'm your cousin and not your…your sister?" Holding the thin cigar in her right hand, she began tapping her left fingers on the seat beside her, playing a faster version of her fingered orchestra.

Resigning to the ominous moment of necessary honesty, Tina took the final plunge. "At grandma's funeral, I overheard mom and Aunt Lilly arguing in a back room. Aunt Lilly was angry because mom showed up to the home going with dad, mad that mom was leaving and not taking all three of us. I mean, furious."

The Limo pulled into the cemetery.

Tina's voice rose, "We may not share the same mother, but we are sisters! We really are!" Hysterically she blurted out, "Dad raped Aunt Lilly!"

Marlene gasped, and her hands flew to her gaping mouth. Motion stopped for Lexy. The limo kept its snail pace.

"T-That's why mom felt guilty!" Tina wailed. "She w-wanted… wanted…to make things right… b-but the drugs…Oh, honey! We are sisters!" Tina crumpled forward, holding her head in her hands.

Marlene continued staring wide-eyed, unable to speak. Lexy's body remained tense.

So, there it is. The reason I'm so fucked up.

A chime sounded, signaling their arrival to the burial plot. Feeling weary, Lexy looked out the window at the cemetery. "This is some fucked up shit," she whispered. The vehicle came to a stop. Without addressing the issue further, Lexy began straightening her clothes before reaching into her purse for a mirror to touch-up her makeup. Tina and Marlene watched the unusual reaction across from them in disbelief, but soon followed suit and began pulling themselves together.

The three emerged from the limo with their heads held high as if nothing had happened. If she could help it, Alexandria Tyson Leigh would not be a spectacle. Her ego would not allow respect to be lost just because life was messy. Lexy stood between her two sisters and held both their hands during the graveside service.

In her heart, she knew Tina had tried to protect them and Marlene had been clueless. From her point of view, the woman she had known as her mother, her aunt Diane, and her biological father, whom she had called Uncle Leroy all her life, were a sorry lot. Being birthed by Lillian explained some things about herself. Lexy watched Lillian's casket descend into the ground, understanding it all, yet knowing nothing.

KAT
Thursday - 3 p.m.

On the late-afternoon day, Kat's car service pulled up to the valet at the Crown Royal Hotel. She knew the lock-down at the five-star establishment meant no drugs unless you liked to snort or pop pills, neither of which held her interest, so she had to be content with the marijuana she had smoked after leaving her shopping excursion with Beverly.

Working the White Out Ball meant being at your best, so she almost appreciated the forced discipline. This was her fourth ball, so she felt secure enough to smoke weed before arriving, especially since she planned to see Taz afterward, just in time to stave off minor withdrawal symptoms; that is if TL did not interfere. The valet opened the door, and Kat floated out of the car on her marijuana buzz.

Behind her sedan, luxury vehicles continued pulling into the covered driveway. Young women piled out. Some arrived alone; others arrived in groups, and most were without make-up and dressed in casual attire. Seasoned dancers knew to wait until the evening of the ball to transform, unlike a few of the new girls who were glammed up.

Despite looking like plain Janes, they were all attractive. They conversed in various languages—chatting without concern about the effect they were having on the men in the hotel entryway and the lobby as they made their way to their floor. To these women, men were invisible unless they were paying customers.

In the posh penthouse suites, the dancers enjoyed what little personal time they had before the lock down and stringent rules were enforced to prepare for the ball. They swam in a rooftop swimming pool, consumed alcoholic beverages, ate at an over-the-top food buffet, enjoyed massages, and watched movies in the media room. The more level-headed women unpacked and tended to the meticulous job of checking wardrobe and jewelry, got manicures and pedicures, or rested and napped.

Feeling like a senior employee, Kat watched a few newbies look around in awe, one of which kept staring at her. Just when Kat got up to confront the rude girl, the dark-haired beauty left the commons area, leaving Kat wondering what the girl's issue was.

CHAPTER 19

THE BALL
Friday- 9 p.m.

At Lexy's, a slow tempo Frank Sinatra song saturated the airwaves, supplying an early evening ambiance of sophistication and a hint of "Rat Pack" intrigue; thus, stroking the egos of the powerful and famous guests who wore expensive jewelry, costly fragrances, and insanely priced custom-made evening wear. Looking distinguished, with his soft gray speckled hair cut in a military fashion and dressed in a classic retro white tuxedo with black accessories, Marcus stood in front of a 1950s inspired microphone on a mini stage that extended from a primary runway.

He tapped the black handkerchief in his outer, left breast pocket and adjusted his black horn-rimmed glasses for no other reason than to go through ritualistic motions while scanning the sea of patrons dressed in white formal attire. His gaze stopped periodically at the strategically placed ten-foot-tall round dance-platforms that held dance poles from which scantily clad entertainers mounted by sliding down them from catwalks in the rafters of the ceiling. Hanging in seductive poses and manipulating the poles in ways only true professionals could, the exotic dancers, secured by nearly invisible safety wires, performed sensual acts from the elevated heights, causing many of the guests' eyes to stay focused up at the strategically placed Vegas-style acrobatics.

Oblivious to Marcus' presence in the winter wonderland themed ballroom, guests chatted under dangling snow-crystals, decorative lighting, and moving body parts. Marcus nodded in the direction of the control booth, indicating to the technicians to stop the music and increase the house lights, which caused the attendees to turn to the bright area on the stage under which he stood. Having captured the crowd's attention, the emcee opened with a few pleasantries before introducing Lexy.

Behind him, against the backdrop of the main stage, a theatre sized scarlet curtain inched open to the sound of an ethereal jazz song, revealing an enormous white screen. The shadow of a temptress and the outline of a large afro displayed on the canvas. The crowd went silent, and Lexy stepped from behind the screen.

To the sexy and haunting music, like an ice skater's effortless waltz across smooth ice, the club owner confidently walked down the runway wearing a sleeveless, white crystal-embedded floor-length gown with a plunging neckline to her waist that left her taut implants to play a sexy peek-a-boo. The back of the dress hung equally daring, exposing her well-defined back muscles. The material began its coverage dangerously low on her derriere and flowed to the ground, ending in a classic mermaid shape at her white high heels. Large diamond hoop earrings hung from her ears and five-row diamond tennis bracelets wrapped each wrist, but her lean neck remained alluringly bare. The woman who was known for both her physique and her auburn micro-braids now wore her natural hair in an oversized auburn colored afro. Smokey eyes and blackberry-stained lips completed her conservative but exotic look.

Lexy's brief journey down the runway ended at Marcus' side on the thrust stage. Once the clapping died down, murmurs continued in the room as the occupants marveled at her exquisiteness. Resting his hand on the small of her back, Marcus kissed her lightly on each cheek and whispered in her ear, "You look amazing, Baby Doll," before bowing and exiting the stage, leaving her before her admirers.

The music stopped. Other than a few hushes, the room fell silent. The lights on her face felt hot, and Lexy hoped she would not sweat and ruin her make-up so early in the night. With her hands clasped together near her tight abs, the host centered herself and put forth the confident woman from within. "Welcome to the Tenth Annual White Out Ball!"

The sparkling, bright room seemed to lift off the floor from the vibration of clapping as guests showed their love to the woman who represented an unofficial historic brand in the Twin Cities. Once the metaphoric earthquake calmed, she continued, "This year's theme, as you can see, is ice."

Catcalls went forth from the crowd, which forced her to smile to show appreciation. Careful not to reveal how she detested such a poor display of decorum during a formal moment, she continued, "Ladies and Gentlemen, it pleases me to have this tenth annual event coincide with the new launch of Lexy's. It is our desire that you enjoy yourself as we usher Lexy's into a new era…"

Another round of accolades went forth, so she waited patiently to allow her prestigious guests the opportunity to show their support.

"…but have no concerns, we still offer the same high-quality entertainment that will please a wide range of tastes. From simplistic bliss to royal extravagance, we have it all." Moisture began to build in the crease of her back. The host took an undercover breath to steady her nerves. "Please, enjoy the remodeled main room, which, as you all know, is Lexy's…"

"Yeah!" A man shouted. Others joined in with enthusiastic shouts and shrill whistles cut through the air. A woman yelled from the crowd, "We love you, Lexy!"

Raising her voice slightly, she pushed on with renewed energy, like a political campaigner bringing home the message. "And, to the rear of the club, we've added our new venue, *Club Black! Club Black* will cater to a rotating music genre of the month. In addition, the private Kingdom suites have been completely reimagined. There are new items debuting on the food menu, and our wine list has been upgraded! From hand-rolled cigars in our specially designed ventilated cigar lounge, to our Michelin rated restaurant, and our professionally managed conference services, every client will find a service at Lexy's that fits their personal or business needs! We have gone through great lengths to secure the proper licensing for all your adult entertainment, and it is my personal pledge to you that all clients will continue to be serviced by qualified staff who will provide five-star guest services!" Her hands came apart and she extended them out to the audience. "And finally, I can assure everyone, there are exotic dancers on the premises that will suit anyone's unique taste!"

While a surge of thunderous ovation erupted, a stunning, curvaceous young black dancer walked on stage in a white crystal miniskirt and matching crystal bikini top and handed Lexy a glass of champagne. Men's mouths, and some women's, fell open as they watched the well-endowed cocoa-butter colored woman turn and walk away, giving them an eyeful of a surgically enhanced rear-end. The audiences' attention turned back to the boss when the heavy-bottomed girl left the stage.

"I want to thank the city of Minneapolis, our sponsors, our local community partners, and staff members. Without you, Lexy's would not be the iconic venue it is today! But most of all, I want to thank you, my guests!" Lexy held up her crystal stemware, causing the bright decorative lights to bounce off the sparkling champagne glass. "You are all an integral part of our success and the reason we can donate all proceeds from tonight's event to the No One Hungry Campaign! Thank you!" With a delicate smile, she nodded to the audience and took a ceremonious sip.

White confetti fell from mysterious locations, and a large crystallized disco ball descended from an opening in the ceiling, giving the party an "ah-ha!" moment by casting shimmers of diamond reflections across the room. An upbeat soul ballad replaced the Vegas music of yesteryears as the DJ continued the trajectory of bringing the music up through decades of music history genres. With Marcus' help, Lexy exited the stage to make room for an array of seductive women who filed out from behind the white screen, each of their shadows highlighted larger than life before they turned the corner to go onstage.

Sexy and self-assured, the women strutted down the runway to the music wearing see-through stilettos, oversized crystal-lined white snowflake wings, and glittery, white mini-skirts. The dancers continued to dispatch themselves throughout the venue. As they did, the cool air from the new HVAC system perked up nipples on both natural and surgically enhanced breasts, all of which pressed against the thin material of the bikini tops that would soon come off. The dancers seductively smiled and went into actor mode as they milled about courting high spenders.

* * *

Greeted by loud music from the seventies, TL walked through the foyer of the club and into the main ballroom. He stopped at the threshold and straightened his gold *TL* pendant with manicured hands, making sure it lay flat against his stark white shirt and tie, which blended seamlessly with his white custom-tailored Italian suit. He sported five-carat white diamonds on each pinky finger and wore white leather shoes that almost out shined his jewelry. His cuff links matched the white gold of his pendant and the gold stitching of his white initialized handkerchief. The height of his tall, chocolate God-like-stature stood out from the crowd, as did his chiseled, handsome looks, which could not be matched by anyone no matter how impeccably dressed they were. And, of course, he smelled insanely delicious.

The poised man walked through Lexy's as if he owned the place. For him, the White Out Ball was the equivalent of a Pimp's Ball. He enjoyed the bravado of the atmosphere and appreciated the ability it gave him to scout international talent. He took in the opulence of the new renovations with tight-set eyes purposely concealing his delight. He approved of the crystal and silver chandeliers that blended seamlessly with the rest of the modern decor and the white pedestal styled conversation tables embedded with lights around their perimeters, which looked like works of arts and brought a sexy kiss to each seating section. The contrast of the deep scarlet carpet with the plush black and white leather furnishings impressed him as well.

TL continued scanning the room, noting the different factions at the party. Towards the rear of room, Teddy Boy sat trying to look as important as he could. Instead, he looked like an old player, a cartoon character in an oversized jeweled and feathered wide-brimmed white hat, a white suit trimmed in black and white plaid, and clownish black and white plaid shoes. The exaggerated clothing made his underdeveloped frame look washed out.

Man, how I hate that niggah and men like him. They give us real pimps a bad look.

In another area, Razor's clique, dressed in white and gold, were causing an inebriated ruckus but were not drunk enough to be of serious concern, yet. Also, easily identifiable were the Bloods dressed in white with red accessories. The elite of other gangs represented their colors in similar fashion. Hmong and Somalia power players represented, too.

These cats look ridiculous. They aren't their own men, but a manifestation of weakness coming together to build strength.

He noted royalty, Hip Hop and Rap stars, actors, politicians, and a host of their entourages.

What a waste of money, entourages.

The upper corner of TL's lip twitched, a sign of his disgust with all that he judged. He continued his survey. Sprinkled throughout the venue were police officers, wearing ill-fitting cheap white suits with standard-issue uniform black ties—badges hanging noticeably around their necks.

At one point, he stood back watching Lexy making her rounds and wondered why he had not slept with her. Liking the thought of the challenge, he mused over the idea of her for a moment. Their sterile relationship spanned a decade, making him feel it was his right-of-passage to bed the accomplished woman. "Just a matter of time, Lexy," he mumbled under his breath.

He then dismissed his weak and vulnerable thoughts of her and continued his assessment of the den of sin before him. He scanned the rest of the area looking for his various investments and stopped when he saw Kat walking down the runway. He did not recognize the sophisticated and mature woman before him who came down the catwalk with a smooth and sexy stride. He noted she sported a new shoulder-length haircut styled in an old Hollywood finger-waved hairdo, which was highlighted with shimmery-gold highlights. With red set lips, golden bronze makeup, and black silk false eyelashes, her ice blue eyes popped against the backdrop of her makeup. The snowflake ornament on her back created a beautiful halo around her willowy figure. It was hard for him to believe she was the teen he copped three years ago. He noticed, too, how the men looked at her. He felt like a proud father.

Unfortunately, Maria trailed clumsily behind her. Her smoldering beauty made it difficult for the average person to see what TL saw—a train wreck. He frowned and set his lips in a harsh line, wishing she would pull herself together. Over the last several days, she had begun to display overbearing neediness. Initially, he was aroused by her dark, exotic vibe, but now she seemed more pathological than intriguing. TL had realized the truth about Maria.

As he looked at Maria with disapproval, he heard a bravado voice shout out over the music, "Whazup up, niggah!"

There was only one person bold enough to call TL niggah, Razor.

"Aw, hell," TL said, embracing the short man in a man hug. Their fists clasped solidly between them as they slapped each other's backs, careful to use their forearms as barriers to personal space.

"Hombre, ¡ Kat se ve muy bien!" (*Man, Kat looks great!*)

"Sí, sí," TL said, careful to keep his eyes on everything in the immediate area while focusing on Razor, too. "¿Te gusta la chica atras de ella?" *(You like the girl behind her?)*

Razor's eyes followed Maria's butt off the stage as the girls exited down into the shark pit.

The narrow slits of TL's eyes opened. "Hablamos de negocios." (Let's talk business.)

"¡Que bien!" (Sounds good!) Razor said, his mouth ending in a lopsided grin.

Like roosters strutting in a pen ready to fight, the arrogant men walked up floating stairs to a member's only V.I.P. area. The two powerhouses ordered drinks and then sat back to observe the overindulgences of the festivities. Razor stood and took off his white silk jacket and laid it on the back of his armchair, his muscles bulged beneath the tight-fitting white, formal shirt. He tugged at his gold tie to give relief from the constriction around his meaty neck. "Bruh, wha'tha fuck? You drinking aqua?" Razor grinned boyishly, the killer in him temporarily hidden. "Fool, that shit gonna kill you!"

TL unbuttoned his suit coat and leaned back like a king on a throne. "You guys just don't get it. That shit you put in your body gonna kill you." He winked at the server and held out forty dollars for his water and Razor's cognac.

"Sir, it's only twenty," the sexy, young girl informed.

"Baby, keep the change. Shit, you deserve more than that." TL winked at her. "Let's talk later."

He did not know the smiling, curvaceous woman but decided that would change. The men sipped while listening to Michael Jackson's "Billie Jean," their body language displaying relaxation, each quietly wired—one from cocaine and cognac, the other from a feeling of superiority.

Razor glanced at Detective Hall, who was sitting at one of the main level bars looking like he was trying not to enjoy himself. Sgt. Watts sat next to him looking like he never wanted to go home. "Them mothafuckas there," Razor said, and nodded his shaved head towards the glass railing, which gave an unobstructed view of the bar below.

"See, niggah," the platinum pimp addressed the gang member, "you ma'fuckas got it all wrong. You gotta stay mentally sharp, ya dig? That's why I don't drink or ingest the man's poison. I don't want to be retired early by some street niggah, some crazy bitch, or the establishment—in this case, the folks over there in homemade suits."

Razor threw his hand in the air and swatted away TL's logic.

TL sipped water. "You know, 'hands up,' niggah!" He motioned his head upward in a quick, short jerk. The pimp then leaned in with the smoothness of hustler royalty, set his glass down, and adjusted his tie for the umpteenth time. "It's about survival." He pointed a long-manicured fingernail on the table between them. "Them and us; those are some big labels. At the basic core, it's me against you. I'm not waiting for some order from some punk ma'fuckas." His lip turned up at the corner to signify disgust. "End up serving life for a cause that ain't about me…for some other ma'fucka behind bars calling the shots cuz his punk ass is supposed to be the boss cuz he is hiding behind idealized ranking." Leaning back in the soft, white leather chair, his dark skin stood out against both the chair and his suit, the pimp fingered his diamond pendant that was worth the cost of a small car.

"How ya figure, amigo?" Razor's eyes followed an Asian dancer as she strutted by trying to catch TL's attention.

TL ignored her. "Listen." TL sat erect and leaned in towards the lighted round tabletop. "Everything is relevant. You feel me? You could be a bitch, a trick, a doper, a cop, district attorney, or a banger. Shit, hands up or not, there is no them and us. Therefore, it is either you or me. Hence," he held a long index finger in the air, "a pimp soars solo." TL spread both open hands out, palms facing up. "We are boundless. Being boundless requires a clear mind." TL winked and picked up his glass of water.

Razor thought for a moment, trying to soak in the logic through a hazed mind and then slapped his pant leg and laughed. "Aw, fuck you chulo (pimp) niggah!" With a lopsided sneer, Razor threw up a gang sign. "Pimps are pussies. Fuck that solo shit, niggah. I'll never be in an alley alone. There's nottin' betta than an army behind you." Razor watched Lexy step off the glass elevator. "And some good pussy. Like Lexy's, along with a stiff drink and a little white girl (cocaine)." Razor gave a devilish look.

TL scoffed, secure in the knowledge that Lexy would never have sex with Razor, especially before him; therefore, with money on his mind, he decided to dispense with the small talk and began to sell Maria to Razor. He figured two Spanish locos deserved each other.

* * *

In the dressing room, Kat sat in a makeup chair feeling annoyed. A few seats over, the same Spanish girl from the hotel kept looking down the row at her, so she got up to confront the rude dancer.

"What's your problem?" Kat questioned, with her hands on her bony hips, a scowl on her face, and her wide blue eyes glaring intently at Maria.

Like the eclipse of the sun's rays shut out by mid-noon clouds, a silence fell over everyone in the area. Maria's male hairdresser paused with one hand on his hip and the other holding a brush in the air, ready to soak in newsworthy gossip. Maria looked at Kat through the mirror and put on a "who me" expression, touching her cleavage with her white acrylic claws.

Kat's voice rose, "Yes! You know what's up! You almost tripped me out there!"

In a throaty Spanish accent, Maria feigned ignorance. "I don't know what you're talking about." She batted her long dark lashes and tossed her hair, hitting the hairdresser with it and causing the sensitive man to throw an "Oh, no, you didn't!" look her way.

"You know what I'm talking about!" Kat's baby voice took on a shrill tone. "I saw you back at the hotel. I ain't stupid!" Kat towered over her seated Spanish rival waiting for an answer.

"Is there a problem here?" shouted Angie, the dressing room supervisor and former dancer, as she made her way over to the girls.

Innocently, Maria replied, "No, not at all."

"You'z bitches looking real unfamiliar right now. You'z can both get the fuck ou'da here if you gonna cause some damn drama!" Angie waved off two security guards headed in their direction. "You'z bitch'ez ain't getting me fired today! Hell-to-the-no! I'll kick both ya motherfuckin' asses!"

Kat walked away. The last thing she needed was TL pissed at her over petty locker room mess. Sorrow seared her heart and the desire to get high came out of nowhere. The ecstasy of the time in the shower with TL seemed a distant memory, the joy of spending money to prepare for the ball now a hangover of regret. The illusion of her opulent lifestyle fell away in an instant. Her mind felt scrambled and she longed to understand why. Trying not to bring attention to herself, she hung her head low and pushed back tears before heading out of the dressing room. Back on the floor, despite the extravagance surrounding her, she viewed it all with disgust.

* * *

With the party proceeding on track, Lexy took a moment to step into her office to rest her feet and have a glass of wine. Sitting in her private fortress, she debated whether to drink something stronger, but the professional in her settled on an appropriately aged Pinot Noir. As she poured the dark red liquid, Marlene walked in.

"Don't you know how to knock?"

"Aw, Sis…," Marlene paused, kicking herself for using the word "Sis." The last thing she wanted to do was remind Lexy of the previous day's revelations. "I wanted to see you before it got late. You know I don't stay at these events long. At the witching hour, it gets too chauvinistic for me." Marlene frowned to give her statement weight.

"I understand. Thanks for the support," Lexy said, trying to sound enthusiastic but failing.

Marlene eased around the office as if it were her first visit, pretending to look at the various objects and paintings, fingering items as she moved about. She stopped at a full-length mirror and checked her appearance, making sure her ultra-short dress still covered the right places. "Are you alright?"

"Yes, I'm fine," Lexy dryly replied, busying herself with the work before her.

"Really?"

Without looking up, she replied with neutrality in her voice, "Yep, nothing has changed. Everything is fine."

"I know it's…it's…"

"Now is not the time, Marlene."

"So, everything is fine?" Marlene repeated with a pained expression on her face.

Lexy felt sorry for Marlene. Marlene could not understand that, in an odd way, the discovery of the true family dynamics was helping to define old pain, repair deep wounds, and strengthen their relationships. Lexy got up and walked over to the delicate woman, putting her arms out in a motherly gesture. Marlene walked into her open arms as Lexy encouraged, "I'm okay. I promise. We will get through this." Pulling apart from her, she added, "Now, where is our other sibling?"

Marlene perked up. "Man, you know Tina is a total stick up the ass; her lame-ass ain't coming, and she is not going to let…wait for it."

Together, both girls exclaimed, "Chad come!" Marlene laughed wide-mouthed, and Lexy smiled.

Tina's husband, Chadwick Earl II, was a continuous source of mockery for the two. They could not believe they knew a black man named Chad. Even more amazing, his name matched his deep financial pockets and his avoidance of all things beneath him, such as a strip club.

"I know. I know." Lexy rolled her eyes in mock jest. "If she prefers to sit at home with Chad Earl II, then that's her perogative. I know deep down he wishes he could be here, and Tina wants a night away from him, too."

Marlene released a free-spirited laugh, relieved that Lexy was dealing with things so well. After another round of hugs, Marlene confirmed their standing Sunday workout appointment before leaving Lexy anchored at her desk where she had found her. Lexy turned her attention to the new security system and began viewing test footage. The meeting between Marcus and Vincenzo lay before her.

Frowning, she watched the activity with focused eyes. “Marcus, poor bastard. Hmmm. Shit, Vin, what are you up to?” she whispered, taking a small sip of wine and watching Marcus wipe the sweat from his brow, which reminded her how much he did not belong in the industry.

At that moment, Marcus looked like he did not have a friend in the world. It pained her to see the gun pointed at his head. Not wanting to believe he betrayed her, she reasoned there was the possibility that he was busy with the ball and did not purposely conceal the information. She trusted Marcus with her life but could not help but wonder how he could forget something so important, such as the unscheduled meeting and the fact he had the money in his possession. The possibility that he did not want to add pressure to her on the day of Lillian’s memorial service came to mind but rationalizing this did not change the fact of what she saw. Lexy could not help but wonder if betrayal was in the process.

* * *

Admittance to the ball required strict security measures. All attendees were subject to heavy scrutiny; therefore, no one made it on the premises without being searched and electronically scanned. To do their jobs, some of the mammoth security staff had to be careful not to step, shove, or bump into patrons as they made their way about the lavish spaces to enforce their version of martial law.

Unlike those that had to navigate cautiously in the crowded venue, it was easy for a man of medium build to ease his way around the human bottlenecks—in this case, a man with an athletic physique, dressed in military whites, who slid into a spot at one of the crowded bright acrylic bars. He leaned on the art and twirled a toothpick in his mouth, his strawberry-blonde mustache stopping the sliver of wood every so often as he waited for the opportunity to catch the fast-paced movement of the bartenders.

With combat medals decorating his uniform, it did not take long for the Navy SEAL veteran to capture a bartender’s attention and obtain a drink. Starlet, one of Lexy's seasoned dancers, sauntered up to the not so close-shaven thirty-something man—using the upbeat tempo of the music as a tool to sway her ample hips. The hustler leaned close and spoke into his ear, "Hi, handsome!"

Without replying, the man pulled back, trying not to let her breast, or any part of her body, touch his.

"What's wrong, baby?" Her hand stroked her honey blonde weaved hair. "My skin too dark?" Starlet batted her feathery lashes and continued to sway with the music.

He ignored her and turned his body in towards the bar before downing the shot. Standing, he lifted his glass in the air to signal for another. With hooded green eyes, he glared at the attractive, aging stripper. There was something about the look. Instinct told Starlet to back away and redirect her attention to more favorable company. Once served, the brooding man downed the second shot, abruptly negotiated his way through the crowded club, and went out the front door.

THE BALL
PART II

TL knew it was a matter-of-time before Lexy resurfaced. He spotted her large afro in the crowd when she emerged from her private elevator and watched her maneuver through the club with feline grace and agility. Impressed by her achievements, thus far, he felt he could ascend them both to higher levels of success with his divine direction at the helm. However, there was one problem. Though not openly expressed, TL knew Lexy did not like him.

Lexy looked up at him from her location on the lower level. TL tipped his glass to her. His expression said nothing. Her expression said less. Looking like the club mogul she was, he watched her diplomatically make her way towards his location, stopping to acknowledge guests along her route.

"Game on," he mouthed, keeping his eye on her.

When Lexy reached the top of the stairs, he extended a hand to assist her onto the top landing. He then took a step back and ran his hands over his suit to smooth invisible wrinkles like a child trying to please his mother.

"TL." She nodded gracefully.

Stepping toward her, he guided her to the glass railing. Standing side-by-side, they stood over the party from the upper-level tier.

"We have another successful ball," he claimed as if it was his achievement.

"Yes, it is, but where does it end?" she replied.

"This paradise," TL spread his arms out toward the debauchery before them, "end? Why on earth would we want this to end?"

They both continued their straightforward gaze.

"Have you been taken care of? How is the suite?"

"No complaints," he answered.

Silence between them filled the space of the loud music around them before TL asked, "So, what do you think of Jordache?"

"Who?"

TL turned towards Lexy's strong profile. "The new one I sent over. Hmm, you're slipping, Lexy."

She eyed him from her peripheral. *He sounds like Marcus.*

"Oh, Maria, she's doing okay. A little green, but nothing that can't be improved upon."

"How is Lisa?"

This asshole. "Lisa is fine."

"That's not what I heard," he challenged.

Lexy's attention remained on the club.

"I also heard there are going to be ownership changes here."

Dammit!

Now he had her full attention, but she remained silent.

"I supply a lot of good talent for you. I would like to think I'd be the first to know of any major changes." TL waited for a response but got none, so he continued, "After all, we're practically partners." He licked his full lips and shifted his weight to stand taller. "Investing…"

Her eyes locked on Vincenzo entering the club. He and his entourage wore black. She assumed Marcus gave the approval to let them past security. Turning to TL, and cutting him off mid-sentence, she said, "Please, let the staff know if you need anything. Excuse me." She walked away, leaving the pimp standing alone and seething.

* * *

Before Lexy could get downstairs, Marcus intercepted Vincenzo and his men and took them to a newly constructed conference room located at the back of the club. The room was ablaze in monochromatic whites and delicately blended with balanced touches of red and black. The centerpiece of the space, a massive white, rectangular glass and chrome conference table, with embedded swipe computers and white, leather padded chrome chairs, took up the front half of the room. The rear of the conference room served as an office area with work cubicles and a bar and beverage station. However, to remind the occupants of where they were, nude black and white portraits of exotic dancers graced the walls, as well as nude silhouetted figures decorated the drinkware, stationery, and other office supplies.

With her large afro eerily resembling that of a Black Panther member from the early seventies, Lexy walked into the room with two security details and stood at the helm of the table looking powerful. Vincenzo's elderly lawyer sat at the other end, Vinny and two bodyguards walked about admiring nude portraits, and, appearing chummy, Marcus and Vincenzo stood at one of the beverage stations talking. Lexy took note of their camaraderie before addressing the occupants.

"Gentlemen."

All eyes went to the masterpiece in the room, Lexy. The lawyer stood. A red-faced Vincenzo started laboring toward her taking short, shuffled steps. It was painful to watch the obese man navigate his way. No one spoke as he left a trail of outdated, over-saturated cologne behind him. When he reached his destination, he embraced Lexy and whispered something in her ear before releasing her. He then cumbersomely made his way to the other end of the table and took a seat between his lawyer and son. The other two men stood behind the trio. Marcus positioned himself near Vincenzo's end, which surprised Lexy. She waited to measure the pulse of Vincenzo's temperamental mood while she stood wishing she had a cigarette and tried not to tap her fingers on the side of her dress.

Vincenzo spoke loud with cheer. "Bella Bambino! Of course, white is not for me, but you look...uhm...like a tasty morsel!"

He placed his fingers at his lips and then smacked them, letting them fly apart when he did so and followed the gesture with a perverted chuckle.

Lexy sat down without acknowledging the offensive compliment and without addressing Vincenzo's lack of respect by not wearing white. With a phrase repeated millions of times over the last twenty years, she spoke to the men as if they had never met. "Welcome to Lexy's, gentlemen. How can I help you?"

Vincenzo's smile faded. He grunted and stared at her with hostility. "The contract and…um, an ashtray."

"There is no smoking in this conference room," she replied, holding eye contact, and forcing herself not to tighten her jaws.

Vincenzo glared at her before lighting a cigar. Marcus grabbed a Lexy's branded coffee mug from the beverage area and placed it in front of him.

Before anyone could broach the subject of what happened, security opened the glass conference room double doors and escorted two men in. They took seats on each side of Lexy. One of the men took several electronic drives out of his briefcase and held two up for one of Vincenzo's men to retrieve.

Vincenzo barked, "What is this?!"

"You know my lawyer, Mr. Townsend, and this is Mr. Banks." A hint of a grin graced her lips at the pun intended. "They will be involved with investment negotiations."

"Negotiations?"

The skin on Vincenzo's forehead wrinkled. The puffiness under his eyes occluded his vision as he squinted. His lawyer placed a hand on his suit coat sleeve, silently coaxing him to remain calm. Vincenzo leaned his bulky frame back, stuffing himself into the chair and scowled. An uncomfortable silence followed.

"Ms. Leigh?" Vincenzo's lawyer inquired.

With her hands folded delicately in her lap, Lexy sat with the poise of a trained ballet dancer and spoke in an even tone. "Gentlemen, Marcus and I have just completed the Preparation of Registration Statement and are ready to open our books for financial auditing to prepare for an IPO. The business climate is perfect for it. As you know, many major clubs in the nation are going public. Stand-alone clubs are finding it hard to compete with franchised clubs and often struggle to raise needed capital to expand branding."

Her jaws relaxed a little.

"That's why you have me," Vincenzo countered, trying to keep a business composure in front of the men he did not have in his criminal pocket.

Lexy clasped her hands tighter in her lap to refrain from releasing her musical fingers on the tabletop. "Times are changing in our industry. The independent contractor work classification for dancers is no longer practical. They want and need employment benefits. Unions are starting to form. Going public will assist us in the various areas of transition, along with raising needed capital," she concluded.

Vincenzo's face flushed.

"Workplace benefits! Are you shitten me?!" he boomed. "Unions?!"

Lexy knew she had him.

"It's a new business environment. Are you not following lawsuits and rulings on these matters?"

"You'z kidding me, right?"

"And the proposed ownership structure?" Vincenzo's lawyer asked with professionalism still in his tone, unlike his boss.

Lexy proceeded at a relaxed pace, despite wanting to speed things up so she could go back to overseeing the ball.

"It's all there." She pointed to the table monitors.

Lexy sat and watched the changing expressions on the men's faces as they viewed the requirements and the limitations. In the meantime, Marcus reached under the chair he stood in front of and pulled out a black vintage briefcase.

"Mr. Abela, I do believe you left this here on your last visit. Our staff found it in the V.I.P. suite you were in." Marcus slid the black briefcase across the table toward Vincenzo.

Vincenzo's face went a third shade redder.

Marcus continued, "Here at Lexy's, we make it a point to protect our clients and their livelihood. You wouldn't want something like this lying around."

Lexy looked at Marcus and smiled through her eyes. On the contrary, Vincenzo had enough. His fist hit the table hard. Lexy abruptly stood. Hastily, he struggled to escape the armchair and shouted in Italian. Before his men could carry out their orders, the glass doors and the wall behind Lexy exploded from a powerful blast of volcanic force, rocking the room and sending debris shrapnel in every direction. Instantaneously, the occupants in the room flew off their feet.

THE BALL PART III

Kat felt better. Earlier, she had left the dressing room pushing back tears but then decided to focus on what she did best—dancing—which yielded positive results—money. Besides, instructions from TL to join him during her break had her feeling back on top of the world; thus, causing her to rationalize that the situation in the dressing room was a minor incident blown out of proportion.

With optimism, now dressed in a crystal-adorned bustier with sheer silk, white panels cascading from her waist to the ground, Kat made her way to TL. She was glad the peculiar short man, Razor, and her boss had moved on from his company. The gentle pimp in him stood when she approached. He knew small gestures that made his women feel special went a long way in controlling them.

"Pony."

His smooth voice caused her female parts to stir. She drew in his intoxicating scent when he brushed her cheek with his lips, a light gesture to draw her in, but discreet enough not to appear weak to onlookers.

"Hi, babe," she replied in a whispery voice.

He took her hand and guided her into the roped-off area. The self-proclaimed royal couple sat in his secure section, her looking more like a gold statue than an exotic dancer and him looking like the owner of Lexy's. At one point, a patron approached the pair and inquired about Kat's availability. TL motioned for one of his girls to intercept the investor. Happy and feeling exclusive with her man, Kat sat confident and poised, determined to show TL her unspoken loyalty.

After a couple of songs played, the two went downstairs to his private suite. Before sitting on the black leather couch, he took off his jacket and his tie and unbuttoned his shirt. Kat stood waiting with downcast eyes, trying not to bite her lower lip. Once seated, he twirled his finger slowly in the air, and she responded erotically by stroking her hands over her body.

"Pony, I'm ready to ride."

She nodded her head, closed her eyes, and internalized the sensual music playing in the suite. Her hips swayed, and she danced for him, grinding away as she peeled off her clothes.

It did not take long for him to unbutton his pants and beckon her over. Rolling up from the spread-eagle position she had danced herself into, she seductively crawled on the floor, positioned herself between his legs, and began pleasing him, causing him to grab her by the back of her head as he lay his head back on the plush couch backrest. Just when he was about to release himself, he placed his hands on her frail shoulders, signaling her to stop. It made her think something was wrong, which was farthest from the truth. He stood and pulled her to her feet before turning her around. Then, using his index finger—with the lightest of touch—he guided her down onto the couch, her upper torso resting on the backrest and her knees on the cushions, before sliding her G-string over and entering her from behind in one explosive movement.

During their intense sex, they did not hear an uninvited individual enter the room via a stolen key card. Now, the intruder stood watching and listening to him tell Kat sweet things, the same sweet things he had whispered to her, the promises he had made to her. Out of breath, Kat looked over her shoulder to tell TL how good it felt but stopped abruptly and gasped. Maria stood behind them with anger anchored on her face.

TL looked over his shoulder but did not stop. "Bitch, get the fuck ou'da here!" he growled and turned back around to release himself.

With arms outstretched in disbelief, the unstable girl yelled in Spanish.

TL withdrew from Kat and methodically wiped himself off with a handkerchief to the sound of Maria's tirade in the background. With urgency, Kat struggled to get her garment back on, not caring if she lost a crystal or two in the process. TL zipped up his pants and calmly walked over to the enraged woman. Upon reaching her, he cocked his arm back and punched her in the face, sending her reeling backward as blood erupted from her mouth and splattered across his bare chest and onto his open shirt. The voluptuous young woman bounced off the bar and hit the floor with a thud.

"Fucking bitch!" he spat and kicked her in the stomach, hoping to dislodge the baby she had just professed to be carrying.

Shaking as if she were having a seizure, Kat hit her personal breaking point. A series of traumatic memories flashed in her mind with fury. She saw in Maria's place herself and various other unfortunate women TL had knocked to the ground during their one-sided relationships with him. A queasiness churned in her stomach and began to find its way to the top, sending vomit forcefully spewing out of her mouth, thus giving her much needed relief from the sick feeling that had been plaguing her for days.

With a hard-set face and eyes ablaze with anger, TL shot her a look. "What the hell's wrong with you!"

Kat felt the room spin.

"I-I'm f-fine."

"What?" he scowled, not caring how she felt. He started taking off his shirt.

"P-Probably too much champagne," she quietly replied and wiped the corner of her mouth with the back of her hand, willing the room to stop spinning and simultaneously bemoaning the fact she had to clean up the mess she created.

TL went into the bathroom, and, for the first time, Kat scrutinized the girl lying on the floor, noting how stunning she looked with her jet-black hair, porcelain skin, long lashes, and huge breasts.

"That shit ain't going to clean itself up!" he shouted from the bathroom.

With the specialness of the night wearing thin, Kat retrieved paper towels and began cleaning up her stomach content. TL appeared from the bathroom with a fresh shirt on. "Throw some water on that bitch," he said, as he stepped over Maria's body and left the suite.

Kat stood dumbfounded, wondering why she had to deal with the situation. Feeling lightheaded, she went to the en suite supply closet to get cleaning supplies and a bucket while muttering about her misfortune and cursing the resurgence of the queasiness at the base of her slender stomach.

When she returned, the spot once occupied by the unconscious girl was empty. Thinking TL had retrieved the dead weight, Kat went about the task of sanitizing the floor, working hard to avoid ruining her outfit, and wishing TL had gotten the staff to do the job instead of her.

Wham!

Pain shot through the back of Kat's head as she pitched forward and fell to the floor. Blood oozed out of a deep laceration in her head, causing her fine angel hair to mat instantly. Dazed, Kat rolled over and gazed up through blurred vision at a hostile Maria. The enraged girl screeched an animal type sound, jumped on top of Kat, and began raking her nails across Kat's delicate Scandinavian face and along her neck.

Kat's arms went up in defense as the scratching continued, but, with each stinging assault, she realized the only choice was to fight back, but it was too late. Maria had the upper hand. Maria pulled a fist full of Kat's paper-thin hair violently, causing Kat's torso and head to lift off the ground before sending her crashing down into the wood floor repeatedly.

Wham! Wham! Wham! Kat went limp. Breathing hard, Maria backed off the weakened girl and began walking in circles, looking and behaving as if she had just had a fight with herself. Kat moaned and rolled to her side, simultaneously grabbing a piece of busted marble artwork and hid it in the fold of her cradled body. Catching the movement, Maria dove at her. Kat reacted by crashing the weighted item into the side of Maria's head, knocking the deranged woman back. Bright red blood dripped down Maria's face, creating an artwork of horror. "You can't have him!" the crazed girl screamed.

Maria rose and staggered towards Kat, who sat panting on the floor holding her head. Kat scrambled to her feet and tackled Maria. The two began tumbling about. Kat threw random punches, her lean arms pummeled desperately, which turned the tables in her favor by the time TL and Razor entered the room.

"Oh, shit!" Razor shouted, laughing as he followed TL over to the fighting women.

The men pulled them apart, causing Kat to lose an astonishing amount of hair in the process. TL slung Maria into a wall. "Shut up, bitch!" he roared.

This did not stop Maria from unleashing a new slew of murderous threats in both Spanish and English.

"What tha'fuck's wrong with this bitch?!" Kat yelled, wiping the blood dripping into her eyes from the gouges in her forehead and ignoring her own physical trauma as she stood trying to get oxygen into her lungs.

TL's anger boiled as he prepared to enact his justice on the two for jeopardizing his money. Razor continued laughing, but Maria abruptly stopped ranting and wailed, "Nooooo!" and then pulled aside her ripped dress to reveal a flow of crimson blood running down her thick, shapely leg. Maria doubled over in pain while the release of the life forming in her womb flowed with the blood. "My baby, my baby!" she cried out in English, holding her stomach and slumping to the floor.

Kat's eyes widened in disbelief.

"Ah, man." Razor started. "Bruh, you were selling me soiled goods. You'z fucked up, bruh!" He hooted and slapped his leg in amusement.

"Is it yours?" Kat yelled, still out of breath and limping towards TL.

TL ignored her.

"Is it yours?!" Kat screamed, sounding as crazed as Maria had been, her once coiffed hair in disarray on her head with bald patches exposed on her scalp and her eyelids starting to swell.

TL did what came naturally. He advanced on Kat and slapped her to the ground. Now, both girls lay on the floor.

"See," Razor chuckled, "this pimp shit is too much, niggah." He picked up a cognac bottle off the floor that had survived the fight and began drinking out of the bottle, laughing in between sips at the pimp's misfortune.

TL saw nothing funny about the situation. His investments could not make money on the floor.

"Get that bitch to the ER. I'll pay, but after that, that trick is all yours," TL said, motioning to Razor with the flick of his hand.

Still laughing, Razor pulled Maria up off the floor and put his arm up under her to support her weak legs as they made their way out of the suite. TL looked around the ruined suite and made phone calls while he waited for Kat to regain consciousness. When she did, she rose slowly, looking at TL with hatred. He began to scold her. "You stupid, bitch! Sit your punk ass down before I whoop your bitch ass, ho ass."

With a contorted, wild expression on her face, Kat sprang through the air and lunged at him, screaming like a soul on fire. Her broken acrylic nails tore into his clean-shaven face.

It was then that the explosion hit, sending shards of wall and furnishings in all directions. The impact caught TL and Kat just as she landed on him. They both flew back in the direction Kat had leaped from, sending them across the room and into a wall as one unit, causing fragmented wall pieces to tumble down upon them.

Covered in debris, TL came to consciousness in a dark void filled with smoke, soot, and intense ringing in his ears. Underneath him, Kat lay motionless. With unbearable pain racking his body, he painstakingly inched his way up and out of the construction grave. It hurt to breathe, and his bones felt shifted out of place in all areas of his once strong physique. As carnage continued around him, the arduous process of standing took time.

When he finally stood, another blast shook the club, throwing him back on top of the debris and pinning Kat deeper into it. Shakily, he repeated the same torturous process of getting up. Believing death imminent, the once confident, indestructible man focused on an escape route and made his way into a blackness lit with terror-filled screams and cries while Kat lay buried in the toppled building materials with one large blue eye uncovered and staring blankly into the nightmare in which she lay.

THE BALL
PART IV

The calm summer night was the perfect condition for the mission of the combat war veteran. From a nearby rooftop, Jason, the young man that had worn the white officer's naval uniform, now wore black and watched the chaos he had created unfold through high-powered lenses. At three hundred meters, the rocket-propelled grenades had worked well. In an instant, portions of Lexy's had dissipated into piles of wreckage. Now, lying on his stomach and peering through a scope, he waited for movement from the smoky rubble.

"This is for you, Sandy," her brother whispered and then fired off rounds from his M24 rifle from atop the Crown Royal hotel building.

* * *

The gates of purgatory had opened for the souls at Lexy's. The first explosion blew Lexy off her feet as bits and pieces of building materials flew in her direction, temporarily rendering her deaf. Frosted glass from the meeting room door lodged in her back, but she did not feel the misery of the sharp objects because her senses were overwhelmed from the chaos unfolding around her.

Dazed and confused, she tried to stand, but before she could gain her balance, a second explosion hit and sent her tumbling back to the ground. It was at that point, she felt an agonizing pain in her back and in her left arm, along with more intense ringing in her ears.

Coughing and gasping, Lexy fought to gain control of her faculties. The first clear thought she had was of Marlene, wondering if she made it safely out of the club; her second thought was of Marcus. Ignoring the scorching heat in the flesh of her back, she sat motionless among the large chunks of roofing material, letting the smoke dissipate into the open night while scanning the hopelessness of the dark and listening to the wails and cries of sufferers and the silence of the dead in the demolished club.

A body—heaped in what used to be the corner of the room—came into view, which propelled her to move out of her temporary spot of security. It was difficult to traverse the rubble, but she groped around the floor, incurring more cuts, scrapes, and bruises as her lungs filling with carcinogenic particles from the smoke. She made her way, hoping to find Marcus.

* * *

When the metal and cement of Lexy's gave way from the impact of the two rocket-propelled grenades that screeched through the air like banshees in a dawn of horror and set the night ablaze, Sgt. Watts' body shot through the air like a missile and landed among other victims such as Detective Hall. Miraculously, Teddy Boy survived both explosions but suffered the fate of losing his eyesight from the compression of the shock waves. He whimpered around like a child, extending his hands to feel into the darkness of which he now knew so intimately.

Zzzzz, thunk!

A sniper round picked Teddy Boy off, easily penetrating his bony temple and creating an exit wound out the other side of his tiny head. In a different area of the pandemonium, smoke and fire raged beneath Jordan Glass' feet. He stumbled on the upper portion of a set of stairs near the back of the club, feeling them sway, signifying impending collapse. Before Jordan could navigate to safety, a bullet hit him in the chest and ended his confusion. Other survivors stumbled around, bewildered about the onslaught that unfolded around them before they too felt the heat of the piercing of their flesh, never realizing they were being hunted down one-by-one.

Scantily clothed or nude, some of the women in the rear of the dressing room were able to escape out the back door and avoid the fate of the hunter's wrath. A few collided into Razor and Maria, who had made it to the alley too. The women navigated their way through the commotion and into the smoke-filled blackness, lending their screams and yells to the madness around them; their desire for a night of money-making ending in the payment of a debt none of them had been prepared to pay.

* * *

Hearing sirens getting louder, the lone figure on the rooftop took a moment to revel in the revenge enacted on his sister's behalf before gathering his tactical equipment. He descended the concrete stairwell with the pride of having done something noble. He loved his baby sister and never believed that she was the cause of her own demise. In his mind, Lexy's killed Sandy.

CHAPTER 20

BEVERLY
Saturday, Day 9 – 6 a.m.

Beverly awoke with a desire to remain grounded. Instead of turning electronic devices on, she opted to pray, read the word of God, and meditate before working out. Having not heard from TL since Wednesday and not wanting to send the wrong message by calling him, the reality of Sister Sarah being right rang painfully true. The fluttering in her stomach and weakness in her knees were starting to diminish, and she laughed at herself for acting like a schoolgirl with a crush.

Making matters worse, when she had tried to tell Kat about her new love interest, Kat had said that her friend sounded too much like TL and to stay away from him. Kat then apologized for her lackluster response and blamed it on a "man thing." Beverly now agreed with Kat and Sister Sarah. She planned to call Sister Sarah and tell her how much she appreciated her guidance and vowed to herself to be more vigilant in Christ and not relinquish herself to the desires of her flesh so easily.

By seven a.m., Beverly stood in the cardio area at the hotel gym. She would be on her own for the better part of the day before meeting Kat for dinner. Walking towards the equipment, she noticed people gathering around and looking up at the wall-mounted television monitors. Snatches of conversation reached her ears.

"Do you think it was terrorism?"

"I don't know. Could have been a disgruntled worker."

Looking at the screens, she noted they all displayed similar, if not the same, breaking news. Getting closer, Beverly's knees went weak as she realized the demolished building on all screens was Lexy's. Thick black smoke billowed over the destroyed club as local and mutual aid fire departments deployed a surround and drown tactic for the multiple alarm fire. With eyes wide, the water bottle and towel in her hand dropped to the floor, and her hands flew to her mouth in fear as she processed the images before her.

"Bird!" she mouthed.

The name choked in her throat; bile churned in her stomach. Beverly turned the music off she was listening to through her earphones and called Kat with trembling fingers. The call went unanswered. With a nauseated stomach, and without thought, she ran out of the gym on wobbly legs to retrieve her purse and then ran to her rental car, taking off towards Kat's condominium. When there was no answer, and she could not get the concierge to let her up to Kat's floor, she got back in her car and drove towards downtown Minneapolis.

During the ride, she called as many people as she could who might have known of Kat's whereabouts. Joanne informed her she had not heard from Kat since Tuesday and kept asking what was wrong. Beverly did not have the heart to worry her unnecessarily and promised Joanne she would call her back. Feeling like an irresponsible friend, she cursed herself for not having TL's phone number. Little did she know, she did.

* * *

Beverly could not get close to the club. Considered a hot zone and a crime scene, first responders impeded her movement by routing her out of the area. Like an inmate on the last day of death row, her anxiety increased by the minutes. Soon, morning turned into afternoon; afternoon turned into evening; and evening turned into night. It was difficult for her to sit in her hotel room with her phone in her hand and glued to the television, waiting for news. Periodically, she checked Kat's social media accounts, called metro city hospitals, and stayed in contact with Joanne.

BEVERLY
Sunday, Day 10

Beverly did not make her flight back to California that evening. The following day, she joined Joanne in her St. Paul home, finding herself locked in a situation where they were both overly kind to each other, trying to be strong for one another, and hiding their true feelings of fear and helplessness behind their proclamations of faith.

Initially, law enforcement ruled the incident at Lexy's a terrorist attack. Emergency responders transported victims to trauma level metro hospitals, including Kat. Once staff identified Joanne's daughter, a co-worker called and informed the distressed mother.

A ventilator, a host of tubes, I.V. bags with numerous medications, and monitors sustained Kat's comatose state. A variety of specialists concurred that there was no hope of her recovering; however, Joanne would not consider taking her daughter off life-support. Instead, she set up a prayer vigil next to her unresponsive daughter's bedside.

* * *

Beverly walked into the hospital chapel to find Joanne sitting in the first-row pew with her head bent down in prayer. Not wanting to disturb her and wanting her own space, Beverly took a seat in the back row. Struggling to hold on to their faith, each woman prayed as their religion had trained them to do. Beverly looked up when she heard a sorrowful moan come from Joanne. "Please, Jesus! Please, Jesus! Bring my baby back!" the shattered woman cried out.

Beverly got up and joined Joanne, placing her arm around the woman's shoulders and drawing her into an empathetic embrace.

"I can't do this, Lord! I can't!" Joanne cried out, "Birthday…I-I didn't…pushed her…a-away…Oh God!" she babbled, her rail-thin body shaking uncontrollably.

"Shh, it's going to be okay," Beverly tried to console her while stroking her hair.

Like a switch turned on, Joanne pushed Beverly away and stared at her. "What do you know?!" she hissed, taking her misery out on

Beverly. "I have served the Lord faithfully, and this is what I get!" The sad woman wailed and broke into another round of sobs.

Beverly sat bewildered, not knowing how to react or what to do.

Joanne hugged her body. Rocking back and forth, she muttered, "I prayed for her. I gave it to the Lord. I did everything I was charged to do and for what?" and then she tried to stand on unsteady legs, dropping something in the process.

Seeing the unsteadiness, Beverly got up to support the distraught woman, helping her take a few steps before realizing that Joanne did not have the strength. The younger girl eased them both to the paper-thin chapel carpet and placed the item Joanne dropped back in her hands. With her hands clasped around Joanne's, Beverly began humming the spiritual song "Eye is on the Sparrow." Her own tears spilled over her swollen eye rims and onto her youthful face. Slowly, Joanne's cries quieted, and she joined in. The two hummed, letting their spirits recharge. Finally, Joanne whispered, "Thank you."

"You're welcome."

"I'm sorry."

"For what?"

Joanne responded in between sniffles, "For not being a good example of a woman of faith."

"I don't think God expects us to be perfect. You are a woman of faith," Beverly said, hoping she was saying the right thing.

"Beverly, I feel like a hypocrite," Joanne quietly confessed. "I spent many years thinking I was higher and mightier than I was. You know, praying for others when they had devastating things happen to them, always giving out spiritual advice, and practically living in the church. I neglected my only child." Joanne sniffed, hung her head, and ran her hands over the massage gift card she held, her last gift from Kat.

Beverly tried to think of an uplifting scripture, but verses tumbled together in her fatigued mind.

What would Sister Sarah say?

Beverly's spirit told her to speak from her heart.

"I know you, Ms. Joanne. You're always there when needed. You faithfully serve on the prison ministry. You work with the homeless, and you're always helping around the church. I've seen you give food, money, and prayers without hesitation."

"Yes, but I let my baby down," Joanne whispered.

Beverly thought back on the luncheon she and Kat shared, and her eyes lit up. "I led Kat in the prayer of salvation!" she blurted out.

Joanne lifted her head and stared at Beverly.

"What?"

"We had lunch last Sunday," she said with enthusiasm. "Kat rededicated her life to Christ and asked Jesus to come into her heart, professed he was the son of God, and asked for forgiveness for her sins."

"She did?" Joanne asked.

"Yes, she did." Beverly smiled.

It took a moment for the words to sink in, but then, like a slowed frame sequence in a movie, the expression on Joanne's face shifted from sorrow to spiritual hope before she stuttered, "Oh, oh, oh t-thank you!"

Beverly finally remembered a scripture and paraphrased, "God is always on time."

"Yes, he is," Joanne smiled and gazed at Beverly with the warmth of the love of a mother and used the moment to find temporary solace.

* * *

The rest of the week went by in a painful blur for Beverly, a week spent moving about in a fog while helping Joanne the best she could. Her parents and twin brothers flew in for the funeral service, which was a welcoming relief to have the strength of her family to lean on, but, despite the support, a black hole remained in her heart.

The home going for Katherine Renay Olson took place on Friday, June 14, at 10 a.m. On the day of the service, Beverly thought back to remember if she missed something important with Kat. Being supportive to her friend was always a priority and she recalled a slight look of sadness in Kat's eyes when she tried to share the possibility of falling in love with Terrell. Questions lingered now, making Beverly wonder if Kat had needed her.

After the service, teary-eyed and sitting alone in Joanne's kitchen Beverly vaguely registered the activity of the other guests in the living room and dining room. Beverly thought about the stash of liquor Kat kept hidden in her stepfather's shed in the backyard, something she kept on-site in case her parents got on her nerves during one of her infrequent visits. Without analyzing the decision, she left the kitchen.

In the shed, she sat on a rusty, metal folding chair, surrounded by dirt-covered tools and old vehicle parts, with a red plastic cup in her hand. The first gulp of vodka went down painfully, but after a few more shots of the faceless brand, it slid down her throat like water. Sitting in the cobweb filled shack, her year of sobriety slowly wasted away as she convinced herself life would never be the same without Kat.

Time ticked away as the weight of the alcohol anchored her heart to the isolation of false comfort in the tears of the booze. At some point, Beverly could hear her name called from someone standing on the back door stoop, but the fog of her mind left her where she sat. Then, a set of strong arms guided her upstairs and onto Kat's bed with the gentle voice of a woman in the background providing instructions. The voice sounded sweet, like the feathery softness of Kat's. The next morning, she awoke to a massive hangover, surrounded by Kat's belongings. Overwhelming sadness returned. Beverly pulled the covers over her head and resumed grieving.

BEVERLY
Sunday – 7 Days Later

A week after what would have been her original return flight, Beverly stood curbside at the airport and said goodbye to her parents and the twins. Her mother's excessive fussing was becoming overkill, and to her surprise, heading back to California seemed a welcome relief.

On the plane, upon viewing a pair of young girls excited about their trip to fly West, thoughts of her childhood with Kat came to mind. Beverly's waterworks started flowing as she silently cried. A flight attendant hovered around her, offering tissue and water to the grief-stricken young woman, fussing over her as people often did without knowing why they felt so inclined.

* * *

Upon arrival at her apartment, Beverly retrieved her spare key from her neighbor and tried to be as polite as possible when she did not stay to elaborate on her trip, promising the older woman they would catch up over lunch.

Back at home, the familiarity gave her some needed comfort but also magnified her pain as she looked around the modern, minimalist space. Jetta followed her, displaying subdued happiness, and jumped on top of a carrier Beverly had set next to her suitcases. A rapid firing of soft meows to get out of the container came forth.

"Oh! I'm sorry, Moochie!"

Beverly reached for the carrier and placed it on the dresser. She took a tiny, black fur-ball from the traveling case and cuddled it in her arms, trying to secure the squirming baby. Her eyes watered over as she pictured Kat holding the same kitten that she had purchased from the Grand Avenue pet shop in Kat's honor. She placed Moochie in the bathroom with food, water, and kitty litter and closed the door to provide a safe place for the new family member until she could properly introduce Jetta to her.

Despondent, Beverly sat on her bed and absentmindedly surfed television channels. Calamity presented itself everywhere. Falling stock markets, earthquakes, famine, and terrorist attacks dominated the news. The President of the United States addressed the nation on yet another mass shooting in America, and on another channel, two major political parties argued over whether the presidential candidates had the ability to lead the nation.

She turned off the television and went back into the galley-sized kitchen where she noticed the snail mail stacked on the kitchen counter and realized how sweet her neighbor was. "I should get Ms. Pam a gift to bring to our luncheon," she said to Jetta, who walked close under her heels.

Mindlessly, she opened the refrigerator and looked at the empty shelves. The absence of food did not matter. At this point, her lack of appetite worked in her favor. Arlene would be happy to see her at an all-time-thin from not eating. Hearing her cell phone ring, she made her way slowly to the bedroom, figuring it was either Sister Sarah or Arlene. Looking at the incoming call, her eyes lit up.

"Hello, Bambi," the deep voice on the other end of the phone said.

Beverly smiled for the first time in over a week.

VINCENZO ABELA II
Three Months Later

In a little Italy section of Chicago, a scarred face Vinny made his way out of a black sedan using a customized cane and limping his way into a nondescript deli shop with two of his men trailing behind him. Inside, behind a tall glass display counter, two workers tended to customers while flies buzzed boldly about—the insects landing on their intended targets to get easy food before the fall weather killed them off.

Vinny did not make eye contact with the men as he hobbled by with his head tilted to the right to hide his disfigurement from the blasts. As he passed, the two men behind the counter looked at each other and then went back to their tasks at hand. Vinny and his men made their way towards the back of the shop, where they gained permission to access a set of stairs from three men playing cards at one of the last tables.

The sound of footsteps from the past echoed as the narrow, antique staircase bore the weight of the three men. At a snail's pace, Vinny led the way, struggling with the condition of the new disability that no amount of physical therapy could cure.

At the top of the stairs, using a leathery skin-grafted hand, the leader signaled for one of them to stay outside the door while he and the other waited for a response to his knock. A young boy opened the door.

"Vinny, Vinny, come in, come in!" An elderly, short, stout woman motioned to him when he stepped into the hot, cramped kitchen. The silvered haired woman used her apron to dry her age-spotted hand before reaching out to grasp one of his slender snakeskin-like covered hands that told a condensed story of his stay in a burn unit. "You eat?" she asked in an Americanized Italian accent.

"No, grazie. No, grazie," Vinny replied humbly and then motioned to his companion to stay in the kitchen, which the man did not mind because it allowed him to eat and avoid the stress of the meeting.

From the kitchen, Vincenzo II stepped through a door and into a dark dining room sandwiched between the kitchen and an overcrowded living room that had intricate, dark-colored wallpaper; small angelic figurines throughout; walls covered with nineteenth-century oil paintings in antique frames and more lamps and statues of biblical saints than necessary for the pint-sized rooms.

Four middle-aged men in dark suits, sitting at an oblong wood table, stopped talking when he entered. He could barely meet their stares; his slouched body language expressed words not spoken. Guilt for the way things turned out at Lexy's showed on his face.

After twenty minutes, Vinny left the butcher shop. To his astonishment, the meeting did not go as expected. The Capos brought him word of a rare reprieve. Despite no proof of Lexy having a hand in the death of his twin and though the blast was not her personal doing, the head of the family, his advisor, and the under-boss concluded Lexy's act of defiance to a partnership with the organization communicated insult and disrespect. It was concluded, had she signed the paperwork, the deaths of Vincenzo Sr. and Junior could have been avoided. Vinny left the deli charged with finding Lexy.

CHAPTER 21

LEXY
Three Months Later – Sunset

I stood shaking, knowing I was in trouble. Aunt Lilly glared at me through eyes that looked like mine. It was as if I was glaring at myself. Mixed feelings flooded my psyche. I didn't know what to concentrate on, the imminent thrashing or the feeling that my stomach wrapped around my spine from hunger. How unfair for a ten-year-old. I handed her the green, leafless, thin switch from the bush...my lips trembled... waiting for the first lash.

The pain cut through me like a hot iron forged in fire. I winced and clenched my jaws. I tried; determined not to answer the call of the breaking of my spirit; another lash caught me on my wrist. My wrists were always the catcher. I clenched my jaws harder, but I couldn't hold out. My cries cut through the air; the blood dripped from my wrist ... The shrapnel cut through my back as the blast thrust me forward, causing me to land on the shattered acrylic table. My ears rang, and dust and dirt rose around me. I couldn't move. The fire in my back. Was Aunt Lilly beating me? No, the blast. Where is Marcus?

With a gasp, Lexy awoke from her nightmare with the sun beating down on her as she lay in a poolside lounge chair. She had not meant to fall asleep in such a vulnerable position and appreciated that the disruptive dream jarred her awake. Increased sleepless nights and reoccurring dreams haunted her because recovering from the recent devastating events continually challenged her mentally, thus adding to the list of vivid scenes already present in her nightmare repertoire.

The ramifications from the ball presented themselves in all areas of her life. Though apprehended fast, Sandy's brother felt justified in his reasoning to crush the entity that killed his baby sister. The delusional man would have the opportunity to plead temporary insanity due to Post Traumatic Syndrome Disorder as his defense, which, in this case, was the absolute truth.

Her arm fractures, still in a cast due to reconstructive surgery, and the scars on her back were reminders of the horrible night; however, the physical injuries would never compare to the losses of Marcus, her staff, and guests. The thought of them, him especially, caused her heart to ache, and made her feel responsible for placing everyone in harm's way. In addition, many civil lawsuits followed the catastrophe, which kept her in continuous litigation.

On a different note, Marlene made it safely out, which gave Lexy a moment to admit to herself that God might just care about Alexandria, having spared her sister. More puzzling, Marcus left his assets to her, which both amazed and saddened the love of his life. A few of Marcus' relatives, ones she had never heard of, were coming out of black holes to fight her and claim the small fortune he had amassed, thus resulting in more lawsuits.

In the end, she canceled the attempt to find the woman known to her as mom, telling the investigator to close the case after his first dead end. It became a moot point after all that had happened. With the permission of the courts, Lexy recovered from her injuries on the island of Oahu while waiting for court dates. Often, the now-retired club owner lamented over whether she made a major mistake by not excepting Marcus' proposal to sell the business and move on to a serene life.

With the sun starting to set, two Asian men in black suits approached her. "Excuse me, Ms. Leigh, Ms. Alexandria Leigh?"

Lexy slipped her hand under her cast and gripped the pistol in her lap while simultaneously swinging her braids out of her face with a toss of her head.

The men gave courteous head bows.

With a smooth and calming voice, the taller man spoke. "Ms. Leigh, please excuse the interruption. My name is Akio, and this is my business partner, Li." Li extended his hand to give her a business card. When she did not accept it, he placed it back in his suit pocket.

"What can I do for you, gentlemen?"

"We represent Mr. Fumito, owner of an island in Fiji." Akio paused and waited for a response. There was none, so he continued, "He would like the honor to meet with you."

Lexy discreetly slipped the pistol in her bag and stood. After a courteous bow, she replied, "I doubt there is anything I can assist Mr. Fumito with."

"On the contrary, Mr. Fumito would like to contract with you as a consultant."

Lexy replied, "Gentlemen, I know of Mr. Fumito's reputation. I know he can afford the best business consultants in the world for any venture; I doubt he would want to retain my services."

Both men remained reserved.

"Respectfully," Akio and Li bowed their heads slightly before Akio continued. "He is opening an exclusive casino and gentlemen's club on his private island. If you could make time on your calendar unless you are free now? We have access to his helicopter. It would be an honor to have you join Mr. Fumito for dinner."

Lexy took in what was said and stood silent for a moment. Her jaw softened. A rush hit her like addiction emerging from the abyss of recovery. The spontaneous thrill of a challenge, of the work, of the lifestyle, tugged at her from within, despite her internal battle to rationalize all that had just happened. The desire to do what she did best pulled at her professional strings. The gamble of the unknown heightened her senses. Lexy's eyes narrowed as she thought. The men waited.

"Has construction begun?"

They looked at each other, confused. They were not sent to discuss details.

"The project is in the planning stage," Akio replied.

"Hmm…so much to do."

They did not know if she was talking to them or to herself.

The sun dipped behind clouds giving the overdressed men much-needed relief from the tropical rays as they waited for her to speak.

"Excuse me, gentlemen. If you could give me a moment, I must make a phone call. Just a moment."

"Why, of course," Akio answered as Li stood beside him with an unreadable look on his face.

Upon completion of the ten-minute call, Lexy beckoned the men from the shade of a poolside table they had found refuge at from the heat.

"I'd be honored to accompany you gentlemen, but to talk…talk only."

"Yes, talk only," Akio repeated.

"I'll need to retrieve some personal items. May I meet you in the lobby, please?"

"Yes, certainly."

The three left the pool area and walked into the hotel lobby. As they did, they passed Aadhya Raja—the exotic woman from the gym in East Lake, MN. With a golden chain running from her nose ring to her gold ear band, the stunning woman passed by the trio wearing colorful, silk flowing cultural garments and high-quality colored diamonds, which hung from her ears, fingers, and neck. Her silky jet-black hair lay straight and secured under a jeweled headband, giving her the image of an Arabic princess.

Her billionaire father, along with a security detail, personal assistants, and administrative staff, accompanied her. The women's eyes locked, and Aadhya discretely nodded. Lexy returned the gesture. After passing the group, Lexy completely relaxed her jaws. Life felt normal again.

* * * THE END * * *

RESOURCES

Substance Abuse and Mental Health Services
Administration Hotline [SAMHSA]:
https://www.samhsa.gov/
1-800-622-HELP (4357)

National Council on Alcoholism
and Drug Dependence, Inc [NCADD]:
https://www.ncaddesgpv.org/
1-800-622-2255

National Domestic Violence Hotline
https://www.thehotline.org/
1-800-799-SAFE (7233)

National Suicide Prevention Lifeline
https://suicidepreventionlifeline.org/
1-800-273-TALK (8255)

National Human Trafficking Hotline
https://humantraffickinghotline.org/
1-888-373-7888

ABOUT THE AUTHOR

Born in St. Paul MN, T.R. Gray spent her childhood as a military dependent, which allowed her to travel extensively. Her travels continued when she served as a U.S. Army soldier and as a military spouse. Following those years, she served 12 years as a professional firefighter and nationally certified paramedic.

Gray holds a bachelor's degree in Business Management. She enjoys writing poetry, dancing, exercising, and researching random subjects. Her life experiences have given her the opportunity to write about the concerns of her heart, humanity. She hopes you will enjoy this book and that you will take away encouragement, validation, direction, or clarity to what touches your spirit and your heart as you mitigate your own personal crossroads.

To purchase the novel, visit www.trgray.com.

Email: author@trgray.com

Instagram: @author_trgray

CPSIA information can be obtained
at www.ICGtesting.com
Printed in the USA
BVHW072039090820
585854BV00004B/27